Charles Burnett

The publisher and the University of California Press Foundation gratefully acknowledge the generous support of the Robert and Meryl Selig Endowment Fund in Film Studies, established in memory of Robert W. Selig.

Charles Burnett

A CINEMA OF SYMBOLIC KNOWLEDGE

James Naremore

UNIVERSITY OF CALIFORNIA PRESS

University of California Press, one of the most distinguished university presses in the United States, enriches lives around the world by advancing scholarship in the humanities, social sciences, and natural sciences. Its activities are supported by the UC Press Foundation and by philanthropic contributions from individuals and institutions. For more information, visit www.ucpress.edu.

University of California Press
Oakland, California

Library of Congress Cataloging-in-Publication Data

Names: Naremore, James, author.
Title: Charles Burnett : a cinema of symbolic knowledge / James Naremore.
Description: Oakland, California : University of California Press, [2017] |
    Includes bibliographical references and index. |
Identifiers: LCCN 2017016678 (print) | LCCN 2017019353 (ebook) |
    ISBN 9780520960954 (ebook) | ISBN 9780520285538 (pbk. : alk. paper) |
    ISBN 9780520285521 (cloth : alk. paper)
Subjects: LCSH: Burnett, Charles, 1944—Criticism and interpretation. |
    African American motion picture producers and directors—United States.
Classification: LCC PN1998.3.B865 (ebook) | LCC PN1998.3.B865 N37 2017
    (print) | DDC 791.4302/33092—dc23
LC record available at https://lccn.loc.gov/2017016678

Manufactured in the United States of America

26 25 24 23 22 21 20 19 18 17
10 9 8 7 6 5 4 3 2 1

For Darlene Sadlier, who helped in more ways than I can count; for Jay Naremore (who writes novels under the name Jim), Amy Rubin (memoirist and photographer), and Alexander and Patrick Naremore (budding filmmakers); and in memory of Phyllis Klotman.

CONTENTS

ACKNOWLEDGMENTS

My thanks to the Motion Picture Academy of Arts and Sciences, which awarded me a scholar's grant in support of this book. Thanks also to Michael T. Martin, Brian Graney, and the staff of the Black Film Center Archive at Indiana University; to John Vickers and the staff of Indiana University Cinema; to Linda Harris Mehr, Matt Severson, and Elisabeth Cathcart of the Herrick Library in Los Angeles; and to Mark Quigley and the staff of the Research and Study Center at the UCLA Film and Television Archive. For individual help and advice, I'm especially grateful to Edward Dimendberg and Robert E. Kapsis, who read and supported the manuscript. Thanks also to Janet Cutler, Julie Dash, Allyson Field, Jonathan Rosenbaum, and Craig Simpson. As usual, I could never have written the manuscript without the help of my wife, Darlene J. Sadlier, a talented scholar and writer who read each chapter, gave me invaluable suggestions for improving things, and was always there with love and moral support.

Mary Francis, a former editor at University of California Press, initially contracted the project. Her successor, Raina Polivka, has been a great gift to me; unfailingly patient, intelligent, and encouraging, Raina provided editorial support beyond the call of duty when it was most needed. Her editorial assistant, Zuha Khan, cheerfully guided me through the production process; Sharon Langworthy was a fine copy editor, and the designers at the press did their work skillfully.

Portions of the book, in different forms, appeared in *Charles Burnett, a Troublesome Filmmaker*, edited by Maria Miguez and Victor Paz (Cantabria, Spain: Play-Doc Books, 2016); the March 2017 issue of *Black Camera: An International Journal*, edited by Michael T. Martin; the Summer 2017 issue of *Cineaste*, edited by Gary Crowdus; and the September 2017 issue of *The*

Ryder magazine, edited by Peter LoPilato. I am grateful to these publications for their help.

One of Charles Burnett's best producers, Carolyn Schroder, answered my e-mail questions and gave me permission to quote her; she also made it possible for me to talk with Burnett in Los Angeles. And I'm especially thankful for the help of Charles Burnett himself. I've never written about a filmmaker whom I have had the pleasure of meeting. In this case I tried to maintain a certain distance because I didn't want to distract him from his work or make my book seem "authorized." We had only a couple of conversations, and he kindly answered the factual questions I asked him via e-mail. (In the text, whenever I mention things Burnett told me, I'm referring to the e-mail remarks he gave me permission to use.) He also gave me a copy of his unproduced screenplay for *Man in a Basket* and a video of his seldom-seen *The Final Insult*. As anyone who knows him can probably tell you, he's a modest, generous man, always ready to give credit to others, whose considerable knowledge and strength of character are clothed in an unpretentious, gentle personality. He's not responsible for any errors in this book. It was an honor to meet him, and I hope I've done him justice.

ONE

A Cinema of Symbolic Knowledge

CHARLES BURNETT, WHOM CRITIC Jonathan Rosenbaum has described as the country's most important African American film director, is relatively unknown outside the world of committed cinephiles. One of the many reasons he deserves greater attention is that virtually the whole of his remarkable career has been devoted to the proposition that Black Lives Matter. His feature pictures have dealt with poor black families struggling to survive in Los Angeles (*Killer of Sheep* [1977]), generational or social-class tensions that threaten to split black families apart (*To Sleep with Anger* [1990]), police murders and incarcerations of innocent black men (*The Glass Shield* [1994]), black attempts to achieve literacy under the nightmarish conditions of plantation-era slavery (*Nightjohn* [1996]), and the bloody Namibian war for independence from South Africa (*Namibia: The Struggle for Liberation* [2007]). His experimental documentaries and short films have concerned the Nat Turner rebellion (*Nat Turner: A Troublesome Property* [2003]), the poverty of a black single mother (*When It Rains* [1995]), urban homelessness (*The Final Insult* [1997]), and the displacement of blacks in the wake of Hurricane Katrina (*Quiet as Kept* [2007]). Even his lively, semidocumentary celebration of blues music (*Warming by the Devil's Fire* [2003]) is filled with archival material showing that behind the music is a history of lynching and enforced labor of blacks in the American South. As I write he's at work on two documentaries, one about the 1960s civil rights movement to end segregated hospitals, and the other, in cooperation with the Watts Community Action Center, about chemical poisoning of water in South Central Los Angeles. He recently told Spanish interviewers that the "stand your ground" law and the wave of police shootings of unarmed blacks in the United States are reversions to pre-1960s terrorism directed against the black community. "I live in fear every day," he told the interviewers. "Every time my sons leave their house, I worry about them coming back" (Miguez and Paz 2016, 68–69).

To frame Burnett only in these terms, however, is to limit and potentially ghettoize his importance. Burnett is a major film artist whose work involves a nuanced representation of conflicts and affectionate bonds not only within black communities but also between blacks and whites; his films demonstrate generosity of spirit, defamiliarizing power, and general relevance as social criticism. "[T]o call yourself a black filmmaker," he has said, "is a political statement and has the effect of causing less opportunities to work or have your film produced. . . . People ask why I call myself a black filmmaker and I respond by saying that I was given that title because I didn't fit with the mainstream. The fact of the matter also is I do make films that focus on the black community. I'm like a subset because in actual fact I make films about America" (Miguez and Paz 2016, 65).

Unfortunately cultural, social, economic, and political conditions in the United States are such that a filmmaker of Burnett's integrity and sense of purpose is given few opportunities to reach a large public and sometimes even to practice his art. There's nothing obscure about his work (several of his pictures are straightforward history lessons aimed at teenagers), but he resists melodrama; doesn't traffic in sex and violence; and assumes a caring, thoughtful audience. Hence, his work doesn't appeal to your average Hollywood producer. In an era when "independent film" in the United States has become a signifier of niche marketing, Burnett has remained about as authentic an independent as one can be and is faced with all the disadvantages and disappointments such a position entails. Filmmaking, he has pointed out, requires "people who can finance a film and understand what you're trying to do and agree and sympathize with you and who feel the same passion you do and want to help you get it done. In this business, it doesn't happen that way. You have to take an idea and try to sell it to people . . . Some people don't get it and you go in knowing it's going to be a hard sell" (Martin and Julien 2009, 29).

Burnett's 16mm *Killer of Sheep*, completed in 1973 as an MFA thesis at the University of California, Los Angeles (UCLA), and shown at a few theatrical venues in 1977, has been listed as one of the one hundred essential pictures in U.S. history by the National Society of Film Critics and was among the first films to be designated a "National Treasure" by the Library of Congress, but it wasn't widely available for viewing until 2007, when it was restored by UCLA preservationist Ross Lipman and produced on DVD by Steven Soderbergh and Milestone Films. Burnett's next feature, the 35mm *My*

Brother's Wedding (1984), was completed with the partial assistance of a Guggenheim Fellowship and was well received by critics but took three years to make and was given only limited release. During the late 1970s and 1980s Burnett produced, wrote, directed, and photographed his films, plus photographing Haile Gerima's *Bush Mama* (1979), contributing photography and editing to Julie Dash's *Illusions* (1982), and writing and photographing Billy Woodberry's *Bless Their Little Hearts* (1984), all the while supporting himself by teaching filmmaking and working at a script agency in Los Angeles. A MacArthur "genius" grant and collaboration with Danny Glover and producer Edward Pressman helped him raise more than $1 million for his first widely exhibited picture, *To Sleep with Anger*, but digital versions of this extraordinary film were unavailable in the United States for many years. Burnett subsequently directed two films that might be described as Hollywood genre projects, *The Glass Shield* (1994) and *The Annihilation of Fish* (1999), although the results were unconventional by any standard; the first was handled unintelligently by Miramax and the second never found a distributor. He has also made several brilliant shorts and documentaries, as well as a series of made-for-television movies for such organizations as Disney, the Hallmark Channel, and Oprah Winfrey. He avoids the sleek comedy style made popular in recent years by black directors Kevin Rodney Sullivan and Tyler Perry, and this, together with his interest in emotion rather than blood-and-sex spectacle, has resulted in his finding only sporadic work at the margins of the marketplace, including the outstanding Disney TV movie *Nightjohn*; several short films; some documentaries; and the half-documentary, half-fictional *Nat Turner: A Troublesome Property*. Burnett's career has involved more than the usual battles to maintain financing and artistic control, even in the case of *Namibia: The Struggle for Liberation*, a wide-screen color film shot in Africa. The development of digital cinema has helped him in certain ways but has also required that he move away from the fundamentally photographic aesthetic with which he began. "I never really call myself a filmmaker," he once told Bernard Weintraub, "because of the fact that it's so infrequent that I do it" (interview in *New York Times*, January 30, 1997).

Since Burnett made that statement, he has directed fifteen films of varying lengths under varying production conditions for movie theaters or U.S. and European television, thus building an important if not widely known career. In this book I have tried to present a straightforward, reasonably comprehensive critical study of his work in roughly chronological fashion. I write for those who already know Burnett's films, but also in hopes of piquing the curiosity of those who may not know them. Because some of the films are difficult to see, I've interwoven detailed description with commentary. I haven't discussed several pictures that seem to me relatively unimportant. For example, I've omitted the ninety-minute PBS-TV documentary entitled *America Becoming* (1991), which he directed, photographed, and cowrote with the aid of a Rockefeller grant. It's a competent film about how immigrants have contributed to the national imaginary, but Burnett was bitterly disappointed by the restrictions PBS placed on him. He and his producer, Dai Sil Kim-Gibson, had to fight to include a segment on a black community in Philadelphia and were prevented from doing a segment on Native Americans; whenever their on-site discoveries conflicted with scholarly research, they were distrusted, and they had to follow predetermined dictates. "In the end," he has said, "it became a nightmare" (Miguez and Paz 2016, 67). I've also omitted discussion of one of his TV films, *Relative Stranger* (2008), which he directed for the Hallmark Channel. It tells the story of a former football star who has abandoned his middle-class family and been reduced to driving a cab in Chicago; when this character's father dies, he returns to the family for the reading of the will and gradually confronts his shame, healing old wounds. The sentimentality of the story is exacerbated by an almost wall-to-wall musical score, but Burnett does a fine job of keeping the acting understated, and gets an especially good performance from Eriq La Salle in the leading role.

Certain aspects of Burnett's work that I have emphasized in this book should be mentioned at the outset and can be described in terms of artists or films he has publicly praised. He once remarked to Michael Sragow at the *New York Times* that William Faulkner (like Burnett, born in Mississippi) was important because he "put race on the table" and because "the right to exist, how to exist, the power to endure were always part of his theme" (January 1, 1995). As Faulkner had put it in his Nobel Prize acceptance speech, he wanted to help readers "endure and prevail." Several of Burnett's films involve a physical and psychological struggle to endure under circumstances more impoverished and cruel than those in Faulkner's novels, but through an exact attention to suffering and a rueful sense of humor that Burnett's critics have underemphasized, they dramatize endurance and offer a measure of redemption. Burnett also shares something of Faulkner's reverence for preindustrial or agrarian culture: in his case, the arts, religion, and satirical folklore that blacks brought with them from the South into the northern and western cities. One of his recurring themes is the country versus the city, expressed through family traditions or manners that once helped enslaved or segregated communities survive but were later threatened by urban discrimination.

Much of Burnett's early work was shot in the streets using nonprofessional actors, and for that reason some commentators have assumed that Italian neorealism influenced him. When asked about this in interviews, he has praised Roberto Rossellini's *Paisan* (1946) and *Umberto D.* (1952), Pier Paolo Pasolini's *The Gospel According to St. Matthew* (1964), and Allesandro Blasetti's little-known *1860* (1934). He has also said that he admires the contrast between the neorealists' spare simplicity and underlying complexity, and that "you can't find any other form as poetic as neo-realism" (Martin and Julien 2009, 10). He usually adds, however, that he had no special interest in the Italians when he began. (More likely candidates for influence were the early films of Nelson Pereira dos Santos and Ousmane Sembene, which Burnett saw as a student at UCLA.) Armand White, in liner notes to the DVD edition of *Killer of Sheep*, emphasizes that "Burnett's astringent view of poverty and quotidian meanness is the opposite of DeSica's plangent sentiment." I agree, but there's something pertinent in Burnett's avowed interest in the "poetic." This may account for the fact that Jean Vigo's *L'Atalante* (1934) is one of his favorite pictures (Kapsis 2011, 66). Vigo's film achieves a mix of naturalistic asperity and surrealism, and in a somewhat analogous way Burnett's *To Sleep with Anger* infuses the story of an ordinary black family in Los Angeles with oneiric, magical, and folkloric qualities. *Killer of Sheep* is a more realistic kind of film, but its power derives in some degree from its beautifully selected music and almost magical images of poor children at play in the streets.

Children and young people are especially important in Burnett's films (another characteristic he shares with the neorealists, not only in Italy but also in Latin America). They function sometimes as onlookers, sometimes as leading characters or central points of view, and sometimes as the target audience. Significantly, his first student film with a synchronized sound track, the twenty-nine-minute *Several Friends* (1969), opens with a shot involving a child. The setting is a sunlit, dusty alleyway running behind fenced houses in the Watts area of Los Angeles. (It's the alley behind the house where Burnett once lived.) At the right of the screen a drunken soldier in a U.S. Army uniform staggers a few steps, gripping a whiskey bottle in one hand and weaving as if his legs are about to give way. At the left a little girl in a bright Sunday dress, not much older than a toddler, stands almost as unsteadily as the

soldier and looks on in mute confusion. Cut to a low-angle shot from over her shoulder as a car suddenly drives up and stops. Two young men lean out the car's window and one of them shouts, "Where's your daddy at?" The little girl awkwardly points a finger toward the drunkard. The car drives off, and from over the little girl's shoulder we see that the soldier has fallen to the ground and is barely conscious.

Several Friends isn't as bleak as this may sound; it has comic scenes, although it repeatedly emphasizes the characters' inability to deal with the social forces that determine their lives. A film of symptomatic vignettes, it was photographed in the neighborhood where Burnett grew up and is more typical of his early work and instincts as a filmmaker than are his more tightly plotted later films; like *Killer of Sheep*, it has the raw, nonjudgmental quality of a fly-on-the wall documentary, a loving sensitivity to quotidian speech and gesture, and the elliptical structure of jazz. In a larger sense, it's symptomatic of Burnett's abiding interests. Like everything he has done, it conveys an unpuritanical but moral concern. Unlike the face-on-the-barroom-floor melodramas of the D. W. Griffith era or the social-uplift films of Oscar Micheaux, it has less to do with individuals than with a community in need of a compass. The characters' loss of direction is the result of mostly unseen conditions outside the black ghetto (the uniformed black soldier gives indirect evidence of those conditions, especially when we realize that *Several Friends* was made at the height of the Vietnam War) but is intensified by the difficulty of achieving transformative consciousness from within the ghetto.

In "Inner City Blues" (1989), a short essay that serves as a kind of manifesto of Burnett's aims during the early period of his career, he compares poor American blacks to the Italian villagers in Ignazio Silone's novel *Bread and Wine*, in which a revolutionary tries to explain "that certain things—food and shelter and the right to happiness—belong to everyone, but the villagers can't conceive these things as a part of their reality" (223). In the ghetto, Burnett says, daily life is ruled by immediate, elemental responses to pain and pleasure; furthermore, "politically speaking, there is a large reactionary and/or chauvinistic point of view in the inner city" (224). The child in *Several Friends* is heir to an environment in which the ground for social action has been so deeply eroded or crushed by racism that it barely exists.

Conditions in U.S. cities have in some respects grown worse since Burnett began his career: black children are shot dead in the crossfire from neighborhood gangs, and innocent young black men continue to be killed by cops. In *Ghettoside: A True Story of Murder in America* (2015), Jill Leovy, a reporter for the *Los Angeles Times*, points out that although African American males make up only 6 percent of the U.S. population, they account for 40 percent of U.S. deaths by murder. They're also, as Ava DuVernay's 2016 documentary *13th* shows, by far the largest group of incarcerated prisoners in what amounts in many cases to a new form of slavery. The criminal justice system in most of the country has never properly served the black population, economic inequity has reached grotesque proportions, and forms of de facto segregation still exist. "One of the features of my community," Burnett writes in his 1989 essay, "is that it does not have roots; in essence it is just a wall with graffiti written on it" (225). The attempt to exert influence through cinema is inhibited or blocked, not only by the commercial marketplace but also by the larger culture's systematic attempt to destroy the black consciousness of history and tradition. "The situation is such," Burnett grimly observes, "that one is always asked to compromise one's integrity, and if the socially oriented film is finally made, its showing will generally be limited and the very ones it is made for and about will probably never see it" (224).

Even so, Burnett wants to do whatever he can to restore his community's values and show that "we are a moral people." This requires, he argues, "humanizing" stories, modern analogs to "the negro folklore which was an important cultural necessity that not only provided humor but was a source of symbolic knowledge" (1989, 224–25). Burnett does not mean "symbolic" here in the way symbolist poets or semioticians do. He means simply that folk wisdom and knowledge are often communicated through the images and actions of stories, and his emphasis on knowledge, especially moral knowledge, is significant because Burnett is in many ways an educator. I have used "symbolic knowledge" in the subtitle of this book as an indicator of what seems to me his primary aim. As we shall see, virtually all his work—even the films set in middle-class environments and modern periods—aspires to the humor, social purpose, and moral lessons of the old folklore. Whatever the style or mode of his films, whatever audience he addresses, whatever production circumstances he works under (they have been various), and whatever degree of artistic success he achieves, he deals with the basic social concerns of America. He offers us a cinematic repository of moral narratives and symbolic knowledge that tries to hold communities together and enable them to endure.

TWO

Beginnings

BURNETT WAS BORN IN VICKSBURG, MISSISSIPPI, on April 13, 1947, but when he was age three, as part of a diaspora of blacks from the Deep South who were seeking employment in West Coast industries, he and his family moved to Watts in South Central Los Angeles. The area takes its name from a farmer who bought a small amount of acreage in 1886 and sold it when it was about to become an important railroad hub (the Watts train station is a historic landmark). The earliest population was made up of Hispanic rail workers and black Pullman porters, but in the 1940s a huge number of southern blacks moved to Watts to raise families in specially built housing projects. Los Angeles was blatantly racist, and many black people in Watts were confined to their neighborhood. Yet there was work to be had in the community until the early 1960s; in the summer, for example, the young Burnett could get jobs with carpenters or construction crews.

By the mid-1960s the railroad was rusting away, the heavy industry was gone, and much of the black population had become grimly poor. In 1965 the Watts riots broke out: a chaotic explosion of violence prompted by the arrest of a single youth by the California Highway Patrol after years of systematic police brutality against residents. (The young man's name was Marquette Frye, and he and Charles Burnett had been in junior high school together.) In the mid-1970s, at the time when Burnett made *Killer of Sheep*, Hispanic gang culture was on the rise, stimulated by the growing drug trade, but it was not until the late 1980s that the notorious battles between the Bloods and the Crips made Watts a war zone. The warring factions signed a peace treaty in 1992, the same year as the Rodney King riots. By that time many poor blacks were moving back to the South, and Chicanos were becoming a larger presence in a community of mostly single-parent families who lived in rented housing.

Burnett was raised chiefly by his mother and grandmother. His father joined the military and was seldom seen. "He didn't have any impact at all," Burnett told Manona Wali in 1988 (Kapsis 2011, 15). His mother, who worked as a nurse's aide, left home at four in the morning and usually didn't return until evening; therefore, his grandmother quit her job and watched over Burnett, requiring him to go to church before she would let him go to the movies. He never became truly religious, but his grandmother's sense of right and wrong was a lasting influence. Her love of spirituals, together with his mother's love of blues, eventually shaped his taste in music. As a child he learned to play the trumpet and became interested in photography and films. The "race" pictures of Oscar Micheaux and Spencer Williams predated this period and were no longer available, but he saw old adventure serials, Universal horror films, and Tarzan movies. He remembers that he and his friends cheered when Tarzan wiped out a whole village of black warriors (Kapsis 2011, 16).

Like most boys in Watts, Burnett had to learn boxing as a survival skill, but at least he didn't have to worry about armed killers or dangerous drug addicts (Kapsis 2011, 14). He managed to stay relatively clear of gang activity and unlike some other kids never became an alcoholic or a pill popper. In high school he grew increasingly aware of institutionalized racism because of the way teachers tacitly assumed their students were never going to amount to anything and tried to shove boys into shop class. (They resembled Supreme Court Justice Antonin Scalia, who in 2015 argued that affirmative action should be overturned; the poor black students, he said, should go to schools where grading was less strict.) After graduation, partly because he wanted to avoid being drafted into the military, Burnett earned a practical degree in electronics from Los Angeles Community College (LACC). He soon realized, however, that he was never going to be happy in a technical job. Fortunately, while at LACC he took a writing class taught by Isabelle Ziegler, who became the next major influence in his life. Her students were working class, experienced, and aspirational; Ziegler had them read widely in European and American literature and write short stories, novels, and plays. Burnett has recalled that she asked him, "'What is your ax to grind?'" (Miguez and Paz 2016, 74).

Although Burnett had become interested in photography while in high school, the only motion picture lens he could look through was attached to an old 8mm movie camera owned by a friend. He remembers using it once to photograph an airplane in the sky as it approached Los Angeles International

Airport. For a while he considered becoming a photojournalist. "I spent time at the library looking at old black and white photos of people and events," he told me. "I wanted to capture what was going on in my community. I bought an old 35mm still camera and went out immediately to start documenting things. . . . The first thing I came upon was a lady who had died of an overdose lying in the doorway of an apartment. Police were standing around keeping people away, but they didn't bother me when I started taking pictures of the lady. When I had to stop to change film I stood under a tree on the sidewalk reloading. A young, attractive teen-age girl who had cerebral palsy slowly made her way up to me. I saw her out of the corner of my eye. She stopped in front of me and very politely asked me why I was taking pictures. I didn't know what to say. I said something stupid, like, 'Oh, for fun.' She said to me, you take pictures of tragedies for fun. I put my camera away, and that was the end of my attempt at photo journalism."

He was much happier in Ziegler's class. Intellectually curious and possessed of an artistic temperament, he got a night job at the main branch of the LA public library and began going to movies in his spare time. As he grew older, the first film he saw with which he could identify in a strong personal sense was Robert M. Young and Michael Roemer's *Nothing but a Man* (1963), a love story about a railroad section hand and a preacher's daughter, which deals intelligently with conflicts of both class and race and features an exceptional music score by Motown artists. In 1980 Burnett told a French interviewer that he especially admired this film because it was about "a young man and his wife working hard to survive in a racist environment. The movie is full of anger but without hate" (Kapsis 2011, 3–4). Other films he liked when he was young (all of them re-releases) were Delmer Daves's *The Red House* (1947), a rural melodrama about class tensions; Rudolph Mate's *D.O.A.* (1950), a noir thriller with documentary footage of San Francisco streets; and especially Jean Renoir's *The Southerner* (1945), a harsh but lyrical film about the lives of dirt-poor southern tenant farmers. At least one critic has compared Burnett to Renoir, because both men are skilled directors of ensembles who tend to give all the characters their reasons (Kim 2003, 8–9). What Burnett especially admired about *The Southerner* was its tendency to treat all the poor with equal dignity: "They were all sharecroppers, white and black, and sharecropping was hard for everyone. The rich landowners were the ones who benefited. Not the poor whites who were fighting for the same scraps from the master's table. Renoir showed it" (Kim 2003, 9).

The 1960s were at least in some ways good years for the arts in the black community of Los Angeles. "The Watts Writers Workshop [inspired by Malcom X] was booming," Burnett told an interviewer. "Until—it was rumored—an FBI informant burned it down" (Kapsis 2011, 16). Burnett wasn't involved in the workshop, but he had a growing awareness of the political determinants of life in Watts and was preparing to examine that life through writing and filmmaking. It was against this background that he gained admission and financial support to study film at UCLA, an inexpensive school at the time, with $15 per quarter tuition for in-state residents. Burnett enrolled in 1967, earning a BA in theater arts and creative writing in 1971 and an MFA in 1977. One reason for his long stay there was that he could make excellent use of UCLA's free cameras and equipment, and he became important as a student instructor. He had arrived at the right moment. While at the university he was a leader and facilitator of what was arguably the most important black cultural formation in the United States since the Harlem Renaissance.

THE L.A. REBELLION

In those days Los Angeles was, and to a considerable degree still is, an unofficially segregated city, but Burnett found the atmosphere in Westwood strikingly different from the world he had known in Watts, which resembled a semirural extension of the black South, or what he described as a "displaced" community. One of his strongest memories as a schoolchild was when his teacher wrote "poor," "middle class," and "rich" on a blackboard and asked the students in which category they belonged. Burnett assumed he was middle class, but the teacher told him he was poor; he had never seen life outside his neighborhood and didn't know his own condition.

It would have been difficult for him to acquire that knowledge, because Watts was rather like an apartheid area in lockdown. As a teenager Burnett was occasionally stopped by members of the Los Angeles Police Department (LAPD) as he walked down the street; his pockets were searched, and had he been carrying as much as a seed of marijuana, he would have gone to jail (Martin and Julien 2009, 23). At UCLA in the late 1960s and 1970s, however, he moved freely and lived in an apartment where the hallways were filled with the smoke from burning joints. "I was terrified," he recalled. "But the campus police would pretend like nothing was going on" (Martin and Julien

2009, 23). Some of his anxiety was well justified. In 1970 he was mistakenly arrested and held in jail for a weekend because he had been traveling in an automobile that was used in a robbery.

During those years antiwar protests were spreading, feminist and black-power rebellions were gaining media attention, and the impulse toward national liberation was taking root throughout the "Third World." At the same time, the civil rights movement and affirmative action were helping make institutions like UCLA somewhat more multiracial. There were nevertheless potentially explosive relations between privileged white students and students of color. In 1968, a year after Burnett's arrival, a small group of students and faculty formed the ad hoc Media Urban Crisis Committee (MUCC, also known as the "Mother Muccers') and staged a series of protests that caused the university to establish a pilot program in "ethno-communications." As David E. James has explained, this program, which began with thirteen students from a variety of ethnic and racial backgrounds and remained important not only for blacks but also for Asians and Chicanos, "was modelled on the film school's main production training, which required a number of 8 and 16mm shorts, followed by a thesis film, and the production courses were supplemented by seminars on Third World aesthetics and community involvement. Elyseo Taylor, a former U.S. Army cinematographer and one of the first blacks hired in the film school, played a leading role, and Charles Burnett, one of the few blacks in the film school proper, was engaged as a teaching assistant" (2005, 304).

Elyseo Taylor was a key figure in the education of Burnett and other black students, among them Ben Caldwell, Larry Clark, Zeinabu Irene Davis, Julie Dash, Jamma Fanaka, Haile Gerima, Ali Sharon Larkin, Barbara McCullough, and Billy Woodberry. He was already training teenagers in Watts in amateur filmmaking, and at UCLA he taught a course called Film and Social Change that was especially important for Burnett because its objective was "to get people of color to tell stories about their community" (Kim 2003, 9). Taylor's seminars in Third World aesthetics, and similar courses later taught by Teshome Gabriel, introduced students to the twin manifestos of Latin American "Third Cinema": Glauber Rocha's (1965) "Aesthetics of Hunger" and Julio Garcia Espinosa's (1969) "For an Imperfect Cinema," both of which argued that revolutionary, socially liberating films made by and for oppressed people must willingly embrace the standards of low-budget production, avoiding slickness, spectacle, and the formulas of commercial entertainment. (As Rocha put it, "Wherever there is a filmmaker prepared to stand up against commercialism, exploitation, pornography and the tyranny of technique, there will be the living spirit of *Cinema Novo*.") Taylor hosted a campus visit by Ousmane Sembene and a delegation of visiting African filmmakers and showed students examples of "imperfect cinema" by such committed Latin Americans and Africans as Rocha (*Black God, White Devil* [1964]), Sembene (*Black Girl* [1965]), Nelson Pereira dos Santos (*Barren Lives* [1963]), and Fernando Solinas (*Hour of the Furnaces* [1968]).

In 1971 Taylor directed *Black Art/Black Artists*, a fifteen-minute color documentary about black painters that suggests the kinds of ideological and aesthetic issues he was discussing with his students. Centering on a museum exhibit of black painting and fine art in Los Angeles, the documentary is backed by jazz and blues music and features offscreen commentary by Van Slater, a political activist, woodcut artist, and teacher at Compton Community College. Slater argues that the 1960s were the beginning of "black art that represents a black point of view." In the nineteenth century, he points out, black painting in the United States was technically indistinguishable from white painting and was largely overlooked, and in the period of the Harlem Renaissance it was preoccupied with modernist depictions of nightclub highlife—the sort of thing that white patrons found more appealing than, say, paintings of black families and children. Middle-class blacks, Slater observes, tended to purchase black art that had been approved by white critics. True black art, he insists, would emerge only when it began to reflect the ideas and full experience of black people. Such art, whatever forms it might take, could embrace different ideas or attitudes: if two black artists looked at the same dying neighborhood, for example, one might see beauty in decay and the other might see evidence of a failing society.

Partly as a result of exposure to these ideas, Taylor's students began to assume an activist, adversarial role in the film program. Willie F. Bell, a black student from the South, curated a series of films by Oscar Micheaux, a director Burnett had never heard of and was excited to discover. When a white teacher wanted to avoid talking about "sociological" aspects of *Birth of a Nation* and concentrate on formal matters, Haile Gerima and Francisco Martinez carried him bodily out of the classroom and took over the discussion. But at least one white teacher was a positive influence: Basil Wright, a pioneer of the British documentary movement, taught a course that Burnett took early in his student years and greatly admired. Wright had been chiefly responsible for *Nightmail* (1936), the most famous of the British General Post Office films, which has a poetic-realist quality enhanced by W. H. Auden's verse narration. Wright's somewhat earlier *Song of Ceylon* (1935) especially impressed Burnett; neocolonial in politics, it nevertheless has a quietly subversive attitude toward the alienated labor of colonial subjects, a sensitive feeling for daily life among poor Sri Lankan families, and a lyric imagery of children at play. Wright was a fine writer about film (he succeeded Graham Greene as the film critic for the London *Spectator* and wrote two film books, *The Use of Film* [1948] and *The Long View* [1974]), but most important, Burnett has said, he gave the students in his classes a conviction that "'one had to approach filmmaking from a humanistic point of view'" (quoted in Klotman 1991, 95). Burnett also recalls being introduced by Wright to Dutch filmmaker Joris Ivens, whose globe-hopping career began with semiabstract, avant-garde experiments in montage and led to politically radicalized films that mixed newsreels, reenactments, and on-the-spot footage. Like Wright, Ivens was a social activist (he was blacklisted in the United States in the early 1950s) who was possessed of a lyrical temperament. Whether he was exploring the condition of Belgian coal miners (*Borinage* [1934]), the daily life of U.S. rural families in the Great Depression (*Power and the Land* [1940]), or Vietnam's revolution (the collaborative *Far from Vietnam* [1967]), his work had an aesthetic sensitivity to movement, light, and photographic texture.

At UCLA Burnett studied languages (French, German, Italian, Russian, and Spanish), read Georg Lukács and Frantz Fanon, and immersed himself in production. In those days the film school was relatively open to experiment and less geared toward Hollywood than its equivalent at the University of Southern California, which saw itself as a feeder for the industry. The year after Burnett arrived, and when "ethno-communications" was born, Francis Ford Coppola received an MFA from UCLA for *You're a Big Boy Now*, which served as a calling card for his subsequent Hollywood career. But students in Westwood, especially the black students, weren't expected to follow Coppola's path. The school didn't court the studios by creating specializations in producing, directing, writing, or cinematography, and students weren't taught how to get agents or pitch projects; instead they learned the entire movie technology and often shot films on the streets, recruiting amateurs for their casts and crews. In a 1994 interview with Aida A. Hozic, Burnett looked back on the important education he had received in those years and lamented how much things had changed:

If you go [today] to UCLA where everyone is nineteen years old, has seen the same movies, and has the same background, you cannot learn anything from each other. It is no wonder that the kids can only think of selling movies. . . . People are not interested in talking about issues. I have been lecturing at colleges and find it very frustrating. The kids just want to earn a certain number of credit units. It is maddening. At UCLA, the students are not interested in experimenting; they want to learn how to write these very slick movies. When I was going to school . . . one of the great things was that you better not come back with a film that was a cliché or ordinary or something that someone had seen before. . . . It was very competitive in this sense: people were afraid of sharing their ideas and they guarded them like babies. And if you worked on something, you did not do it because you needed a job—you just did it because you had a passion for it. But now, God, I was over there and I was so disappointed. I felt raped. (Kapsis 2001, 84)

Out of the freewheeling, politically aware atmosphere at UCLA in the 1960s and 1970s, a wave of U.S. black independent filmmaking emerged. (At roughly the same moment, a smaller manifestation of black cinema was developing in New York, beginning with Bill Gunn's *Ganja and Hess* [1973] and culminating in Kathleen Collins's *Losing Ground* [1982]; see Klotman 1991.) Historians initially referred to the UCLA group as "the Los Angeles school," but as a result of a 1984 retrospective organized by Clyde Taylor at the Whitney Museum, it came to be known as "the L.A. Rebellion." Burnett was at its forefront, directing his own films and serving as a kind of mentor for Woodbury, Dash, and Larkin (Larkin dubbed him "the professor"). This is not to say, however, that he was the leader of a homogeneous collective or conscious movement. The UCLA group was composed of individual artists with their own interests and was no more stylistically cohesive than a group like the French New Wave had been (in retrospect, Truffaut, Godard, Rohmer, and the others in this group are quite different from one another). Unlike most movements, it never promoted itself via a journal or a manifesto, and when its work was first shown outside the walls of UCLA, it didn't give itself a name. The "Rebellion" might have had somewhat greater success if it had done these things.

Burnett and his cohort eventually achieved significant recognition at European film festivals, where motion pictures were recognized as art. His early work won prizes in Berlin and at a 1980 Paris retrospective of "black independent cinema," where his films were shown alongside those of Ben Caldwell, Larry Clark, and William Greaves. A French interviewer asked Burnett if he belonged to a kind of new wave. He responded, "No. We're not a single school of filmmakers sharing the same ideas. We are very independent. The only points we have in common is that we are Black and we feel close to the Third World" (Kapsis 2011, 3). In 1991 he told Berenice Reynaud much the same thing. He had stayed in touch with other filmmakers from UCLA, "But it wasn't a rebellion. Clyde [Taylor] and I argue about his use of the term. When we went to UCLA, we tried to form groups at different times to facilitate filmmaking. But it wasn't a 'school' of Black filmmakers, or a conscious effort. Things just happened" (Kapsis 2011, 57; for Clyde Taylor's view, see "Once Upon a Time in the West . . . L.A. Rebellion," in Field, Horak, and Stewart 2015, ix–xxiv. See also two other essays in that volume: Chuck Kleinhans's retrospective commentary on the L.A. formation in light of subsequent changes in black cinema and its audiences [57–82] and Michael T. Martin's essay on what he prefers to call "the Los Angeles Collective" or "L.A. School" [196–224]).

Like most other members of the UCLA group, Burnett had no wish to become a Hollywood director; indeed, he had no plans for a career. Much of his work was fashioned in a rough, "imperfect" style that paradoxically required great artistic judgment and considerable technical skill. He eschewed the "well-made" narratives of both commercial and certain types of social realist pictures. Too many films of the Left, he argued, "would present an abstract worker against management. . . . They had this sort of A-B-C-D quality—that if you do A and B, then C would follow'" (Kapsis 2011, 6). In contrast, he emphasized the domestic sphere and the relatively subtle things that happen between people in everyday life. Reacting against cause-effect plots, he avoided stories about growth, change, and the resolution of conflict. Instead he concentrated on the pressures that poverty exerts on families and friendships and the struggle of black families to exist with dignity; as he put it in an interview with Michael Sragow, using a language that has come to be identified with the "survivalist" branch of black sociology, he was trying to depict situations in which "you don't necessarily win battles; you survive" (Kapsis 2011, 98).

Burnett and the other black filmmakers of the "L.A. Rebellion" were nevertheless recognizable as a distinct cultural formation, and like any cultural formation in modern society, they tended to define themselves in opposition to an established standard. The Italian neorealists had been against glossy studio films, the French New Wave against "the tradition of quality," and the Latin American and Third Cinema movements against all forms of Western cultural imperialism. Burnett's group had something in common with all these formations, but Burnett and most of his fellow students reacted more specifically against the blaxploitation pictures of the early 1970s and the films about black gangsters that appeared intermittently in US theaters over the next two decades. The short-lived blaxploitation cycle, prompted by the runaway success of three historically significant black-directed films—*Sweet Sweetback's Baadasssss Song* (1971), *Shaft* (1971), and *Superfly* (1972)—was exactly contemporary with Burnett's years at UCLA and spawned several B-picture, action-genre vehicles for black actors (*The Legend of Nigger Charley* [1972], *Black Caesar* [1973], *Slaughter's Big Rip-Off* [1973], *Blacula* [1973], *The Mack* [1973], *The Black Godfather* [1974], etc.). Popular with certain black audiences and promoted as if blacks had created them, some of these films were in fact produced, written, and directed by whites, and their gestures toward social rebellion tended to be confined chiefly to the image of the hero as outlaw and superstud. All of them had the sensational qualities of traditional exploitation cinema and resembled what could be called a hustler's version of the cinema of poverty. They confirmed Burnett's deepest distrust of Hollywood. As he later declared, "The studios are not interested in depicting life in a realistic way. Films create myths about black people. . . . I think that the studios project this image of being really what they're not, sort of liberal institutions. . . . Most of the films they show are action-packed dramas about drugs and so forth. . . . The only perceptions these people have of us are basically drugs and mothers who prostitute themselves" (Kapsis 2011, 71).

The UCLA group's characterization of its blaxploitation "other" was somewhat oversimplified, and the question of what constituted black cinema was debated for many years afterward (for a recent, postmodern example, see Gillespie 2016). Nevertheless, unlike a later generation of more commercially oriented black directors that includes Spike Lee, John Singleton, and Carl Franklin, Burnett and his cohort avoided making films about dope dealers and gangsters. (One exception to the rule was Jamma Fanaka, but his films can be viewed as critical of blaxploitation; see Horak 2015, 119–55.) Instead they made antigenre films about racism, police brutality, sexual stereotyping, and the quotidian experience of black people. Some of their early films were striking for the way they deliberately broke the formal rules of continuity editing and conventional screenwriting.

PROJECTS ONE, TWO, AND THREE

Like everyone in the production school at UCLA, the black students had to fulfill three filmmaking assignments. Project One, for which the individual student acted as writer/director/photographer/editor, was a short film in 16mm or Super 8, without synchronized sound but with the possibility of magnetic stripe. (Magnetic stripe, or "mag stripe," is a strip of recording tape attached to one edge of a roll of film, allowing for music and post-synch sound, but requiring a special projector.) Project Two was a longer 16mm film with synch sound, made in collaboration with other students. Project Three was a short film with synch sound.

Unfortunately, Burnett's untitled Project One (1968) has been lost. Allyson Field, who researched all the Project One films made by the black students, has found that it was shot with a Bolex camera, a Switar lens, and 8mm Kodak color. (See Field's excellent essay on the Project One films by the students of color, who deliberately set out to "unlearn" the usual codes of narrative cinema, in Field, Horak, and Stewart 2015, 83–118.) Michael Cummings, a friend of Burnett, played a black painter who strangles his white model after making love to her. This plot sounds uncharacteristic of Burnett; it may have owed something to the combined influence of Richard Wright's *Native Son* and Eldridge Cleaver's *Soul on Ice*, the latter of which, with its essay "White Woman, Black Man," was published during Burnett's first year at UCLA.

In chapter 1 I described the opening scenes of Burnett's Project Two, the 16mm, black-and-white, twenty-nine-minute *Several Friends* (1969), which is a more ambitious and original film, signaling a major talent. It, too, deals with interracial sex, but it has a looser, less goal-directed narrative; episodic in structure, it was originally planned as a feature-length picture and resembles a trial run or preparatory experiment for *Killer of Sheep*. Like *Killer*, it was shot in a poor area of Watts using local players and documentary-style photography (the photographer was Jim Watkins, but the compositions are Burnett's). It shares two actors with the later film and has the same affective mixture of grimness, humor, and melancholy. It even has a few incidents that seem to foreshadow *Killer*: a butcher kills, plucks, and strings up the carcasses of chickens; two men spend a good deal of time trying to repair an old car; and the same two men struggle to move a large machine into a house.

The film's action involves several minor characters who provide a relatively broad view of life in Watts. In an early scene, for example, we follow the car that drove past the child and the drunken soldier in the opening shots. Two men are in the front seat, a third is in the back reading a newspaper, and next to him is a young woman wearing a tight miniskirt and a stylish hat. Chattering among themselves with the air of neighborhood hipsters, they're trying to pool their money to buy a bottle of wine. When they drive up to a liquor store, they encounter two drunken men clumsily fighting in the street, one of whom has been dragged from a shiny Cadillac and appears to be taking a beating. A small crowd has gathered, but neither the onlookers nor the men in the car are inclined to intercede. The young woman in the back seat is curious and concerned. She wants to "see what we can do" because there's always a chance "something can be avoided." She steps out of the car and walks toward the fight in her dressy high heels, but she's ineffectual; as the awkward battle in the street continues, a dandified fellow, maybe a pimp, tries to pick her up. The scene ends with a surreal juxtaposition: a young man and woman on a horse ride up to the Cadillac and watch the clumsy fight.

The film chiefly involves three unemployed male friends who spend much of their day in fruitless or frustrating pursuits. Andy (Andy Burnett) has an expectant wife who keeps their small house in good order despite their quarrelsome marriage; when she tries to watch a snowy TV show, he goes to the record player and jacks up the volume on Dee Irwin's soulful 1968 hit, "I Only Get This Feeling." Later, out in the front yard, Andy and his pal Gene (Eugene Cherry) unsuccessfully work on a dilapidated car. Crawling under the vehicle, Andy gets grease and motor oil on himself and remarks that he hasn't had a bath in some time. Just then a ground-level shot shows a new car pulling up and shiny male shoes getting out, followed by female high heels. The male shoes belong to another of Andy's pals, Bracy (Charles Bracy, who was Burnett's classmate in high school and at LACC, and who plays virtually the same loud, boisterous character in *Killer of Sheep*). The female shoes, one of which slips off a nyloned foot and has to be slipped back on, belong to Sharon, Bracy's newfound white girlfriend (Donna Deitch, one of Burnett's UCLA classmates, who went on to become a film director). Sharon asks if she can use the bathroom and goes into the house while the three men stand outside. Bracy boasts that Sharon is a "Hollywood broad" rich enough to own the new car, and proposes that Andy and Gene join him and her along with a couple of her female friends, also "Hollywood broads," for a hot party that evening. Inside the house we see a brief exchange between Sharon and Andy's wife: the younger white woman, wearing a silken dress, pauses as she exits and thanks the unsmiling black woman, who is wearing an old frock. Meanwhile, Andy and Gene have more or less agreed to Bracy's proposal. After Bracy and Sharon leave, however, the two men spend the rest of the day trying to move a washing machine from the front yard into Andy's small kitchen. When Bracy returns that evening, Andy and Gene are shirtless, dirty, and exhausted. The three gather around the kitchen table, and Bracy loudly complains, "I got a couple of fine broads out there waiting!" The night is ruined, he moans, because Andy has no time to shower and would be "goin' out stinking like a damned skunk!" Gene quietly defends himself and his friend: "We ain't hippies, though."

For Project Three, Burnett wrote, directed, and edited a fourteen-minute, 16mm color film, *The Horse* (1973), based on one of his unpublished short stories. Compared with his other UCLA films, *The Horse* is a stylistic anomaly, but it gives clear evidence of his considerable talent as a director of short subjects. The film was shot in the picturesque California countryside of Paso Robles, several hundred miles outside Los Angeles, during a hiatus in the preparation of *Killer of Sheep*, which had encountered a delay because the actor Burnett originally wanted for the lead role was in prison. In an indirect way, *The Horse* was influenced by the interconnected stories in William Faulkner's *Go Down, Moses,* especially by "The Bear," which Burnett had dreamed of adapting. "I wanted to do something on [Faulkner's] personal South," he told French interviewers in 1990, "where everything is said and explained in a symbolic way" (Kapsis 2011, 48).

The Horse ultimately centers on what at first seems a minor character, a young black boy who witnesses the execution of an ill and dying old horse. Beautifully photographed by Ian Connor, it has minimal dialogue and an evocative sound design by Burnett of birdsong, gusts of wind, the minatory creak of an old windmill, and a few moments of nondiegetic music (Samuel Barber's musical setting for James Agee's "Knoxville: Summer of 1915"). In part because of its brevity and minimalism, one might call it a symbolic film, but only in a qualified sense. Burnett was bemused when some viewers tried to decode the imagery as if they were watching a religious allegory. His symbolism, like that of Faulkner and other modern artists, is entirely in the service of a realist, albeit lyrical and relatively ambiguous, narrative; in other words, the characters in *The Horse* are representative of a general culture, but the meanings of their behavior are conveyed obliquely, almost mysteriously, through the connotative force and open-ended suggestiveness of images, gestures, and sounds.

The opening shot provides a kind of signifying map for the entire action. From atop a high hill on a clear, sunny day we look down at a distant car moving along a winding, fenced road and turning into the dusty drive of a dark, dilapidated house. The landscape on the far horizon is mountainous, clearly Californian rather than southern, but the decayed house down below suggests a vaguely Faulkneresque world of dead or dying agricultural plutocracy. There are shabby outbuildings behind the house and a large, dry field in front, where we can make out the tiny, isolated figures of a horse, a boy, and a man. The car stops, and three men get out and walk toward the house.

Burnett cuts from this Olympian viewpoint to one of the closest shots in the film: as in *Several Friends*, he introduces a character by means of a ground-level, tightly framed close-up of shoes, thus conveying information about gender, social class, and aspects of personality. In this case, we see expensive, two-toned Oxfords and Argyle socks. The man wearing them stamps on the front porch of the house, ridding the shoes of dust. Another man, wearing brown dress shoes, goes stomping up rickety stairs to retrieve something from inside the house. Meanwhile, the man out in the field, wearing black shoes, walks back and forth, talking to himself and worrying: "I told them they could have the job. I don't know. I just don't know if it's worth it." When the fellow who has gone into the house returns bearing a box, Burnett reveals all the characters in the scene: three white men are gathered on the porch, looking out on the field, where a white man paces around restlessly and a black boy in jeans and T-shirt gently strokes a gaunt, sway-backed horse.

Most of the film is devoted to a sinister dead time in which everyone waits for the arrival of something that hasn't been explained. The three men on the porch are sharply individuated by their looks, behavior, and costume, but none seems interested in being there. One is quiet and white-haired, wearing a rumpled business suit; another is impatient, preoccupied with maintaining the sharp creases in his pants; and a third, wearing denim work clothes, is bored, sitting listlessly on the edge of the porch. The man in the field, who has a brooding, patrician air vaguely like a character such as Faulkner's Gavin Stevens in *Go Down, Moses,* walks forward to claim something from the white-haired man and then asks the fellow in denim, "You found a job yet?" "That's right," the fellow answers, "you mentioned it yesterday. I'm sorry." The flashily dressed man walks around a corner of the house to piss and returns to bum a cigarette from the white-haired man. "Ain't got all shitting day," he complains. "Where'd that boy come from? Why in hell do we have to wait for some nigger?" The man in denim stretches out to lie on his back. He takes a large pocketknife out of his jeans, opens it, and throws it lightly up to the roof of the porch; the blade sticks in the rotting wood, wobbles, and then falls, barely missing him. "One of these days you're going to find that thing stuck in your forehead," the flashy man says.

The wind blows, the windmill makes creaking sounds, and the black boy in the field keeps stroking the flanks of the old horse. Who are the white men on the porch, and what exactly is their relationship to one another? The film avoids answering but makes them seem old acquaintances, forming a strange, uneasy fraternity. As dusk approaches, they fall silent. In a wide shot we see the lights of a vehicle approaching down the long road to the house. It's an old dump truck, driven by a black man. When he arrives, the boy leaves the horse and runs joyfully to him, meeting his embrace. He's the boy's father (played by Larry Clark) and the figure everyone has been awaiting. The white man in the field removes a revolver from an oilcloth, loads it, and gives it to him. The irony of the situation is now evident: the boy's father has been hired as the horse's executioner, and the relatively well-to-do white men have been concerned about whether it was worth hiring him. For the first time, the film takes the boy's point of view. In close-up, he holds his hands over his ears and closes his eyes; after a moment, he opens them slightly, only to wince at the sound of gunfire. The film ends with a freeze-frame on his face. He has experienced not only the death of the horse, but also an act of killing imposed on his father.

The slaughter of an animal is a key element in the film, functioning chiefly as a kind of metonymic illustration of a society in which the cruelest, most psychologically damaging work is assigned to the poorest and least powerful. The father in *The Horse* is hired to kill a single animal at a moment when his son happens to be present, but the father in Burnett's MFA thesis film, *Killer of Sheep*, which was supported by an L.B. Mayer fellowship and budgeted at roughly $10,000, is hired to kill many animals on an almost daily basis, always out of sight of his family. *Killer of Sheep* is not only the culmination of a theme that had preoccupied Burnett, but also the climax of his work at UCLA. It was shot during weekends in Watts, using the local kids and other residents as both actors and crew. One of his major achievements and one of the most original American films ever made, it opened the way for his subsequent career.

———

THREE

Killer of Sheep *(1977)*

AS THE MAIN TITLE of *Killer of Sheep* appears over a black screen, a chorus of children's voices sings:

> Lull-a, lull-a, lull-a, lull-a by-by.
> Do you want the moon to play with?
> All the stars to run away with?
> They'll come if you don't cry.
> So, lull-a, lull-a, lull-a, lull-a by-by,
> In your mother's arms a creeping,
> And soon you'll be a sleeping.

Just before the song ends we see a tight close-up of a preadolescent boy with tearful, frightened eyes. The song fades into a man's angry voice from offscreen: "You let anyone jump on your brother and you just stand and watch, I'll beat you to death!" A slow retreat of the camera reveals a father berating his son: "I don't care who started what . . . you pick up a stick or a god damn brick!" The father, wearing a wife-beater T-shirt, is ill, fatigued, or maybe drunk; his speech is slurred, and at one point in the harangue he breaks into a coughing fit. Cut to a brief shot of a woman's torso as she stands in a kitchen doorway embracing a young child, his face buried in her perhaps pregnant stomach. A shot from behind the father shows the frightened son standing quiet, tense, trying to remain expressionless and accept humiliation. "Knock the shit out of whoever is fighting your brother," the father says, "because if something happens to me and your mother, you ain't got nobody in the world except your brother!" Cut to a thin old woman seated with her back to us in a poor but brightly lit kitchen, calmly leafing through a newspaper. Return to the father: "And if the son of a bitch is too big for you, come get me! Look, you're not a child any more. You'll soon be a god damn *man*! So start learning what life is about *now*, son!" The heavy woman exits the kitchen, smiling slightly; behind her, seated in the kitchen, we glimpse a teenage boy. In a reverse angle, the woman walks up to the boy who is being chastised and slaps him in the face. The screen goes black, and the rich bass voice of Paul Robeson sings the same tune we heard at the beginning.

This sequence contains seven shots and five camera setups, most of them close-ups. There's no establishing shot, and viewers work a bit to determine spatial and temporal continuity. The only dialogue is the father's angry rant, and some of the shots (the woman holding her child to her belly, the old woman reading a newspaper, and the male teenager glimpsed in the kitchen) generate questions that aren't answered. Burnett leaves it to us to sort out details and decide how the scene and the people in it will relate to everything that follows. The characters don't reappear, although some of the players can be glimpsed later in different roles. There's no causal, spatial, or temporal connection between this and any later scene, and thus the opening of the film takes on thematic or poetic rather than narrative importance. The film deals with the themes it dramatizes: black family life, the growth of black children into adulthood, the problem of becoming a "man," the relationship between black family and black community, and the chances of black survival in a dangerous world.

A great deal of the film centers on children, because, as Burnett has remarked, "without children, there is no survival. . . . In my community, the most important thing is to survive above all else, and children are taught that they have to support their brother, or their family, no matter what they do. . . . When you're growing up, it poses some moral problems. You become more and more insensitive: the only thing that matters is survival. This callousness gradually alienates you, distances you from other people and complicates relations in a peculiar way—survival implies a good deal of mistrust—particularly relations between men and women. That's why I show these children in *Killer of Sheep*, always there, attentive to what their parents are doing, witnesses of everyday drama" (Kapsis 2011, 8).

Throughout the film, music is as important as imagery. Burnett's eclectic compilation score ranges from King Oliver to Rachmaninoff but is chiefly associated with African American culture. The song that frames or bookends the opening sequence, called simply "Lullaby" in published credits for the film, is also known as "My Curly Headed Baby," one of a series of faux "plantation songs" by the classically trained Australian and later British composer George H. Clautsam, who in the early twentieth century wrote light operas and a single movie score. Clautsam's song was intended to be performed as art music, but its lyrics were written in a crudely phonetic, naively racist, appallingly bad imitation of southern black dialect. Paul Robeson later recorded the song, dispensing with phony dialect and giving the words simple dignity. Burnett's choice of it is significant, not only because *Killer of Sheep* concerns black families in Los Angeles who have ties to the Deep South, but also because of Robeson's historical importance as a black artist, star, and advocate for social progress. (Burnett has long wanted to make a film about Robeson.)

Burnett's treatment of music differs from a typical Hollywood picture because he seldom mixes it with diegetic sound, thus giving it a degree of independence and allowing it to function as counterpoint or commentary. But if the song at the beginning is intended as some sort of comment on the action, exactly what does it say? Obviously there's an ironic relationship between the song, which evokes parental love, peace, and celestial beauty, and the scene, which deals with parental punishment, violence, and danger. The song is about a child falling asleep in its mother's arms, the scene about a boy awakening into the duties of manhood and the imperative of survival; the song is comforting, the scene shocking; the song is dreamlike, the scene harshly realistic. But there's also a sense in which the song is coterminous with the scene, so that music and image aren't in complete conflict, and one doesn't take priority over the other. The song bleeds into the visual action in the form of a chorus of children's sweet voices and reemerges at the end in the form of a man's grave bass voice; it joins with and permeates the "plot" of the scene, lingering afterward like a poignant memory or yearning.

Killer of Sheep gradually develops a plot of sorts, made up of a series of vignettes involving the problems of a married black man with two children who works in a sheep slaughterhouse and suffers from depression. Burnett got the basic idea for the film from a man he often saw riding the bus in Los Angeles. "One day he happened to sit by me, and I had the opportunity to ask him what he did. He told me he worked at the slaughterhouse, and what he did was kill sheep. What they did then was they had a sledgehammer, and they would hit the animal in the head with the sledgehammer and crush the skull. And I just couldn't imagine someone doing that every day, day in and day out, without creating some nightmare effect" (Kapsis 2011, 166).

Burnett's central character and his wife have come to Los Angeles from the South and are trying to divest themselves of a "country" background, such as when the father tells his son to stop addressing his mother as "mot dear" (an old expression meaning "mother dear," made fun of in Tyler Perry's films about the character Madea), or when his wife admonishes their daughter for going barefoot. He's a proud man who at one point angrily claims he isn't poor: he's able to give a few things to the Salvation Army, he loans or gives small amounts of money to his friends, and unlike another man in the neighborhood, he doesn't have to survive by eating greens from vacant lots. Even so, he seems perpetually weary and dejected and is unable to make emotional contact with his family. During the film he undergoes a very modest emotional change for the better, but he doesn't achieve true progress; his day-to-day projects—helping a friend repair an old car, a trip to a racetrack— usually end in frustration, and he keeps the same awful job at the end that he had at the beginning.

This is a film lacking a clear resolution or a strong cause-effect relationship between events, centering on a man whose personal crisis is both economic and psychological. Burnett's purpose, he has explained, was to depict a character who works in terrible conditions but whose "real problems are within the family, trying to make that work and be a human being. You don't necessarily win battles; you survive" (Kapsis 2011, 98). Hence, as Manthia Diawara has pointed out, *Killer of Sheep* almost completely rejects the forward momentum of classic Hollywood and the typical social problem picture, "with its quest for the formation of the family and individual freedom, and its teleological trajectory (beginning, middle, and end)" (1993, 10). Like certain other black independent films, among them *Ganja and Hess* and *Daughters of the Dust* (Julie Dash, 1991), its form is "rhythmic and repetitious" and its narrative style "symbolic." It has something in common with "Black expressive forms like jazz, and with novels by such writers as Toni Cade Bambara, Alice Walker, and Toni Morrison, which stop time to render visible Black voices and characters" (Diawara 1993, 10–11).

In more specific terms, *Killer of Sheep* renders visible the 1970s black community in Watts. Burnett doesn't show us the area's most famous landmark: the Watts towers, a notable example of outsider art, constructed by Italian emigrant Simon Rodia in the period between 1921 and 1954. During Burnett's interview/commentary with Richard Peña on the Milestone DVD of the film, he says he wanted to depict more of the local life in the schools, but was unable to do so. He also doesn't show us churches; indeed, his central

character remarks that he hasn't been to church since he was "back home" in the South. Burnett nevertheless gives us documentary evidence of the city streets and produces striking images, some disturbing, some beautiful, of a kind that had never been seen in theatrically distributed movies. Most of his large cast was made up of nonprofessionals, including many children, who lived in Watts; some of them had even participated in or been witnesses to the Watts riots. One of his purposes was to encourage local participation and "demystify filmmaking in the community" (Evry 2007), but he also drama-tized aspects of daily life he had witnessed, creating a more personal sort of film than the Italian neorealists or the Brazilian *Cinema Novo*. Like *Several Friends*, his earlier student film about Watts, *Killer of Sheep* has a scene that was shot directly behind the house where Burnett once lived (it involves the theft of a TV in broad daylight). He knew people who stored car parts inside their houses to keep them from being stolen, just as a character in this film does; in fact, he once walked into a house and saw the entire front end of a car sitting on the floor. The dangerous games played by young people in the film are the same games he played.

Scattered throughout *Killer of Sheep* are short scenes of kids playing in the streets and of sheep going to slaughter. Burnett traveled to San Francisco with his lead actor to find a factory that would allow him to document the killing of sheep, which he photographed without the aid of a crew. He shows us ghostlike crowds of snowy ewes; a Judas goat leading the innocent to their deaths; sheep carcasses strung up on hooks and moved down an assembly line for butchery; sheep heads stuck on pikes and stripped of flesh, eyes, and brains; and sheep blood washed from floors. More often, he shows children running and playing their dangerous games in Watts. Boys throw rocks at one another, jump gracefully from rooftop to rooftop, and race bikes down the street chased by angry dogs. Sometimes they torment girls; when a girl in a sunlit, blindingly white dress starts hanging her white laundry on a sagging wash line, boys throw dirt over her and her clean clothes. Occasionally the girls get back at the boys; as a group of preteen girls dance in an alleyway, as a boy riding a bike enters from behind the camera, rides over to the group and shoves one of them, the girls push him, kick him, and break his bike. In another scene, a boy on a porch watches a couple of girls walk down a sunny sidewalk. "Look at them ol' ugly girls," he says loudly; the girls shout back "Your daddy is ugly!" and stroll off. "Wanna come here and fight?" the boy halfheartedly yells. In still another scene, a rangy girl climbs onto a rooftop and leads a group of boys in a rock-throwing fight; as she aggressively tosses missiles at kids on the street below, one of the boys on the roof suffers an injured wrist and tries to make his way down, wincing and wiping away his tears.

When the kids aren't playing, they're silent, sometimes amused witnesses of rough adult behavior, as when a drunken man in an army uniform is forced out of an apartment by an angry woman bearing a gun. Burnett's treatment of them has a complex tone, often humorous and remarkably unjudgmental. He never sentimentalizes the children or looks away from their occasional cruelty; at the same time, he repeatedly shows their ingenuity, curiosity, and energy. Manohla Dargis has rightly compared some of his images of kids in Watts to the photos of legendary New York street photographer Helen Levitt, who specialized in still pictures of children's games. Levitt's sixteen-minute, 16mm film *In the Street* (1945–1952), a straight documentary photographed in New York's Spanish Harlem in collaboration with James Agee and Janice Loeb, has almost no scenes of raw poverty and far less roughhouse play than *Killer of Sheep*, but it resembles Burnett in its humane respect for the anarchic spirit of children and its awareness of the beauty in their improvised amusements. In *Killer of Sheep*, children have very few things to improvise *with*—a few bikes, an old top, a string of unexploded cap-pistol caps, a gum wrapper, a rubber mask, a beat-up white doll—and they often make do with rocks and rubble. Burnett records the meanness of their life, but he observes them with tenderness and wit.

Killer of Sheep isn't a thesis film that overtly argues for solutions to social problems, but it implicitly compares the children in Watts with the sheep going to slaughter and makes viewers think about what could be done to give them a reasonably secure future. To solve that problem, one needs to confront a wide range of social, political, and economic issues. No doubt Burnett wanted audiences to discuss such things, but his immediate aim as an artist was to objectively dramatize the quotidian struggles of a working-class black family, its attempts to reproduce itself and raise its children against almost impossible odds. Fittingly, he introduces us to the family—Stan (Henry Gale Sanders), Stan's unnamed wife (Kaycee Moore), Stan Jr. (Jack Drummond), and Stan's daughter Angela (Angela Burnett, who is Charles Burnett's niece)—by way of neighborhood children playing daredevil war games in the decaying remains of the Watts rail yard.

The games are gritty and spontaneous looking, staged in a wasteland of dust, dirt, and rocks, but like nearly all the scenes in *Killer of Sheep*, they were scripted, storyboarded, and guided by Burnett's unobtrusively poetic feel for space, time, and tempo. He gives them an overarching design, moving from a tightly framed montage of a dangerous rock fight to an exhilarating wide shot of boys running alongside a passing train, and finally to an elliptical series of shots conveying dispersion and restless boredom. As he often does elsewhere, he starts with a close-up—in this case a boy using a piece of plywood or metal as a shield from rocks thrown at him—and gradually reveals the environment. Once the rock fight ceases, we see a kid's legs and feet standing on a patch of grimy, paper-strewn dirt. The kid knocks dust off his pants, and the offscreen sound of a train serves as lead-in to a wide, expansive traveling shot from the point of view of a railroad car as it traverses the dusty rail yard, making the entire space visible. On the far horizon are palm trees (this is, after all, sunny California), a few houses, and industrial power lines marking the outskirts of Watts. Suddenly, from over a mound of dirt, the boys run energetically into sight, racing the train and gradually passing it. Open-air exuberance ends with a stationary, reverse-angle telephoto of the slowing freight train as the boys line up along the tracks and throw rocks at it.

Once the train passes, we become aware of individuals: a boy stands beside a railroad sign, bored or sad, while another boy behind him listlessly throws rocks at a metal shed. An older boy with a cap and glasses suggests that they all go to a local bar and watch "hos" go in and out. One of the kids says no; if his mother were to see him there, "my ass is hers. You'd have to call the police to get her off me." In the next shot the boy with cap and glasses is lying on a rail track, his neck against the wheel of a freight car, laughing and daring the other kids to push the train over him. (Burnett has said that in his neighborhood when he grew up, "most kids did not believe they would live longer than twenty-one." In 1994, he added, "they do not believe that they will live longer than sixteen" [Kapsis 2011, 79].)

A wide-angle, deep-focus shot positioned at ground level shows a boy walking down the tracks toward the camera away from the railcar. He reaches the foreground, ties one of his sneakers, and tells everyone that he's going home to get his BB gun. We don't know it yet, but this is Stan Jr., nearing his teen years and entering a rebellious, troubling phase. He's a sometimes-angry kid and virtually drops out of the later parts of the film. The camera follows him home as he walks down an alleyway behind houses, combing his Afro and observing the local sociology. Strolling along, he turns to look at two young men climbing over a fence, boosting a TV set. An elderly gentleman in shirt and tie who is watering his back lawn also sees this, and the thieves chase him off: "What you looking at, punk?" they shout. "I'll kick your heart out!" Stan Jr. warns the thieves that the old gent is going to call the cops. (The call would do no good, because the LAPD was notoriously indifferent to black-on-black crimes.) One of the thieves tears a board from the fence, waves it like a weapon, and flies into nearly hysterical rage as his pal struggles to restrain him. Stan Jr. laughs. The thieves pick up the TV set, and the camera tracks backward as they race wildly down the alley carrying their loot, backlit by an afternoon sun. On the sound track, as counterpoint, we hear Cecil Grant's 1945 "race" record, "I Wonder." ("I wonder, my little darlin', where can you be, while the moon is shining bright?")

The sequence is characteristic of Burnett in its mixed emotional effects: a blend of humor, violence, beauty, and sadness, roughly like the great blues songs. The humor and beauty are underappreciated by commentators on Burnett's films; without them, *Killer of Sheep* would be unbearable. In the closing shot of the sequence, for example, there's a momentary beauty in the light of "the magic hour"; a crazy violence and comedy in the thieves' run with the TV set; and a wistful sadness in the tune, which continues as Stan Jr. walks farther down the alley and passes a group of silent children looking over a wall at the theft.

"I wonder, my little darlin'" bleeds into the next sequence, which introduces Stan and establishes his depression. We look down at his shirtless back as he kneels on the floor of his kitchen, laying linoleum and talking with a big fellow named Oscar, who stands mostly offscreen, restlessly slapping his fists together. "I'm working myself into my own hell," Stan says. "I close my eyes and don't sleep at night." (As one of Stan's friends later observes, trying to count sheep would do him no good.) The big man offhandedly asks, "Why don't you kill yourself?" Stan looks up—he's a handsome man with a slight bald spot and sad eyes—and wanly smiles. "No, I ain't going to kill myself," he says. "Got a feeling I might do somebody else tomorrow, though." He glances offscreen, and we cut to a surprising, almost surreal close-up of a child of about four or five, standing in a doorway, wearing a rubber Droopy-Dog mask, sucking a finger through the mask's mouth hole. She's Stan's daughter, impressively acted by Angela Burnett and the subject of some of the film's most memorable images. When Stan Jr. enters he treats her roughly, squeezing the mask and asking where his BB gun is. "Mamma threw it away," she says. Stan tells his son to stop acting like he has "no sense" and shoos him off.

If Burnett is underappreciated for his humor, he's equally underappreciated as a writer of dialogue, perhaps because people assume the conversations in his early films were improvised. Some of his lines have what Adrian Martin aptly describes as a "loopy" quality (2008, 73). A good example is when a woman named Dolores remarks that Stan would be good-looking if he didn't frown so much. Hearing this, a nearby fellow boasts, "Some sister told me I look just like Clark Gable!" Dolores looks wearily at him and mutters, "You about as tasteless as a carrot." Many of the speeches in *Killer of Sheep* have this wry, hard-boiled quality. In the scene at hand, Oscar notices two men approaching the back of Stan's house and makes a quick exit: "Here come Bracy and Ernie Cox. I don't want them asking *me* for money." The two men enter, and Bracy (Charles Bracy, a longtime friend of Burnett who was also responsible for the sound recording in *Killer of Sheep*) observes Stan scraping the floor with a kitchen knife: "I see your wife got you towing the cart. I see Oscar must have been here. . . . He's the only one I know wears that Old Spice aftershave."

Bracy is a bumptious type, unmarried and unemployed, whose raucous personality makes Stan's depression more evident. (In his commentary on the Milestone DVD, Burnett emphasizes that the poor have little if any possibility to get medical treatment for depression.) Before the contrast between the two men is fully established, however, we briefly leave the kitchen for a sweet and humorous encounter. Stan's daughter Angela hears a whistle and runs outside, where she meets a shy little boy standing against a hurricane fence;

she sucks her thumb through the hole in her mask, moves a little closer to him, and quietly bounces against the fence. Brief scenes involving her will become a motif. She's a key witness to adult behavior: innocent, not yet marked by the harshness and traumas of life in Watts, but coming to an awareness of her family's troubles.

When we return to Bracy and Stan, they're seated alone at a table in the poor but well-kept kitchen, sipping tea. Stan presses a warm teacup against his head and wearily remarks that it reminds him of "making love, how warm her forehead get some time." Bracy laughs; he thinks warm tea is nothing but "hot air" and doesn't care for "women with malaria." He and his pals have been walking the streets at night, he explains, hesitating to drop in; Stan says not to worry, he never sleeps. Another of Burnett's elliptical cuts shows the two men later in the evening, playing dominos as somewhere in the night a dog barks (the sound design of the film is as effective as the photography, establishing an ever-present offscreen environment). Stan's lovely wife, who has apparently been ignored during all this, appears in the kitchen doorway without speaking, her hair wrapped in a bath towel and an angry expression on her face. She turns and exits. Whatever nostalgia for intimacy Stan might feel, he doesn't act on it; he simply rubs his face in fatigue and says it's time to go to work. Bracy yawns and looks at his watch: "Maybe me and Ernest can luck up on a slave [i.e., a menial, part-time job] if we's lucky."

Each episode in the remainder of the film is relatively autonomous, illustrating typical events in the life of an ordinary but admirable man who is trying to cope. Like certain forms of jazz or modernist narrative, these episodes could be somewhat reordered without disturbing the fundamental unity or meaning of the film. The first two, however, are in dialectical contrast, representing male industrial labor versus female domesticity. To the music of William Grant Still's "Afro-American Symphony," we're given a montage of Stan at work in the slaughterhouse, hosing the floor and carrying sheep parts; then at home, we see his wife awaiting his return. The wife applies makeup while Stan's daughter, wearing a dress, sits on the back porch floor next to an old phonograph, playing with a white doll that has no clothing, happily singing along with Earth, Wind, and Fire's recording of "Reasons."

The next sequence, also without dialogue, shows Stan at home and makes clear that his depression has affected not only his libido but also his will to express affection. The postures of the actors in Burnett's films are always communicative, and are especially so here: Stan slumps in a kitchen chair, one arm dropped to his side, while his wife, wearing an attractive African print dress, sits across from him and leans forward, her legs crossed and her chin cupped in her hand. Angela enters, gets a glass of milk from the refrigerator, exchanges glances with her mother, puts her glass down hard, and exits. The wife stares at Stan, her head tilted, trying to get him to return the gaze. Stan lifts a teacup (a reminder of the earlier scene in the kitchen), and she reaches out to him. He rises, turns his back, and resumes work on the kitchen floor.

Burnett was fortunate in the casting of Stan and his wife. The man who was supposed to play Stan wound up in prison, and Burnett came across Henry Gayle Sanders by accident in an elevator. "I thought Henry was [the] saddest-looking man I'd ever seen," Burnett has said. "I asked him if he'd ever done any acting" (Kapsis 2011, 143–44). Sanders had recently returned from two tours of duty in Vietnam, where he was injured, and was attending college under the GI Bill; his original ambition was to become a writer, but in Los Angeles he had begun to take acting courses. In *Killer of Sheep* he radiates gentle strength and thoughtfulness, performing in a quietly naturalistic style. Kaycee Moore, on the other hand, had appeared only in theater (after

Killer of Sheep, she acted in two films directed by Burnett's "students": Billy Woodbury's *Bless Their Little Hearts* and Julie Dash's *Daughters of the Dust*). She's a more vivid, ostentatious performer, and the slight difference in acting styles helps bring out the contrast between Stan's depression and his wife's vitality.

Moore's intensity is evident in one of the more improvised moments in the film, when a couple of gangster types—characters who seem to have entered from one of the blaxploitation pictures Burnett disliked—try to recruit Stan for one of their jobs. A shiny Cadillac with whitewalls comes to a lurching halt in front of Stan's small house, and in comic but sinister fashion, two slicked-up dudes named Scooter and Smoke exit the car and strut up the walk, calling out, "Hey, Stan, can you come out and play?" Laughing, bumping fists, acting cool, they knock on the door until Stan grudgingly emerges. They're wearing shades, leather, and bling; he's barefoot and wearing an undershirt and shabby pants. He sits on the front step, frowning while they gather around and tell him he's been recommended as a "third man."

In a ghostly close-up, Stan's wife is seen through the screen door as she watches Stan telling the two men he doesn't want to hear about their

proposition. Scooter says he and his pal are looking for somebody "who wouldn't blush at murder" and asks to borrow Stan's "roscoe." When Stan says that he doesn't have a gun, the wife emerges. "Why do you always want to hurt somebody?" she asks loudly. Burnett frames the four actors as a group, and their postures and movements tell us everything: the wife stands in an assertive position, arms akimbo; Stan sits on the step, his head hanging down, lighting a cigarette, and picking at his toe; the two hoods sway almost like dancers, gesturing with an air of flashy, easy confidence. Scooter speaks to the wife in a patronizing tone: "That's the way I was brought up! A man got scars on his face for being a man . . . me and Smoke are going to take our issue [i.e., what's ours]." Turning to Stan, he says, "You can be a man if you can, Stan."

At this, the wife marches down the steps and gets in Scooter's face, gesturing passionately and making a fiery speech, much of which Moore made up on the spot: "You wait just a minute! You talk about being a *man* if you can . . . scars on your mug!" Her finger points assertively. "Where do you think you are? In the bush or some damn where? You are *here*! You use your brain, that's what you use. You're not an animal. And both of you nothing-ass niggers got a lot of nerve coming here to ask him to do something like that!" When Smoke reaches out to grab the wife's arm and turn her toward him, she becomes nearly wild with anger and fear, jerking free and wordlessly rebuking Stan for doing nothing. Smoke and Scooter give up and wander off, complaining: "All we trying to do is help the nigger."

A threat of violence against the woman hovers throughout the scene, becoming evident in the veiled contempt Smoke and Scooter feel toward Stan's wife and their attempt to shame Stan into ignoring her. Ironically, the domestic male is the true "man," even though he looks shabby, passive, and worn down (we may recall that the theme of manhood was introduced in the film's opening sequence). Stan's job and his consequent depression have sapped his energy; he's in an inferior, seated position when his wife takes charge. There's also irony in the wife's speech. She passionately criticizes certain ideas about black manhood, but does so with the same language and imagery racists use: Smoke and Scooter, she says, are primitives who think they're in the jungle "bush." They're "nothing-ass niggers" with ugly mugs. They're "*here*," meaning the big-city United States, far away from Africa or the South, and they should be using their small brains. Smoke and Scooter deserve this abuse, but the wife has internalized racial images and language created by a long tradition of oppression.

Stan has better sense than to join up with thieves and killers, but it isn't clear that Stan Jr. will grow up to think the same way. Soon after Smoke and Scooter leave, the boy unsuccessfully asks his father for a dollar; in a later scene he broods about the rejection of his request. We see Stan's little daughter putting on a dress in the bathroom and going into the kitchen, where her brother is eating cereal. "How clean I must be," she says, then sits at the table watching him. He scowls, pours what looks like half a box of sugar on the cereal, munches ferociously, and in close-up mutters, "I need some money." "What?" his sister asks. He pauses, stares at her with near hate, and speaks distinctly: "I need some money!"

Lack of money determines everything in the film. At one point Stan confronts a man who owes him money, and the man walks away, saying, "I ain't got anything but my good looks." At another point Stan gives a dollar and a can of peaches, wages he's received from "Miss Sally" for "cleaning up behind the garage," to his poor friends Gene and Dian. But the local economy is most evident when Stan goes to the only bank available to him—a liquor and convenience store—and tries to cash his paycheck from the slaughterhouse. Burnett introduces the episode with a striking image and a sad joke about the people hanging around on the street outside the store. A drunken man is reflected in a bewigged young woman's aviator sunglasses. "You a no-good woman," he says. "You get yourself in line," she sneers, and a close-up of her high heels shows her walking away to the sound of blues music. He follows, and the two squeeze into a beat-up car where four others are already sitting; there's a beer can on the hood of the car, and a fellow in the front seat reaches straight out to get it, revealing that the car has no windshield.

The only white person in the film is a big, tough-looking woman who manages the store. (Burnett found the woman working in a post office.) When a customer asks to cash a check, a middle-aged clerk behind the counter calls to her and she emerges from a back room, seen in a floor-level shot that makes her look imposing. Shoving the clerk aside, she glances at the man's check and says "hell, no." Then the younger, better-looking Stan comes in with the same request, to which she responds with a sexual come-on. She *might* be able to cash the check, she says with a smile, and asks, "Why don't you come work for me?" Henry Gale Sanders does a nice job of conveying Stan's struggle to hide his discomfort and remain politely subservient; he shyly smiles and looks away, saying that he fears getting held up and shot. "Oh, *I'll* protect you," the woman promises. "You'll work in back with me." She nods toward the middle-aged clerk: "*He* takes care of the register." A close-up shows her hand stroking Stan's wrist. Stan doesn't pull away and manages to get out with his check cashed.

Possessed of a little money, Stan tries to help his friend Gene buy a used auto engine. This results in the longest episode in the film, a self-contained drama that serves as a virtual allegory of Stan's precarious situation in life. It's by turns bizarre, comic, sweet, suspenseful, and almost tragic. At the beginning, we see the two men, accompanied by Stan's daughter, drive an aged pickup to the edge of Watts and park on a steep hill outside a three-story stucco apartment house. Gene enters the building, heading up the steps to the top apartment. Before joining him, Stan worriedly counts cash from his paycheck and puts bits of it in different pockets to hide the amount. Stan's daughter, whom he leaves behind, sucks on a plastic toy. In the ambient street sounds we hear the shouts of kids and faint music from an ice-cream truck playing "Yankee-Doodle Dandy."

Inside the apartment is a strange collection of characters. Burnett introduces the scene with a close-up of a man with a bandaged head, lying on the floor. Gene knocks, enters, and asks what has happened. A wide shot reveals four other people: a slender, flashily dressed man playing with a deck of cards and consulting a hand mirror; a sullen young woman and her little daughter; and a teen-aged boy picking his toes. According to Burnett's screenplay (published in Klotman 1991), the man on the floor is named James and the woman is named Dolores, although we never hear these names. We eventually learn that they're the nephew and niece of Silbo, the fellow playing cards. The boy's exact identity is unclear, but he seems to be part of the dysfunctional family. He explains to Gene that James was hurt when "Adolph and Boulevard jumped on him." Just then Stan arrives, winded from the long climb up the stairs. "What's happenin' ol' dude?" the boy shouts in welcome. Silbo unsuccessfully tries to get the morose Dolores to join him in a card game. Gene tells Silbo, "All I got is ten dollars." James, groggy from the head wound, complains of the noise and tries to go back to sleep. Burnett waits until this point to slowly zoom back and reveal that sitting on the floor next to James is an automobile engine atop a bunch of newspapers.

A large close-up shows Dolores, chin in her hand, quietly asking herself, "How did I ever get married to such a damn silly-ass family as this?" Before the zany situation can develop further, however, Burnett takes us outside with Dolores's daughter, who has gone to meet Angela in the truck. As in an earlier episode, we have a brief glimpse of childhood innocence apart from the adult world. The two girls sit together, chew gum, and play with the gum wrapper. "How come you don't come to school?" Stan's daughter asks. "I have been sick," the other little girl says. "You gotten far behind," says Stan's daughter.

Back in the apartment Dolores, seated in a chair and wearing a short skirt, rubs lotion on her ample, attractive legs. The wounded James leers from his position on the floor and tries to make a pass, which results in bickering and then an angry quarrel between the two. During this, Gene confers with Stan and announces to Silbo, "All I got is fifteen dollars." He can barely be heard over the exchange of insults between James and Dolores, which escalates until James yells, "You just an all-day sucker, bitch," at which point Dolores gets up and kicks him (like most of the sequence, this is framed in a close-up—we see Dolores's face, but not where the kick lands). James cries out, Stan rushes to him, and Gene holds Dolores back. "Hey, Silbo," Stan says. "Take care of your nephew here, man! . . . He's bleeding!" In response, Silbo picks up his hand mirror and studies himself. "I've got more important things to do," he says. "My hair's falling out." Then he half rises, disgusted with his niece and nephew, and accepts Gene's offer of $15 for the motor.

The remainder of the episode concerns Stan and Gene's grueling, reverse-Sisyphus attempt to get the engine down to the street and load it onto the pickup. Burnett devotes nine shots to the journey, negotiating the tricky space of a long stairway, creating a downward spiraling movement, and

generating a fair amount of suspense. (The sequence was shot on two different stairways, making the trip down look especially complicated.) Given the
world of this film, we fear disaster—and not the comic disaster of Stan and
Ollie moving a piano. Burnett begins with a close, handheld view as the two
men struggle to get the engine out of the building. They move through the
apartment door, out a hall entrance to a stairway, and then start down. Good
Samaritan Stan is predictably at the heavy end, moving backward along the
rickety steps. They reach a landing, turn slightly, and encounter another
flight of steps. Slowly they continue down, pause, turn, and face a third set of
steps. Stan, wearing work gloves, is beginning to wince from the effort. "One
more," Gene says as they reach the bottom. They put the engine down for a
moment's rest, then pick it up and struggle toward the truck. Arriving, they
heave the load up onto the flatbed, which lacks a gate, and Gene, who has no
gloves, cries out because his finger is caught. He extracts the finger from the
engine and winces, "Just leave it there. It'll stay there." Stan disagrees, and
they shove the engine forward a bit. Still nursing his finger, Gene insists that
they've done enough—no more pushing.

On the sound track there are ambient sounds of a passing airplane and
kids at play. A low, street-level shot shows the two men walking up the hill-

side toward the doors of the truck. Dolores's daughter gets out, and the two men get in, Gene taking the driver's seat. He starts the truck, but when he puts it in gear it lurches, causing the engine to tumble off the flatbed and crash into the street. (The engine nearly hit Burnett and his camera when it rolled toward him as he lay on the ground for the street-level shot.) The truck stops and the two men get out, silently surveying the wreckage. Without speaking, they climb back in and drive off, to the poignant piano music of Scott Joplin's "Solace." Burnett ends the episode with Angela looking sadly out the back window as the truck moves away. From her point of view, we see the engine lying dead in the street, receding into the distance.

The sexual problems between Stan and his wife reach a crisis sometime later, when they're alone at home, embracing and slowly dancing. For this sequence shot, Burnett originally used Dinah Washington's sensual, hauntingly romantic rendition of "Unforgettable," but he was unable to secure the rights for distribution; instead we hear Washington's hit 1960 recording of Clyde Otis's "This Bitter Earth," which creates a sensual mood tinged with lament, pain, and sorrow. ("What good is love that no one shares? . . . My life is like the dust that hides the glow of a rose.") The music is mixed in a style that makes it seem nondiegetic, yet it collaborates with the expressivity of the actors and the choreography. Stan and his wife are framed in profile, half silhouetted against a lighted window; at left, atop a table, are a lamp and a pair of preserved baby shoes. The actors only slightly change their position, and the camera doesn't move. Stan, shirtless and wearing loose pants that almost expose his buttocks, stands slightly apart from his wife; she looks lovingly at him, but he doesn't return the look. They slowly turn to the music so that his bare back is to the camera; she runs her hand along his back, puts her head on his shoulder, and moves close. As they continue to turn, we see that his hands are held loosely and his expression is zombie-like. She strokes his chest and moves a hand behind his neck. They turn again, and she seems to reach down into the front of his pants. Then she embraces him with both arms, kissing his neck and cheek. When the song ends, she kisses his chest, grasping him tightly, subtly grinding against him, on the verge of tears. He pushes her gently away and exits, leaving her alone.

Stan's wife moves to the window and strikes a somewhat melodramatic pose of grief that suits the inherent musicality of the scene. Turning, she sits on the windowsill, and we're given one of the film's most unusual narrative

devices, a brief internal monologue that also has musical or lyrical qualities.
The monologue deals openly with themes that until this point have been
treated only indirectly, revealing the wife's deep memories of the rural South,
an impoverished world she and her husband had left behind for the sake of
opportunity, only to find alienation and struggle: "Memories that don't seem
mine, like half eaten cake: rabbit skins stretched on the back-yard fences; my
grandmother; mother dear, mot dear, mot dear, dragging her shadow across
the porch." (An insert shows the wife picking up the baby shoes on the table.)
"Standing bare-headed under the sun.... Cleaning red catfish with white
rum." As she embraces the shoes and walks off, the plaintive sounds of
Rachmaninoff's "Piano Concerto Number 4" form a sound bridge into a
montage of sheep being herded to slaughter.

When Stan returns from work on a subsequent day, tension is conveyed
by a silent tableau around the dinner table. He once again slumps in his chair,
and his wife looks dejected. Stan Jr. stretches his arms, rises, slams his chair
against the table, and walks out, barely noticed by his father. As Angela tries
to clear away the dishes, Stan breaks the silence by glancing at his wife and
asking, "So, what'd you do today?" She smiles sadly, shakes her head, and
worries the napkin in her hands. "Got to find me a job," he mutters. She

grasps his wrist, gently reminds him that tomorrow is Saturday, and suggests they go to bed. He doesn't respond. The remainder of the scene is played silently through an exchange of gazes between husband, wife, and child. Stan shifts his chair around toward his wife as she clears the dishes, and Angela comes to him, standing between his legs. He gives her a gentle touch and one of his rare, halfhearted smiles. His wife exits, looking back as he embraces his daughter, who looks offscreen toward her mother. The wife goes to the next room, sits on a couch, anguished, and looks toward the kitchen. Angela looks at her mother and softly strokes her father's face, taking on a maternal role, trying to comfort both parents.

The catalog of frustrations and disappointments carries over into the next phase of the film, which begins with a richly detailed deep-focus shot: Stan's skinny friend Gene leans far over the open hood of his car while his enormous wife Dian watches him and complains that he's spending too much time and money on the project; in the foreground, a boy straddles a bike decorated with an American flag and tries to push it forward as another boy pushes back against the handlebars; and in the far distance, Stan comes around a corner and jogs uphill toward Gene and Dian, bringing them a dollar and a can of peaches. A close-up shows the freckle-faced Dian smiling in tender gratitude. "It's getting late," Gene says, "Let's go have some coffee and see what my guests are doing." He and Stan load a battery and a spare tire into the car's trunk, and the camera pans as they head toward the house, passing a stray dog. Then the camera pans back to the closed trunk, portending trouble.

In Gene's kitchen the guests are having a party: blues music is playing, a crap game is in progress, and the camera is set almost level with the floor, looking up at the large posterior of a woman who embraces a fat man. The man proposes marriage and then joins the crap game. Dian approaches the woman, smiles, and asks if she's happy. A big fellow on the floor grins and winks at another woman as he rolls the dice. Stan and Gene stand apart and look miserable.

The theme of gambling continues into the next episode. It's a bright Saturday morning, and seven characters—Gene, Dian, and their baby; Stan, his wife, and his daughter; and Stan's pal Bracy—prepare for an outing at the racetrack. Dressed in their good clothes, they begin packing themselves into Gene's car, which is now in working order, while a bunch of kids play and fight in the far distance and the apparently drunken Bracy, sporting 1970s-style stacked heels, shouts incoherently about his last night's adventures. In the backseat Stan's wife fixes Angela's hair and wipes her face. Once everybody squeezes aboard, the car drives off to the sound of Louis Armstrong's rendition of King Oliver's "West End Blues," upbeat in tempo yet also mournful. On the road, Dian tells Gene to slow down, Bracy studies a racing form, and Stan's wife enjoys the air from an open window as her weary husband sleeps on her shoulder.

Soon trouble strikes. Out in the countryside, the car gets a flat tire, and Gene discovers that his spare has been stolen from the trunk. Angela gazes sadly out a window, just as she did in the sequence involving the wrecked engine. We look down the side of the car as Bracy paces back and forth on the road, gesturing wildly and berating Gene: "Look, man, I told you to have a spare tire and don't be comin' out here in the middle of nowhere. . . . In the ninth race, man, I got me a nag that I *know* is going to come in! I got me some money, man! And you ain't got no spare! Look, aw shit!"

Here Burnett makes excellent use of offscreen space. Stan's wife, nicely coiffed and made up, slowly emerges from below the frame into a big close-up, looking grimly down at the wheel of the car, while behind her Bracy (whose voice sounds post-synchronized) breaks into rap: "Man, I'm out here singin' the blues, got me a horse that can't lose! Always told you to keep a spare, but you's a square!" Gene studies the situation and softly replies, "I guess we have to ride back on the rim, that's all. Ain't got no spare." Everybody gets back in the car, which makes a U turn and drives off on the rim; once again Gene's fixation with his auto has resulted in a kind of tragicomedy. Despite all the discord and trouble, however, there's a sweet quality in the scene: the sharply delineated, flawed characters remain friends, moving through life in the same boat (more accurately, car), facing disappointment together.

We are now at the closing moments of the film, in which Burnett emphasizes the theme of survival and creates a modest sense of ongoing strength. After arriving home from the abortive trip to the racetrack, Stan slumps wearily on a couch as his wife remarks that rain is coming and the roof needs repair. Angela stands with her arms akimbo and then turns and opens the screen door. "Daddy," she asks, "what makes the rain?" Stan softly replies, "Why, it's the Devil beating his wife." Angela smiles and a large close-up shows Stan's wife also smiling, happier than she's been at any point. She crosses to Stan and sits close to him. They share a soft smile (his third in the film, and the most genuine), and he touches her knee.

I grew up in the South not far from where Burnett was born, and whenever it rained while the sun was shining, my white father would remark that the devil was beating his wife. It's an expression peculiar to the deep South, and Burnett's use of it here is significant. Stan is making a slightly dark joke, but also acknowledging his roots in the folklore of a world he's been trying to escape. For the moment, father, mother, and child feel a happy bond.

The only member of the family who isn't present is Stan Jr., and in the next scene we see the wife standing behind their house, calling him. "I know you hear me calling you, boy," she says loudly, and then talks to herself: "I know that boy heard me calling him." As she goes inside, the camera pans up to the roof and reveals Stan Jr. and another boy. Cut to the front of the house. On the tiny porch, a girl sitting in a chair is having her hair arranged by Angela, and two other girls are perched on the steps. A pretty young woman enters the shot, supporting herself with a cane, and as she moves up the front steps we see that her right leg is in a brace. She knocks at the screen door, and Stan's wife welcomes her, giving her a delighted hug when she whispers something. Inside, two women are visiting. One of them brandishes a cigarette and asks the new arrival why she's wearing a pretty smile. The lame young woman looks down at herself shyly. Stan's wife beams and announces, "She's going to have a baby!" One of the women remarks, "Well, I thought her old man was shooting blanks, but I see he's dropping bombs on occasion, I guess." Stan's wife laughs and the young woman looks proudly at her stomach, moving her hand in an arc over it, indicating how it's going to grow.

This is the first scene involving female friends of Stan's wife and the only scene, apart from a brief early one between Stan's wife and daughter, made up entirely of women. It's also a rare example of a scene that ends on a happy note. Unlike a typical Hollywood movie or "well-made" drama, it doesn't identify the new characters and doesn't explain the pregnant young woman's disability. In fact, the disability motivates nothing and isn't necessary to the scene; it's simply there: an undiscussed, unusual, harsh fact that will probably complicate motherhood. The scene is pregnant, one might say, with unstated meanings that have little to do with plot. It celebrates new life and the endurance of the community, but at the same time, partly by means of the young woman's leg, dramatizes an ongoing struggle.

Burnett ends with a montage of Stan and his fellow workers on the killing floor of the slaughterhouse. Once again we hear Dinah Washington singing "This Bitter Earth," this time as a background to images of dead and bleeding sheep. There's a small flaw that Burnett was unable to correct. As Stan herds animals to their death, he's broadly smiling, almost laughing; during the shooting, Burnett has explained, Henry Gayle Sanders split his trousers wide open and couldn't control his amusement. Even so, the somber music and the montage are anything but uplifting, and the film leaves Stan in virtually the same circumstances as at the beginning. The screen goes dark, and over the closing credits we hear Paul Robeson's rendition of Antonin Dvorak's "Going Home," a hymn inspired by what Dvorak called the "great and noble music" of nineteenth-century African Americans. Like the film, it's pathetic, tender, passionate, and melancholy; it bestows grace and importance on Stan, his family, and his community.

FOUR

———

My Brother's Wedding *(1983)*

KILLER OF SHEEP WAS FIRST exhibited in the late 1970s and early 1980s, mostly at festivals, museums, and black film series. Its reception wasn't entirely adulatory. In the *New York Times*, Janet Maslin gave it an astonishingly wrongheaded review, describing it as "arid," with nice moments but without "the kind of coherence that might give them larger meaning." She even complained that "the slaughter of the sheep is numbingly uneventful" (1978, C10). *Sight and Sound* proclaimed it "sincere but fatally scrappy and meandering" ("On Now" 1982, 216). In Europe, however, it was much admired, and in 1981 received the Critics' Award at the Berlin Film Festival. This opened greater possibilities for limited theatrical distribution, but at the time Burnett was still trying to secure rights for the music. In October 1981 *Variety* declared that "marketplace possibilities are slim outside of specialty and festival situations for this admirable effort." The film's reputation nevertheless grew, and in 1990 it was among the first pictures selected for the National Film Registry of the Library of Congress. Nearly thirty years after it was made, UCLA's Ross Lipman restored the print and converted it to 35mm; Milestone Films raised $150,000 ($75,000 of which came from Steven Soderbergh) to acquire music rights and bring it to a wider public via cinemas and DVD. By that time, *Killer of Sheep* had become legendary, influencing not only films of the L.A. Rebellion but also such later pictures as David Gordon Green's *George Washington* (2000) and, in a less pronounced way, Barry Jenkins's *Moonlight* (2016). Decades earlier, working as what he describes as a "callow third-stringer" at the *Village Voice*, J. Hoberman had given it a short, relatively dismissive review, but when it was reissued by Milestone, Hoberman (2007) confessed his error, praised the film, discussed its influence, and remarked that its reputation was now so great that it threatened to overshadow some of the impressive work of Burnett's subsequent career, much as *Citizen Kane* overshadows the popular conception of Orson Welles's later work.

Burnett's less well known second feature, *My Brother's Wedding* (1983), has suffered relative neglect in part because it encountered production difficulties that hampered its release and critical reception. Like *Killer of Sheep*, it was produced, directed, written, photographed, and edited by Burnett. His wife was a coproducer, and he involved a number of young black filmmakers in Los Angeles in the project: Julie Dash was one of the assistant directors, and the credits for the film list a dozen associate or assistant editors. The $80,000 budget was funded chiefly by German public TV (ZDF, or Zweites Deutsches Fernsehen), Canadian investors, and a Guggenheim fellowship. Burnett had trouble meeting a deadline imposed by his German backers due to delays caused by weather and by the film's leading actor, Everette Silas, who disappeared in the middle of shooting. Burnett eventually tracked Silas down in the South, where he claimed to have become an ordained minister, and flew him back to Los Angeles; Silas disembarked wearing a Dracula cape and demanding more money. As the German deadline drew near, Burnett tried to cut the film's rough assembly by thirty minutes but was unable to find the $8,000 he needed for the job. As a result, *My Brother's Wedding* had very limited showings, and Burnett's production company had to declare bankruptcy. It was not until the Milestone/Pacific Film Archive restoration, supported by a grant from the National Endowment of the Arts, that he was able to edit a version more to his liking. "It was difficult to get back to it because I didn't have access to all the material I had shot," Burnett explained to James Bell of *Sight and Sound*. "It was a matter of trimming rather than being able to take scenes and make them work by using [alternative takes]. I was able to cut a lot of the bad performances, but if I'd had all the original material it would have been a lot better. It's not what I originally intended" (Kapsis 2011, 184). Both versions of the film are included as extras on the Milestone DVD set of *Killer of Sheep*. I've chosen the shorter, "director's cut" for the following discussion.

Killer of Sheep was shot in grainy, documentary-style, 16mm black and white and was concerned with the lowest levels of the 1970s Watts economy. As we've seen, it took the form of a series of vignettes without strong narrative closure, portraying the quotidian life of a black husband, wife, and two kids. Generational conflicts were only hinted at, such as the rebellion of Stan's son or the attempts of the parents to divest their children of southern manners. Black religion played no part, and there were no evident class conflicts in the community. In contrast, *My Brother's Wedding*, which Burnett hoped would reach a larger audience, was shot in Academy-ratio 35mm color. It deals not only with the Watts working class of the 1980s but also with black small business owners and the black bourgeoisie. Throughout, it dramatizes sharply delineated class and generational conflicts, among them conflicts between a religious older generation and a secular younger generation, and it has a relatively strong closure. Burnett describes it as a "satiric" and "didactic" film, and Amy Corbin rightly observes that it has a mixed effect, shifting between realistic scenes that encourage the audience's emotional involvement and more or less Brechtian or broadly comic scenes that create a distancing effect (2014, 34–56).

The film opens with a brief autonomous shot: a close-up of elderly singer/harmonica player Dr. Henry Gordon, dressed in formal attire, standing in a dark limbo and mournfully performing "Amazing Grace." (The credits for the film incorrectly identify the song as "The Old Rugged Cross.") Gordon's location and narrative function aren't clear, but he seems to be in a church, foreshadowing the two religious ceremonies—a wedding and a funeral—that climax the film.

When the story proper opens, it centers on thirty-year-old Pierce Mundy (Silas), who, we eventually learn, has gone to trade school in hopes of becoming a heavy equipment operator, only to discover that "everybody was going to school to be the same thing." Since then, he's had a series of low-wage jobs: driving a cement mixer, working as a brakeman on the railroad, and driving trucks that carry explosives and dangerous materials. Currently he lives rent free with his parents and works in their small dry-cleaning shop. Tall, gangling, often dour or sullen, Pierce is both drifting through life and constantly rushing somewhere, figuratively and sometimes literally pulled in two directions by his family and friends. In the opening scene, Burnett establishes his condition by means of a physical to and fro: Pierce is hurriedly walking down a sidewalk on his way to visit the mother of his friend Soldier when a young woman bursts out of a house behind him and shouts, "Come see my sister's baby!" Grabbing him by the arm, she pulls him back in her direction and asks, "What kind of friend are you?" Inside the house, he reluctantly agrees to hold the baby for a few moments and wonders, "Who is the daddy?" Cut to the child's mother, wearing a house robe, sitting at a nearby kitchen table, and gloomily smoking a cigarette. Pierce backs away from what looks like an attempt to recruit him as a father and rushes off to complete his original mission. As he walks along, he passes two girls on the cusp of adolescence, standing on a street corner. One of them (Angela Burnett, almost grown and still a charming actor) calls out to him. He stops, turns, and unhappily walks over to her. "There's something I had to tell you," she says flirtatiously, squirming and grinning, "but I forgot." She and her friend giggle. Almost rolling his eyes, Pierce silently turns and continues on his way.

When Pierce at last reaches his destination, the ruefully comic tone gives way to a quiet, serious conversation. He and Soldier's mother are seated in her kitchen (many of the key scenes in Burnett's early films take place in kitchens, which function as the heart of the family), and from what they say we can infer that Soldier is about to be released from prison. Their conversation is intercut with shots of Soldier's father outside the house, stomping on a pile of soda cans to redeem them for money, then coming inside to fall wearily into bed. The mother holds a broken china cup—one of several instances when Burnett makes good use of an actor and an object—and sadly wonders, "Will Soldier ever act his age?" Pierce assures her of Soldier's desire to change his ways: "He said he's never going back. He even asked me to help him look for a job. He's never done anything mean or vicious, never used dope. He's nothing like these kids today. If you look at it, we're pretty much alike." But the mother doesn't agree: "You and your brother never got into trouble." Pierce makes a quiet, sincere pledge: "I promise you, I'll do whatever I can to keep him out of trouble."

Pierce's promise to his friend's mother motivates one part of the film's double plot. The other part is motivated by his grudging but equally important promise to his family to act as best man in his older brother's forthcoming wedding. One of the unusual qualities of this structure is that Burnett gives the two intertwined narratives somewhat different styles. The friendship plot is realistic in the manner of *Killer of Sheep* and ends grimly with Soldier's death; the family plot contains a good deal of stylized comic satire, almost like a socially edgy TV sitcom, and ends in the disruption of the brother's wedding. Burnett crosscuts between the two plots in the closing scenes, when Soldier's funeral is held at the same time as the brother's wedding and Pierce's divided loyalties, one based on an old friendship and the other on a sense of obligation, come into stark conflict. He's forced to make a decision, but he waits too long, abandoning the wedding only to arrive too late at the funeral. The mood that results is less tragicomedy than bitter frustration or ironic deflation of two kinds of narrative, one associated with tragedy and the other with comedy.

In a 1988 interview with Monona Wali of the *Independent*, Burnett described the film as the story of a young man who "romanticizes the poor for the wrong reasons" and "hates the middle class for the wrong reasons." Pierce, he said, "is an accident waiting to happen" (Kapsis 2011, 20). He isn't a bad person, although he's having an affair with a young married woman who meets him in the evenings, her entrances backed by the sexy, nondiegetic music of Johnny Ace's 1955 recording, "Anymore." In fact, Pierce has admirable qualities. He's an intelligent, responsible worker, and most of his daily life involves dashing back and forth to help others: he runs errands for his mother; changes a baby's diaper; and babysits for "Big Mamma and Big Papa" (Cora Lee Day and Tim Wright), his aged grandparents. We see him unzipping his grandfather's pants to help him pee, taking the old man's clothes off to bathe him, shining his shoes, giving his grandmother her daily pills, and reading to both of them from their Bible. On the eve of Soldier's release from prison, he not only tries to comfort Soldier's parents but also tries to get Soldier a job. First, he goes to a liquor store manager, who tells him, "If *you* wanted a job, yeah," but nixes the idea of Soldier. He then goes to a local mechanic and carefully leads up to asking a favor by remarking, "You know, Soldier's getting out of jail." Without pausing in his work, the mechanic says, "That's too bad. That's one fellow they should keep in jail till he rots."

Pierce's chief flaws are immaturity and bad judgment, especially in regard to Soldier (Ronald E. Bell), the only person in the film around whom he seems happy. On the day when Soldier is released from prison, Pierce, who has been delayed because of his attempts to find his friend a job, runs breathlessly down a crowded street to a bus station, where he finds Soldier standing outside in a dark suit and two-toned shoes, holding a paper bag filled with his belongings and checking his watch. There are many scenes involving running in *My Brother's Wedding*; a guiding metaphor of the film, Burnett has explained, is "running blindly" or rushing into life without "wisdom" (Kapsis 2011, 20). The two men almost collide and shout with joy and laughter as they punch each other like kids.

In a subsequent homecoming, Pierce stands by while Soldier embraces his mother and father and promises that he's returned to stay. The scene is poignantly staged, with Soldier's back to the camera as he holds his weeping mother for a few moments and then walks toward his father, offering to shake hands and accepting a tight hug. But on the same evening, while Pierce is eating dinner with his parents, a man named Walter (Garnett Hargrave) knocks at the door and calls him outside. In the back seat of Walter's car, another man

is moaning in pain, his face bruised and bloody. "Look, what your friend did," Walter says. "Your friend is sick. Sick! Tell him *I'm* looking for him, to kill him."

This encounter has no apparent effect on Pierce, who, whenever Soldier is around, behaves more like a teenager than a man of thirty. Burnett shows the two running wildly and happily down the streets in sun and rain, not unlike the kids in *Killer of Sheep*. They race one another and engage in an impromptu wrestling match, falling and breaking the front fence of a house on Chico Street, where the homeowner comes out with a gun and chases them away. They stand in an alleyway at night and harmonize with a doo-wop tune. When their singing ends, Soldier turns to Pierce and asks, "Where *is* everybody?" Pierce solemnly replies that there's "just you and me." Their closest childhood friends have presumably left the neighborhood or died young.

In the early 1980s Watts was changing from the relative innocence depicted in *Killer of Sheep* to something more deadly, precipitated by the rising drug trade. Looked at alongside *Killer*, the neighborhood in this film seems comparatively urban, colorful, and in some ways prosperous, but guns are becoming more evident. When Mrs. Mundy sends Pierce to retrieve a kitchen pot from his aunt Hattie (Jackie Hargrave), we see the aunt putting down a big glass of vodka and picking up a gun before she answers the door. A couple of thieves armed with a knife try to rob the Mundy dry-cleaning shop, and Mrs. Mundy reaches for a gun beneath her front counter, forcing them to run down the street to their car. Inside the car, a heavily drugged man and woman discuss going back to the shop; when the man grabs a pistol, the woman tells him in slurred speech to keep it away from "my baby," and Burnett tilts the camera down to reveal that she's holding an infant in a child's car seat. Later Walter, who warned Pierce that he intended to kill Soldier, aims a gun at Pierce and Soldier as they walk down the street in broad daylight. He pulls the trigger, but the gun doesn't work. Soldier draws a knife, and a chase ensues down Arlington Avenue and into a couple of alleyways, the overweight gunman barely escaping Pierce, who has found a club.

The scenes involving Soldier are neorealist in style, but the scenes involving the family and the dry-cleaning business are often humorous. Burnett felt that the humor in *Killer of Sheep* had been too "dry" and insufficiently noticed, and he set out to make it more evident in this film, in the process creating a kind of dialectic between realism and social comedy. Pierce's father and mother, Mr. and Mrs. Mundy (Dennis Kemper and Jessie Holmes, the latter an especially fine performer), are vivid character types: a hard-working, salt-of-the-earth couple from the South who have done a good job of raising their two sons and are devoted to the local Baptist church. She's a thickset matriarch with a big voice and a pronounced drawl, and he's a small, dapper man who is feeling his age. Mrs. Mundy is disappointed by Pierce's aimlessness but ecstatic over the fact that her oldest son, Wendell (Monte Easter), has become a successful lawyer and is about to marry into a wealthy family.

The forthcoming marriage is a prime source of comedy and satire, but so is the dry-cleaning business, which provides a window onto the local culture. Silas amusingly performs Pierce's not-quite-deadpan reactions to a cross-section of folks who appear at the front counter of the dry-cleaning store. Among them is Mr. Bitterfield (Ross Harris), a fat man with a pipe in his mouth who continually mutters to himself and expects Mrs. Mundy to work miracles on a pair of "churchgoing" trousers massively ripped apart at the crotch. (Mrs. Mundy decides to pretend she's worked a miracle and give Bitterfield a pair of unclaimed pants.) Another fellow shows up and can't remember what name he used when he brought in his clothes. "Could have used the name of Bob Walker," he says. Pierce consults the books and can't find that name. In the past, he tells the customer, "You used the name of Jack

Ace." The customer shakes his head. "Look under the name of Korn," he says. Exasperated, Mrs. Mundy tells him, "I'm tired of trying to keep track of all your aliases!" In still another scene, Angela, the girl who has a crush on Pierce, appears wearing a close-fitting dress and relatively high heels. "In a couple of years, I have my prom," she tells Pierce. "I was thinking. . . . If you weren't busy . . ." When Pierce doesn't respond, she announces that she's going to a Smoky Robinson concert. Mrs. Mundy, in the back of the shop, hears this and steps to the counter to remark, "I would think you'd be home watching Howdy Doody." Angela holds her abdomen as if she is having a period and complains that it's uncomfortable being a woman.

A repeated gag involves a zany but affectionate wrestling match that keeps popping up between Pierce and his father, amusing because Pierce is tall and skinny and his father short and a bit stocky. Early in the film Pierce initiates a battle by lightly slapping his father on the back of his head. They start to tussle, and Mrs. Mundy shouts, "You two act your age!" The father gets Pierce in a hammerlock and starts pulling him toward the back door. "Son," he says, "never underestimate an old man!" At this point a sad-faced but dignified fellow appears at the front of the shop and tells Mrs. Mundy that he's looking for work. "No," she says, "I've got two grown men out back to do everything." Behind her, father and son are rolling around like kids. The effect is comic, but notice also that Mrs. Mundy's admonition to "act your age" is an ironic echo of a remark by Soldier's mother in a previous conversation: "Will Soldier ever act his age?" Pierce's childishness around his father has the effect of domestic silliness, but his childishness around Soldier has troubling implications.

The scenes involving preparations for the wedding are permeated with full-scale social satire, occasionally employing cartoonish caricature. As the occasion draws near, class differences increasingly make things awkward or pose a problem. Pierce may or may not suffer from sibling rivalry, but he isn't close to his brother and deeply resents the brother's fiancée, Sonia Dubois (played in over-the-top style by Burnett's wife, Gaye Shannon-Burnett), who is not only a successful lawyer but also the daughter of what Pierce describes as a "big whatchamajig." When Sonia visits the Mundy neighborhood in her fancy car and expensive clothes, he accuses her of "signifying," or using style to indicate she's superior; he can't stand her family, and when his mother wants him to socialize with them he sulks, grumbling that Wendell ought to marry "someone from around here." But Mrs. Mundy is overjoyed that her family is achieving upward mobility and eagerly looks forward to the big

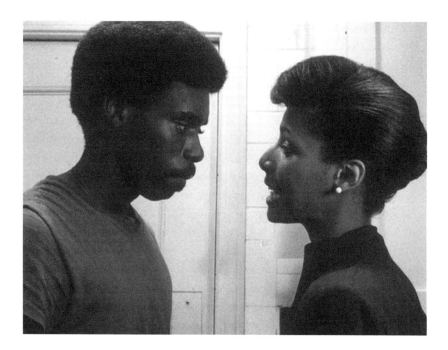

church wedding. She reminds Pierce that he's living with her rent free and orders him to stop behaving like a petulant child.

When Wendell and Sonia visit the Mundy home to discuss arrangements for the wedding, the class differences are glaringly obvious, and the actors project their dialogue with comic theatricality. The very black-skinned Pierce is in the kitchen, wearing a T-shirt and pouring hot water into a washtub so his father can soak his feet, when Sonia, a beautiful, light-skinned female in an expensive dress, sashays through the door to get a drinking glass. "How are you doing, Mr. Mundy?" she asks. Mrs. Mundy enters behind her and beams with pleasure. "You know," she says, "I always wanted girls, but the Lord gave me boys. Have to be satisfied with what you got." She pats Pierce on the arm and he scowls. This leads to a face-off, initiated by Pierce, who confronts Sonia like a prizefighter at a weigh-in. "I bet *you* had a lot to be thankful for," he says. Sonia gives him an arch look and a condescending, exaggeratedly sing-song reply: "I had to worry about *grades*, whether people *liked* me, and oh yes, I had two older brothers I had to compete with." Acting the heroic proletarian, Pierce goes for a direct insult: "They teach you how to pick cotton in Charm School?" She smirks and imitates a southern belle: "Why no, Pierce, Charm School taught ladies how to be ladies and how to be charming in the presence of gentlemen. A man's work was once measured by how much cotton he chopped in a day. And how much cotton have *you* chopped, Pierce?"

When the characters move to the living room, we see Wendell for the first time. More light-skinned than his brother, he wears a business suit and is writing notes with a gold pen. He has only a few lines of dialogue and is a less-developed character than other members of his family; in this scene, he's little more than a social placeholder, providing just the right indications of a recently achieved educational and social status. He tells Mrs. Mundy that his secretary is going to type up a list of wedding guests. Mrs. Mundy turns to Pierce and asks, "When are *you* going to have a secretary?" Sonia airily remarks, "I'm sure that when Pierce makes up his mind what he wants to be, he's going to be quite successful." Mrs. Mundy takes the remark as a compliment and beams again, her voice rising as if she were at a revival meeting: "I got them into church! If they get married and have a family I'll be ready to be called to glory!"

Sonia is so flamboyantly bourgeois that many viewers will completely dislike her and probably also dislike Wendell; nevertheless, the film doesn't take sides in the usual fashion of didactic drama. It has sympathy with Pierce's class position, but it gives Sonia and Wendell chances to defend themselves. As they exit the Mundy house, Sonia turns to her future husband and asks, "Is Pierce retarded?" "No," Wendell says, "just ghettoized." And in fact, Pierce is too self-righteous about his working-class experience and too ready to force arguments with Sonia. He has no political consciousness other than populist hostility toward big shots. His parents, on the other hand, look up to the Dubois family and are deeply conservative, influenced by a mix of fundamentalist Christian charity and worship of individual initiative. Their values are articulated when at one point Mrs. Mundy wants to give a bit of money to a relative who has "the neuralgia." She feels it would be the "Christian" thing to do, but Mr. Mundy objects, launching into a half-senile monologue about self-sufficiency: "If they made cotton like they did when I was growing up, there'd be jobs for everybody." He wishes his relatives were "in a Mississippi field in the hot sun picking five hundred pounds of cotton a day. Old folks used to tell us, 'Boy, you better mind how you walk. There's trouble ahead and your days are numbered.'"

When the Mundy family is invited to dinner with the Dubois family, the stage is set for a parody of social pretentions, ending in slapstick, and employing what Amy Corbin describes as a "Brechtian style" (2014, 40). The comparison is appropriate because Brecht's "alienation effect" has something in

common with satire and broad or crazy comedy. The Brechtian actor and the comic actor are equally antirealistic, concerned less with subtle emotions than with slightly exaggerated representations of social behavior, and the dinner scene fits this model nicely. Corbin notes that the dialogue, excellent for its purposes, has a stilted, unnatural quality (partly, I think, due to the acting style), and all the characters are depicted as social types. The setting, too, is somewhat antirealistic, designed to create an over-obvious air of stiffness, discomfort, and philistine excess. Seven characters are crowded around a relatively small but expensively appointed table in a dining room covered with elaborate blue and white wallpaper, which dominates the image. Burnett photographs the establishing shot with a long lens that flattens perspective and induces a slight claustrophobia. Mr. Dubois (Sy Richardson) sits at the head of the table, presiding over the occasion. A Latina servant wearing a vintage French maid's uniform and cap stands at attention behind him. He begins the meal with a prayer, thanking "our Father" for "these new relationships" in a tone that suggests concealed distaste. Pierce is the only person at the table who doesn't reverently bow his head and close his eyes.

For much of the scene, cringe-inducing comedy is generated by the economic and cultural gap between the Mundy family and the Dubois family.

Mr. Mundy provides most of the laughs when he struggles with his meal. Presented with a small bowl of open clams in their shells, he remarks that it's good you don't have to open them with your teeth. Given a glass of white wine, he makes a face. "Is something *wrong* with the wine, Mr. Mundy?" asks the Dubois patriarch. "I would have liked something stronger," Mundy says quietly, "something like Old Grand Dad." Mrs. Mundy chastises him: "Wine's fine! You don't need nothin' else!" Mr. Dubois smirks and adds, "Well now, if you would like something else, whatever it is, I can get it." Mundy politely ignores this and turns to his son Wendell. Glancing at the bride-to-be, he mutters, "I wish I was in your shoes."

Trouble starts when Mr. Dubois asks the silent, sullen Pierce, "What sort of work do you do?" In an angry tone, the currently unemployed Pierce gives his work history. Asked why he isn't a lawyer like his brother, he becomes hostile. "I don't have the *smarts* for that kind of thing," he says. He leans aggressively toward Dubois and opens his large hands like claws: "You see, I *like* working with my hands!" Mrs. Mundy, seated next to Pierce, leans around him and tries to change the topic by smiling at Mrs. Dubois at the other end of the table and asking about the recipe for the excellent salad. Mrs. Dubois (Frances E. Nealy), silent until now, turns to the maid and asks in mangled Spanish, "Que esta in la salada or whatever you call it?" After getting Mrs. Dubois's translation of the maid's reply, Mrs. Mundy publicly expresses her disappointment with Pierce: "It would have been heaven if both of my children could have been doctors and lawyers like your two children." Hearing this, Pierce rocks back in his chair, puts both hands behind his head, looks at the ceiling, and reflects: "Doctors and lawyers—biggest crooks in the world. The higher up you go the worse people you find."

"You'll have to excuse my dear brother," Wendell says to the Dubois family. "He has a very romantic view of the have nots." Unfortunately, Sonia fills the ensuing silence by giving a nervous, prideful, excessively cheerful account of how she has just won a courtroom victory by devious methods. Her speech gives evidence to Pierce, who attacks her as a typical lawyer and causes her to leave the table in tears. Mr. Dubois pronounces an end to the meal: "This has been a very interesting evening." As the Latina maid removes everyone's dishes, Pierce expresses solidarity with the working class by making a show of thanking her—a gesture she doesn't seem to appreciate. When he and his parents exit the resplendent front door of the all-white Dubois mansion, Mrs. Mundy hauls off and smacks him in the head, knocking him down the steps. Mr. Mundy says, "You want me to hold him while you hit him?"

Amy Corbin notes that the knockabout conclusion to the dinner party functions as "a satire of both Pierce's automatic rejection of the bourgeois and his mother's unblinking admiration of them" (2014, 41). Indeed, the dinner episode as a whole is a prime example of the film's technique of occasionally objectifying the characters and keeping the audience at a certain emotional distance from them. *Killer of Sheep* is a different kind of film (and at least in one respect closer to traditional moviemaking) because its protagonist is an admirable, in a sense heroic, figure with whom the audience can sympathize and possibly identify. In contrast, Pierce Mundy is neither heroic nor antiheroic. More clearly than *Killer of Sheep*, *My Brother's Wedding* demonstrates Burnett's ability to make incisive political/sociological pictures without the emotional manipulation and the good/bad rhetoric of politically tendentious cinema. Pierce has every good reason to dislike the Dubois family, who are perfect snobs; his contempt for the rich is by no means unjustified, but when he says that doctors and lawyers are the "biggest crooks in the world," he's naively overstating the situation and spoiling the evening for his brother and his parents. Just when the audience might disapprove of him, however, Sonia boasts about her tricky courtroom tactics, and Pierce no longer seems so annoying. This is a film in which black class divisions and political attitudes are wisely observed, and the audience is invited to make social judgments that aren't always dependent on the wisdom or likability of the characters. Sonia and her father aren't likable, but sometimes Pierce isn't either.

Close on the heels of the dinner party disaster, Pierce's unquestioning loyalty to Soldier leads to an ugly situation. We see him working at the front desk of the dry-cleaning shop as three pregnant women in a row come in to pick up clothes; he flirts a bit crudely with the third one, who isn't amused and asks why he isn't married, since he's old enough. Just then Soldier arrives with his arm around an attractive young woman (Julie Bolton) and flirts even more crudely with the same pregnant customer. ("I know what you've been doing.") At the back of the shop, Mrs. Mundy is rushing off for her Wednesday prayer meeting at Mount Zion Missionary Baptist Church. When Soldier calls out hello, she asks why he hasn't dropped by since he got out of jail. He tells her he's been busy looking for a job.

As soon as Mrs. Mundy leaves for the meeting, which is scheduled to last a couple of hours, Soldier asks Pierce a favor: he urgently wants to have sex with his woman friend in the back of the shop. The woman protests, offering to pay for a motel room, but Soldier insists, shoving her to the rear of the place among the hanging clothes. She tells him he's "sick" (echoing Walter in

an earlier scene). Burnett poses the couple expressionistically against a red wall as Soldier tosses a plastic bag of clothes to the floor to use as a makeshift bed and begins forcing the woman down in what looks like rape.

Time passes, and Pierce sits listless and alone in the front of the shop. In the rear, Soldier lies naked atop the equally naked young woman and calls out to Pierce to bring him ice water so that he can cool down from his exertions. Pierce dutifully brings the water, which Soldier drinks without offering any to the woman. After a while Soldier calls out again, asking Pierce to bring an aspirin for his "baby," who has a headache. Again, Pierce complies. Then Mrs. Mundy suddenly enters from the back door. She's forgotten her Bible, which is lying on the floor next to the naked couple. Crying out in horror and almost collapsing, she's comforted by two church ladies as Soldier and the young woman pull on their clothes and swiftly exit, followed by Pierce. Out on the street, Pierce and Soldier struggle with the young woman, who slaps Pierce and attempts to run away on a broken shoe. Soldier offers her a perfunctory apology and laughs when she screams at him. He slaps Pierce on the back, and the two friends turn and walk away as the barefoot woman runs off in the other direction.

For the first time, we've been given direct evidence of Soldier's bad character. He may not be a gangster or a drug dealer like some of the younger generation in Watts; he may be handsome, confident, and in Pierce's eyes charismatic; he may even deserve our sympathy at some level (his name suggests that he's representative of a generation of black men who were drafted into the Vietnam War and then tossed back on the street). But he's also a user, a liar, and arguably a rapist. There's probably good reason he went to jail and why he might return there, and Pierce's passive acquiescence to his needs is disturbing. If Pierce and Soldier are "alike," as Pierce has said to Soldier's mother, that's because they're both child-men. Soldier is the bad-boy hero of Pierce's youth; Pierce isn't predisposed to do something mean or criminal, but in his own way he doesn't want to grow up.

Soldier is not only an irresponsible friend but also a dangerous person to hang out with, and Pierce barely misses dying alongside him. On the afternoon of the day of his death, Soldier and a young woman are sitting together in her parked car. He notices Angela and her friend walking past and asks her to go around the corner and tell Pierce that he's waiting for him. But Angela doesn't like Soldier and refuses to be his messenger. Soldier and the woman in the car soon become passionate and decide they don't need a third party, so they drive off. Meanwhile, Pierce is dolefully attending to his grandparents, giving Big Mamma her daily pills. The grandparents are a somewhat comic looking couple: a stooped old woman with silver hair that has been badly abused in the beauty shop and a fat old man with a walking stick. They're normally cared for by the almost unseen, heavy-drinking Aunt Hattie, who, whenever she's away, leaves a black-and-white TV turned on for their entertainment. (In a surreal earlier scene, the TV is showing a prizefight as the characters talk.) Big Mamma calls the broadcasts "the devil's work" and asks Pierce to turn the TV off. Suddenly, out of nowhere, Big Papa asks Pierce if Soldier is religious. Pierce says no and wonders why the question came up. "His name just ran through my mind," Big Papa says.

The remark portends a magical-realist or spiritual effect, foreshadowing the more obvious magic in Burnett's next film, *To Sleep with Anger*. The aura of spiritual coincidence is heightened when Big Papa and Big Mamma ask Pierce to read to them from the Bible. Bored and restless, Pierce grabs the King James Version, flops down on a couch, and wants to know what he should read. The grandparents don't care, so he carelessly flips the good book open, landing on a song of David from Psalm 26: "Judge me, O Lord, for I have walked in mine integrity. . . . I have hated the congregation of evil doers; and will not sit with the wicked. . . . Gather not my soul with sinners, nor my life with bloody men, in whose hands is mischief." As Pierce reads, Big

Mamma and Big Papa, who know the Bible by heart, begin to chant the verses in unison with him, and a slow lap dissolve takes us to a view of daylight sky, apparently seen from the top of an automobile moving down a long straight road bordered by tall leafy trees. The meaning of this shot, which evokes a sense of peace in keeping with the Bible verses, is unclear. Is it a view from the automobile occupied by Soldier and the young woman in the previous scene? If so, it seems incongruous, because it has a pastoral quality and seems far from the city. The voices of Pierce and his grandparents can be heard over the shot and also over the beginning of the next shot, which returns us to a more familiar environment: the Watts skyline seen from a hill as the sun sets and night arrives.

Given his dislike of the black gangster cycle and general contempt for black-themed movies that emphasize sex and violence, it isn't surprising that Burnett doesn't show us Soldier's death, only its consequences. In a night-for-night montage photographed mostly in telephoto, we see an ambulance, flares, and bodies being removed from a pair of crumpled autos, one with bullet holes in its front window. A badly injured woman and her child are carried away on stretchers. Soldier and his date are taken from the bullet-riddled car, and she's placed in an ambulance while medics fruitlessly try to perform resuscitation on Soldier. When they stop, a uniformed black policeman says, "Wrap him up." Walter, or somebody like Walter, has achieved revenge, and Soldier is headed for the morgue.

In the aftermath of the death, a series of brief scenes (and a model of economical storytelling) leads up to the contrasting religious ceremonies that end the film. At night, a telephone rings and lights come on in the house where Soldier's parents live. In the morning, a tall, gangly teenage girl bursts out of another house and runs full speed down the street to where Pierce and a friend are standing on the corner, joking about a recent party. The girl loudly announces Solder's death, and Burnett cuts to an extreme telephoto shot of the astonished Pierce running desperately for three blocks toward the camera, crossing San Vincente, Pico, and the 1300 block of Tremaine Avenue. At Soldier's house, he stands as a mute witness to the grief of Soldier's mother, father, and sister, who is placing a telephone call to an aunt in Natchez, Mississippi. That evening, as he sits alone and weeps at the kitchen table, his mother enters and briefly tries to comfort him with a hug. On the next day he visits Soldier's mother, who, because of her religious faith, seems less distraught than he is.

We see Soldier's body lying in state at a tiny funeral home, visited by a nicely individuated group of working-class characters. Angela makes one of her periodic visits to the dry-cleaning shop and calls out Pierce's name but gets no answer; he's out rushing from one place to another to recruit pallbearers for the Saturday funeral, just as he earlier rushed around in an attempt to find Soldier a job. A man washing a dog in the parking lot of a decrepit motel tells him, "I ain't got nothing else to do." Another man, who is having the ingrown hairs of his beard ministered to by his wife, says he's been working seven days a week and couldn't attend a funeral even if his mother died. A third man (Nate Hardman, the protagonist in Billy Woodberry's *Bless Their Little Hearts*) ponders the request while inviting Pierce to stay for dinner; his wife remarks, "I thought we'd eat like white folks tonight." Pierce explains that his stomach isn't well, and the husband, still trying to think about Saturday, suddenly remembers something: "Saturday . . . ain't your brother getting married this Saturday?"

At this point the to-and-fro rhythm initiated by the opening scene of the film returns at a frantic pace. Pierce rushes off to the Mundy household and finds Wendell and Sonia in discussion with his parents; he's missed the wedding rehearsal and his brother is furious. Without apologizing to anyone, Pierce announces, "You have to change the wedding!" He pleads with Sonia to move the event to another hour but she reminds him that he's never had a kind word for her. Mrs. Mundy tells him, "I've never asked a favor, but I'm calling in my debts now!" Mr. Mundy gives him a lecture about the planning involved in the wedding and suggests that the time of the funeral might be changed. This idea hadn't occurred to Pierce, who now rushes off to Soldier's parents. They're planning for the burial and will soon be dealing with the arrival of relatives; seeing their fatigue, Pierce can't bring himself to ask anything. Both ceremonies will go off as scheduled.

The parallel editing at the closing of the film, which combines crosscutting with a montage of conflicts, is designed to emphasize Pierce's dilemma and create a certain amount of suspense while at the same time highlighting class differences, shifting between moods, and offering a broad, encompassing view of the film's community. Everything is structured by strong contrasts among settings, costumes, music, and typage. First we see Soldier's body being formally dressed by a funeral home mortician in preparation for open-casket viewing. Cut to a large church, where Mrs. and Mr. Mundy smile broadly and pose for wedding pictures: she wears a white dress with a garland in her hair and he's stylish in a tuxedo and black tie. A group of friends in churchgoing clothes gather around the Mundys to offer congratulations, and a Johnny Ace recording ("Never Let Me Go," 1954) seems to reverberate cheerfully and romantically off the church walls. Backstage, Sonia and her bridesmaids laugh and prepare their hair and makeup. Cut to the modest funeral home, where a young man dressed like a minister (Mark Smith) sings a funeral song and a small line of somber but unweeping mourners, nearly all of them in working clothes, sign a register. Back at the church, Mrs. Mundy corners the scowling, tuxedoed Pierce, who is intensely worried about the time, and warns him to behave himself. Just then Mrs. Dubois stands in front of the assembled crowd and announces a short delay because Sonia's favorite uncle hasn't arrived. At the funeral home, a minister can be heard yelling a revivalist sermon as the line of mourners walk past Soldier's parents and offer their condolences. At the church, Mrs. Dubois approaches Pierce and holds out her hand, welcoming him to the family; he pulls his hand away and asks a young man standing nearby if he can borrow his car. At the funeral home, mourners file past the casket. Pierce gets in the car and races down the highway while Soldier's pallbearers, one of them wearing a shirt that identifies him as the driver of a beer truck, walk ceremoniously out of the funeral home with the coffin. At the church, Sonia and Wendell, in their wedding clothes, are seen from a high angle as they join arms and prepare to walk down the aisle. The opening notes of the wedding march are heard, but Pierce can't be found.

Burnett's talent for storyboarding can be seen not only in the previous scenes but also, most vividly, at the end of *My Brother's Wedding*, which consists of two shots of hugely contrasting scale. An extreme long shot from across the street of the funeral home shows Pierce arriving in his borrowed red sports car and skidding to a stop in the empty parking lot; he jumps out and an attendant gestures to him, apparently explaining that the funeral is over. Pierce is a tiny, isolated figure in black, standing alone on barren concrete. Next, an extreme close-up shows his hands: he's holding his brother's wedding ring, which, in his haste, he took with him when he left the church.

The film stops here, at a moment of frustration and failure, with the narrative drive of the double plot exhausted and Pierce suspended between worlds. Percussive African music—a Tarureg medicinal chant from Mali and Hausa street music from Niger—plays over the closing credits. A bit of it was heard earlier, nondiegetically, when a pregnant woman entered the Mundys' dry-cleaning shop. It takes on significance if we remember the autonomous shot at the beginning of the film, when a singer performed "Amazing Grace." The opening music is associated with southern black churches and the history of slavery in America, and the closing music is associated with the ceremonies and rituals of marriage and religious worship in Africa. *My Brother's Wedding* is bookended by traditional signifiers of a black religious and cultural experience that extends far back in time and beyond the American continent. Even though Burnett is a secular artist, in this film he's very much concerned with the way religion can provide coherence and ethical standards to a black community, giving meaning to such fundamental events as marriage and death. In Watts in the 1980s, however, the old religion and folkways were losing their cultural force, and some young men like Pierce were rudderless.

My Brother's Wedding leaves certain problems unresolved, and not just those of an individual who lacks maturity and wisdom. There is a sense in which Pierce Mundy is an allegorical figure representing a generational crisis for black men in Watts. He doesn't have anything in common with what he describes as "these kids of today," and he's alienated from the religion of his parents and grandparents. He isn't the sort of person who might wind up in prison like Soldier, but he has no vocational aspirations (nor, given his misogynistic tendencies, any aspiration to start a family) and is rigidly set against middle-class values. He just wants to stay in the neighborhood. In telling his story, Burnett isn't giving us a sermon about the need for religious revival, nor is he promoting middle-class ideas of progress. His film is in part about the waning of old, familial sources of wisdom in the black community and a contemporary social arrangement that could learn from them. What that arrangement might be, and whether it might have any efficacy without connections with the past, remains an open question. Burnett's next film poses it strongly.

FIVE

To Sleep with Anger *(1990)*

BURNETT'S FIRST TWO FEATURE FILMS were concerned with economic, social, and cultural threats to the survival of black families in Watts. *To Sleep with Anger*, his impressive third feature and the first he made under relatively normal Hollywood production conditions, changes the pattern slightly. The location, unspecified in the film, has moved to the fringes of the Sugar Hill area of Los Angeles, north of Adams Boulevard between Western and Crenshaw. Named after a wealthy part of New York's Harlem, Sugar Hill in the 1940s, 1950s, and 1960s was home to the most prosperous blacks in the city, many of them celebrities of sports and entertainment (residents included Joe Louis, Lena Horne, Louise Beavers, Hattie McDaniel, Pearl Bailey, and Ray Charles). Once populated by whites, it was known for its fine architecture, a good deal of which was demolished when the Santa Monica freeway was constructed, bisecting the neighborhood. The threatened family in *To Sleep with Anger* lives in a two-story Craftsman bungalow outside the borders of the original neighborhood. They seem reasonably secure, although, like the family in *Killer of Sheep*, they came to Los Angeles from the South and have a roof that needs repair. In this case, their survival as a unit has less to do with economic than with cultural, spiritual, and generational forces. More than Burnett's previous films, this one is preoccupied with southern black religious traditions and folkways that once held families and communities together but are beginning to die off.

The title of the film is derived from Ephesians 4:26, which, in the King James Version of the Bible, reads: "Be ye angry, and sin not: let not the sun go down upon your anger." Its plot concerns the extended family of the sixty-something Gideon, named for a mighty warrior of God in the Old Testament (Paul Butler), and his wife, Susie (Mary Alice). As a young man,

Gideon performed John Henry–like labor for the railroad, but at some point he found a job that enabled him to retire and live on a pension. The nature of the job is unclear; when I asked Charles Burnett about it, he said he that he imagined Gideon had found work with the Postal Service. Susie is a midwife who teaches natural childbirth. In cultural terms, the two are typical products of the post–World War II, southern black diaspora: they have southern accents and "country" superstitions, they regularly attend church, they gather the family for Sunday dinner, and they raise chickens and do gardening in their backyard. In a scene that was cut from the film for reasons of length, a policeman arrives at their door and informs them that a city ordinance forbids raising the chickens. Gideon angrily replies that he has always had chickens: "We grow most of our own food. The money I get from social security, my pension and my wife's work keeps us living on the edge. What choice do people like us have?" The policeman says they should move "further out," but doesn't say where. When he leaves, Gideon fumes: "I'll be damned if I get rid of my chickens. I ought to get some hogs and put them out there."

Gideon and Susie's two handsome sons live nearby. Junior, the elder (Carl Lumbly), resembles his father in his evident love for his wife and children and his pride in manual labor. Babe Brother, the younger (Richard Brooks), is a loan officer in a bank who is married to Linda, a real estate agent (Sheryl Lee Ralph), and has a very young son; a rebel against the southern black working class, Babe Brother is troubled by barely repressed sibling rivalry and anger over his father's disapproval of him. This underlying tension is brought to the surface when Gideon's old friend Harry (Danny Glover), en route from Detroit to Oakland, is welcomed into Gideon's home and given a temporary place to stay. At first Harry behaves like a polite, old-country southerner, but he's soon revealed to be a ne'er-do-well who may have magical powers. His name is a sly reference to the mythical "Harry Man" of southern black, Indian, and West African folklore: a trickster who can rob you of your soul if you don't outwit him. Strange things begin to happen after Harry arrives. Gideon falls mysteriously ill, and Harry casts a kind of spell over Babe Brother, attempting to lure him away from home. But there's something morally ambiguous or ironic about Harry, as there is in some versions of the trickster in folklore. Burnett has said that he viewed Harry as a "type of person who is seen as evil, but isn't evil" (1996, 97). The film never attributes truly magical powers to him, and most of the trouble he causes has less to do with malevolence than with a dangerously wild, fun-loving rebelliousness.

His extended visit disturbs the family's status quo and unleashes a hidden rage, yet it creates the possibility for reconciliation and healing.

To Sleep with Anger originated as a television project for the Corporation for Public Broadcasting, an organization that proved almost as intractable and meddling as the big movie studios would have been. Burnett initially approached the CPB because he wanted to tell the story of a real-life character, a heroic young girl named Dimitria Wallace who was murdered by an LA gang because she was going to testify against them in court. The CPB provided money for the development of the script, but when the staff saw Burnett's treatment, they suggested changes that ran counter to the truth of the story. Burnett offered to substitute the purely fictional *To Sleep with Anger*, but the CPB wanted to eliminate the folkloric elements, which the organization thought the general audience (i.e., whites) wouldn't understand, and instead center the story entirely on the buppie couple of Babe Brother and his wife Linda. This was completely against the spirit of Burnett's unusual screenplay. As he later explained, his purpose was "to establish some kind of continuity between the present and the past by using contemporary situations combined with this folklore character" (Kapsis 2011, 23). He was especially interested in a vanishing oral tradition seldom acknowledged in history books and was concerned to show the struggle within black families when the younger generation moves into the middle class. He therefore withdrew from the CPB plans. Fortunately, in 1989 he received the MacArthur "genius" award and a Rockefeller Foundation production grant. That same year, independent filmmaker Michael Tolkin recommended him to LA producer Caldecot Chubb (among Chubb's later films is Kasi Lemmons's *Eve's Bayou* [1997]), who had recently joined forces with Edward R. Pressman. (Pressman's many credits include *Badlands* [1973], *Wall Street* [1987], and *Bad Lieutenant* [1992].) Chubb called Burnett, asked to see the screenplay for *To Sleep with Anger*, and immediately set about raising money.

Chubb and Pressman were model producers and never interfered with Burnett's work. Budgeted at $1,200,000, the film used a nonunion crew and was shot with a three-to-one ratio on location in only twenty-eight days. Burnett's earliest script had centered on conflicts between Gideon and his wife, but in a desire to get a name actor he revised the story to emphasize the conflict between Gideon and his youngest son. Chiefly because of budget and running-time limitations, he ultimately cut some folkloric material, some minor characters who gave a sense of the community, and some evocative details about Harry's past that made him a more complex, ambiguous character. Parts of this material made it into a longer version of the film, which played at Sundance, but they were cut when the Goldwyn Company took over distribution. Otherwise, the finished product adheres to Burnett's plans. (The full screenplay, containing many fine scenes that were altered or omitted, one of them a dream sequence, was published in *Scenario* 2, no. 1 [Spring 1996].) He had the benefit of a photographer he personally approved, Walt Lloyd, who was formerly director of photography for Soderbergh's *sex, lies, and videotape* (1989). He also had a large and excellent cast of actors, all members of the Screen Actors Guild. Most important was Danny Glover, the costar of the *Lethal Weapon* franchise, who was at that time the most successful black actor in Hollywood.

When Burnett and his producers showed Glover the screenplay, they thought he might be interested in playing Babe Brother (it was rumored that he always picked young characters). In the role of Harry, Burnett was planning to cast Julius Harris, a large, imposing, but less well-known actor who had appeared in *Super Fly* (1972), *Live and Let Die* (1973), *The Taking of Pelham One Two Three* (1974), and numerous TV shows. But Glover asked if he could take on the role of the Harry Man. Burnett was understandably quick to approve the idea, and Julius Harris ended up being cast as Herman, an old and ailing member of Harry's entourage. Glover not only brought to the film potential box-office appeal (and financial help as an executive producer) but also gave the most impressive performance of his career, subtly revealing the complex, contradictory aspects of Harry's character: his charm, his guile, his creepiness, his manipulation and seductiveness, his delight in causing trouble, and occasionally his loneliness and vulnerability. In the film his deep, sandpapery voice is compelling, his face can look both kindly and menacing, and his movements are alternately graceful and bent with age.

To Sleep with Anger is a deceptively simple-looking film that takes on added meaning with repeated viewings and has an intriguing, unusually mixed tone. One could describe it as a black comedy (pun intended), especially in its closing scenes, when, as if by some magic concatenation of forces, Harry falls dead in the kitchen doorway and Gideon's family is unable to get city officials to move the body. Burnett told me that where humor is concerned, he was chiefly interested in creating a feeling of the ironic, the absurd, and the contradictory: "Without trying to be funny," he remarked, "humor comes naturally out of ironic situations and the absurd." Not that he would have wanted to, but he could have called the picture *The Trouble with Harry,* a title Hitchcock used in 1955 for a gentle black comedy about a troublesome corpse. (Burnett remembers seeing the Hitchcock picture with his mother and grandmother when he was a child.) Burnett's film, however, is comic in a greater variety of ways. A sweetly amusing view of a community, its dialogue contains funny stories and satirical old sayings, and its ending has the pleasantly upbeat quality of what classical scholars term "New Comedy," which usually has to do with social continuity and the initiation or restoration of marriage. But it isn't a lighthearted movie. As Phillip Lamarr Cunningham has noted, it could also be described as an example of southern and African American gothic, much of which has to do with decaying families, conjuring, and the ghosts of slavery (2011; see also Goddu 1997). Nightmarish moods and family violence emerge during the film and need to be expunged or resolved before comic happiness can be achieved.

To Sleep with Anger was exceptionally well reviewed and won four Independent Spirit awards, a best screenplay award from the National Board of Review, and a Special Jury Prize at Sundance. But it was badly promoted and distributed by the Goldwyn Company and never got a chance to find an audience. A year after it was released, Burnett encountered people who asked him when it would appear. In one city in Texas, it played in a theater so remote that, according to Burnett, you had to make a U-turn on the expressway to get there. Goldwyn was so stingy about the number of prints it made that Burnett had trouble getting prints even for press screenings. There was no attempt to publicize the film in unconventional places, such as black schools and churches, where there was a potential audience. Burnett remembers being in Washington, D.C., when it was playing and not being able to find advertising. It wasn't even listed on the theater marquee; moviegoers had to go inside and ask to find out that it was showing. Burnett recalls that "a friend of mine, Carol Blue, decided to prove . . . that if the film was advertised properly, you could get a full house. So in San Diego, after the film had already come and gone, she organized a series of screenings and packed the house. . . . She just generated a lot of word of mouth, and the film did extremely well" (1996, 203). Recently, the Sony organization has generated a beautiful 35mm restoration, and we can hope it will one day be available on Blu-ray.

Like *My Brother's Wedding*, *To Sleep with Anger* opens with a somewhat enigmatic sequence involving an old black spiritual song, although in this case the enigma is partly explained when we discover that what we're watching is a dream. An overweight man (we soon learn he's Gideon), dressed in a fancy white fedora, a white suit, and white shoes, sits upright and expressionless in a straight-backed chair. On the wall behind him is a large photographic portrait of an elegantly dressed woman from another era (we later see this picture in Gideon's house, but the woman is never identified), and next to him is a table holding a bowl of fruit and a slightly browning half of an apple. As the man twiddles his thumbs, the fruit on the table, the legs of the table, and his white shoes burst into flame. Over this we hear a legendary recording of Thomas A. Dorsey's "Precious Memories" by singer/guitarist Sister Rosetta Tharpe. Burnett conceived the sequence with that recording in mind, in part because his grandmother loved it. Dorsey was a pioneer writer of music for black churches and is often described as "the father of American gospel." Tharpe, a crossover recording success of the 1930s and 1940s, has been described as the "the godmother of rock and roll." The recording's beautiful fusion of gospel and blues—if you like, of sacred and profane—is perfectly appropriate for a film in which tradition and modernity, religion and conjuring, familial love and devilish impulses are intertwined.

At the end of the dream sequence, Gideon's burning shoes dissolve to his bare feet and the camera pulls back to reveal that he's wearing jeans and sitting in a chair near his backyard chicken coop with a Bible in his lap. The film never tries to interpret his dream fully. Was the picture on the wall a relative, perhaps Gideon's mother or grandmother? What's the meaning of the uneaten apple? Why the flames? A possible determinant of the dream is provided when Susie, who has been teaching a crowded Lamaze childbirth class in the living room, meets Gideon in the bedroom. He's anxiously looking through drawers and cupboards and tells her that he's lost his "Toby," a charm his great-grandfather gave him.

The Toby, a homemade, sometimes entirely improvised object with a shape that can resemble a crucifix, has totemic significance in southern black folklore, acting as a shield against the devil or, more rarely, as an instrument of evil magic. As Cunningham explains, the Toby serves to link conjure with Christianity: "Often, conjure is presented as incongruous to traditional religion; however, for many Southern blacks, black magic and Christianity went hand-in-hand" (2011, 127). Hence Gideon's loss of the Toby prefigures the arrival of Harry, who, we subsequently learn, has long ago misplaced his own Toby. The loss of the protective charm also helps partly explain Gideon's dream, in which he's dressed like a dapper gangster or a potentially sinful character about to be engulfed by flames. In an interview, Burnett has suggested just such an interpretation: "Gideon has a dream, a nightmare, born out of anger and frustration. He's lost his Toby. He sees himself burning in Hell for the first time, and then Harry shows up" (Kapsis 2011, 55).

The anger and frustration to which Burnett alludes are also caused by Gideon's unhappy relationship with his younger son, a relationship that immediately becomes a topic of the dialogue. Gideon and Susie, with the assistance of Junior's teenage daughter Ronda (Reina King), are babysitting Babe Brother's five- or six-year-old child Sunny (DeVaughn Nixon), whom we glimpse sleeping in one of their bedrooms. (On the wall behind him is the old portrait we saw in Gideon's dream, and in his hand is a half-eaten apple; he's a silent observer of much of the action and an unwitting agent of the film's denouement.) Gideon complains that Babe Brother is spoiled, utterly different from the responsible Junior; he leaves his child for long periods of time and has forgotten Susie's recent birthday. Mary Alice, who has one of the sweetest faces in the history of movies, does an excellent job of conveying Susie's quiet strength and wisdom while at the same time avoiding the trap of making her look saintly; she defends Babe Brother ("It just takes some people longer to figure out who they are") and calms Gideon in almost the same voice she uses with expectant mothers and fathers in the Lamaze class. Paul Butler is equally excellent at registering Gideon's emotional shift from righteousness to deference. He lies back on the bed and suggests that he and Susie might have time for a bit of sex before Sunny awakes. Susie picks up his house slippers, puts them down on his big belly, and exits, giving him a subtle wink.

One of Burnett's virtues is his habit of departing from the plot to observe details of everyday life in the surrounding world, a habit he's been forced to restrain in his less independent films and to some extent in *To Sleep with Anger*, especially after the Goldwyn Company took over distribution. For example, an early version of the film involved a character named "Old John," who rolls a cart up the alleyway behind Gideon and Susie's house and gives them rabbit manure for their garden. "I was raised a mule and now I'm a rolling stone," Old John says to Gideon. Susie gives him some fresh tomatoes and tells him she's planted a row of vegetables just for him. "I didn't mean for you to pay me," he says. "I know," Susie says, "but you have been so thoughtful." The scene says a good deal about the life of the poor in the neighborhood and about the vestiges of the barter economy that Gideon and Susie brought with them from the South. Along with several other brief and more or less autonomous scenes that gave a sense of the community, it was cut.

A couple of minor digressions survive, however, and appear early in the film when Burnett cuts away from Gideon's house to show kids in the neighborhood. A boy who is raising pigeons releases the birds and throws rocks to keep them in flight; they make graceful swoops and swirls in the blue sky, and the rocks fall on Gideon's roof. Next door, another boy practices the trumpet; when he attempts to hit a high note, he produces an awful screech that annoys everybody in hearing distance. Gideon complains about the noise, and kids out on the sidewalk yell, "Shut up! Go help your mamma wash dishes!" (In the longer version of the film we discover that the early morning crowing of the rooster in Gideon's backyard is equally annoying to the neighbors.) These scenes of children have an autobiographical source—when Burnett was a boy, he both raised pigeons and played the trumpet—but they also become important motifs. We occasionally return to the pigeons, which take on the quality of a magical sign. The boy with the trumpet keeps blowing, at one point causing a little girl on the sidewalk to cover her ears. Later, he intervenes in the plot when the noise of his horn saves a rooster in Gideon's backyard from being murdered by Harry, and at the end of the film he performs a crucial function.

The latent tension in Gideon's house is exacerbated when Babe Brother arrives at one A.M. to claim his son. He and Susie, dressed in her nightgown, have a tender embrace at the door, but Gideon rushes downstairs in a pair of minatory-looking red pajamas and berates Babe Brother for his lateness. Under strain because of the conflict between her husband and her son, Susie is able to partly defuse the situation by stepping between the two men, a position she takes at two other important points in the film. But on the next morning conflict spreads to Babe Brother's home; he awakes to find Linda dressed in business clothes, on her way to work, and when he gives Sunny a sip of his coffee, she accuses him of spoiling the child, just as he was spoiled. He has heard this accusation before, and it touches a raw nerve. He angrily tells Linda that his father, who believed "calluses are the mark of a man," made him do hard labor and go to church all day on Sundays. His family, he says, are "no different from farm animals."

A few days later Babe Brother pays a brief, obligatory visit to the family's Sunday dinner and is publicly called to account by his father and older brother. "When are you going to find time to help me fix the roof?" Junior asks him. Gideon scowls and reminds Babe Brother that he's forgotten Susie's birthday. "Boy, go tell your wife to come in," Gideon orders. Babe Brother goes out to Linda, who is sitting in their car, and tries to coax her into the house. "I haven't read this year's almanac," she says. "What would I talk about?" Inside the house, Junior tells his father, "You all should have been hard on him like you were with me." Susie, troubled, looks down at her plate and quietly replies, "Everybody got the same."

Babe Brother is one of the most interesting characters in the film. He's angry with his father, but hypocritically depends on his parents to help care for his child. He talks disparagingly about Gideon and Susie behind their backs, but in their presence makes lame excuses for neglecting them. He's something of a child-man and becomes less sympathetic as the film goes on. But a grown man who is still being called "Babe Brother" or "Boy" is made to feel like a child, and he may have good reason to nurture resentment. ("Junior," a less condescending nickname, is appropriate for a chip off the old block.) Susie's insistence that both brothers "got the same" carries weight. Babe Brother's repressed fury at being treated as a spoiled momma's boy is understandable. He has repudiated his working-class background, and his father and brother, who treat him with anger, seem partly motivated by a form of class resentment. They and his career-woman wife also implicitly criticize his manhood. All this explains the strange influence Harry will have over him. Babe Brother's male ego has been wounded by his father, brother, and wife; he's mesmerized by the idea of abandoning his middle-class world and becoming not a laborer but an old-time bad man who carries a knife, has lots of women, and lives on the road.

The film presages Harry's arrival with a series of domestic events that have a slightly uncanny or magical quality. The first involves oral storytelling, which has the power to stimulate imagination and create legends. "When I grew up," Burnett once told an interviewer, "everyone told jokes and stories. It isn't that way anymore. Having stories told when you're a kid, organizing perception in symbolic ways, is so important" (Kapsis 2011, 40). The practice is dramatized when Gideon, while working on a household chore, tells Babe Brother's child an elaborate joke. The boy sits on the floor in rapt attention as his grandfather describes a bunch of preachers in a church basement holding a confessional competition to decide which of them has the most sinful habits. Gideon imitates each of their prissy voices as they make their naughty revelations, building up to the last preacher, who is quite sure that he's the worst sinner of all: "My sin is gossip," the preacher confesses, "and I'm going to tell everything I've heard!" Too young to comprehend the joke, Sunny doesn't laugh, but he's captivated by the story and tries to tell one of his own, beginning, "Once upon a time." Just then a wind or some invisible force knocks over a broom standing in a kitchen corner. As the broom falls, it dislodges one of Susie's favorite teacups, which shatters on the floor.

At that moment, Harry arrives. As Burnett had done in previous films, he introduces the character with a close-up of a pair of shoes, which in this case are large and well worn. Then we see Harry in a wide shot, viewed from behind, standing at Gideon and Susie's door and carrying his belongings in large paper boxes bound with string. Gaye Shannon Burnett was costume designer for the film, and her unobtrusive work enhances this and other characterizations: Harry wears a brown, ill-fitting suit and a grey hat with an upturned brim that sits squarely atop his head. From behind, he looks like a weary traveler from the country who is trying to maintain humble dignity. But there's also a touch of the door-to-door salesman in the way he prepares to ring the bell. As the film proceeds, we discover that he has a flashier wardrobe in those paper boxes: loud ties, suspenders, and suits, all redolent of earlier times and rowdy places.

"Harry! I can't believe it's you!" Susie cries as Harry wipes his shoes on the doormat and enters the house. "Good God Almighty, man!" Gideon shouts. "Susie, we haven't seen Harry since we left home!" But after a round of joyful hugs and reminiscences, the mood briefly changes. Sunny, who has been sweeping shards of teacup from the kitchen floor, shyly approaches and accidentally touches Harry's shoe with the broom. Harry's ingratiating smile vanishes and an expression of mingled anger and fear passes over his face. He seizes the broom and spits on the brush end. "Boy," he says quietly, with a forbidding look, "that is bad luck to touch a fellow with a broom." Susie tells Sunny to apologize and brings salt for Harry to throw over his shoulder.

(This is another scene that has autobiographical resonance; as a boy, Burnett was reprimanded for touching an old man with a broom and for years afterward was cautious when he swept the floor.) From virtually the moment Harry enters the house, southern black superstition comes to the fore; domestic objects become charms, things to conjure with, capable of creating or warding off evil. Harry explains that he's just stopping over until his next bus connection late in the evening, but Gideon and Susie urge him to stay. "Well, I don't want to put you out," he says (the words of somebody who, once inside, becomes a semipermanent guest). Susie points out that because their sons are grown the house has empty bedrooms. Harry smiles and says he doesn't need a mattress: "Always make me a pallet on the floor."

The next morning, a Sunday, Harry rises from his pallet, dresses, and goes deferentially to the kitchen, where most of the important family scenes of this film are set. Gideon, in his underwear, is ironing his pants for church. Susie, working on the after-church meal, turns and smiles with delight at Harry's politeness: "One can sure tell you're from back home!" Harry strikes an aw-shucks attitude but has a devilish glint in his eye. Back home, he says, "you have to know how to act right, have to say yes sir, no sir—have to know your place" (a hint of why Harry has become the sort of character he is). Just then Junior arrives with his daughter Ronny and his wife Pat (Vonetta McGee), who is in a late stage of pregnancy. Gideon introduces them to Harry, and when Harry shakes Pat's hand her baby gives her a mighty kick: "Oh! Must be turning over," she says.

When the family goes off to church, Harry stays behind, claiming fatigue but using the opportunity to explore the house. The sequence is backed nondiegetically by Rosetta Tharpe's cover of "Precious Memories," which we heard during the dream at the beginning of the film. Valerie Smith has observed that the first occurrence of the song "suggests something of Gideon's southern past in his northern life," but the second provides ironic background for Harry's search through that same past (2003, 875). His silent actions range from apparently simple curiosity to sinister intrusiveness. First, he studies a large group of family snapshots inserted in the frame of a dressing-table mirror. Pausing at the photo of a child, he holds a hand over it in a weird gesture, temporarily blocking it from view. (Later we get a possible explanation for this gesture.) Next, he inspects a handsome old clock on a mantel. Smiling to himself, he puts a finger on the minute hand, gives it a revolution, then slowly moves it back to where it was. (This slightly chilling bit of business was improvised by Glover as the scene was shot; no Method actor, he approached the role by thinking a good deal about how Harry should look, sound, and behave.) Upstairs, in Gideon and Susie's bedroom, he looks through drawers, finding a gold pocket watch and a group of letters, one of which he reads.

At church, Gideon, Susie, and Junior's family listen to the preacher read a speech by Christ to his disciples from Matthew 10:34–35: "Think not that I am come to make peace on earth. I come not to bring peace, but a sword. For I am come to set a man at variance against his father.... And a man's foes shall be they of his own household." Commentators on this passage usually explain that Christ's mission is in fact peace, but by believing in him his disciples will create violent discord between members of their families. Where *To Sleep with Anger* is concerned, the Bible verse serves to foreshadow the violence that will result from Harry's manipulation of the already tense relationship between Babe Brother and his family—a "variance" of son against father and brother, which will involve a knife rather than a sword.

A knife figures prominently in the next sequence, in which Danny Glover gives a virtuoso performance. While Gideon, Susie, and Junior's family are still at church, Babe Brother and his family have arrived at Gideon's house, presumably for Sunday dinner. Harry is with them in the kitchen, playing cards with Babe Brother while Linda and Sunny look on. (Their conversation is intercut with two brief scenes of young people being baptized at the church, creating a montage of conflicts between the Holy and the devilish.) Linda remarks that Harry seems different from Gideon's other friends: "They think if you're not hard at work you're hard at sin." Harry takes out a big crab-apple switchblade with a rabbit's foot dangling from the hilt and begins cleaning his fingernails. "I'm more modern," he tells her in a whispery, gravelly voice. "I don't believe in sin. I believe in good and evil, and evil is something you have to work at." Fascinated, Sunny moves around his mother's shoulder and tries to touch the knife. Harry shoos him away. The rabbit's foot, he says, takes the place of the Toby his grandmother gave him, which he lost some years ago. Babe Brother reacts with troubled interest, but Linda, amused by Harry's quaint habits, arches a brow, smiles, and asks, "What's a Toby?" Harry explains the nature of the charm and warns that "you don't want to be at a crossroads without one." His remark is rich with implication: it links up the cross-shaped Toby with the troubled, metaphoric crossroad at which Gideon's family has arrived, but more specifically, it alludes to the founding legend of blues music, in which Robert Johnson and Tommy Johnson supposedly met the devil at a crossroad and sold their souls to become masters of

a mean, down-and-dirty style. (Burnett will return to this legend in his later film, *Warming by the Devil's Fire*.)

Harry laughs, shows his winning cards to Babe Brother, and gives him a friendly slap on the shoulder. Then he turns to Linda and asks if Sunny was born at home, like the rest of Susie's family. "No, indeed," she says, looking proudly at her son, "I had my baby at Cedars Sinai." Babe Brother, increasingly interested in Harry's knife, asks, "You ever use this thing?" Harry laughs and says the knife is for "bad monkeys." He squeezes Babe Brother's shoulder and smiles, relishing an opportunity for storytelling.

He begins ambiguously, unwilling to say whether the tale is real or imagined. "I seem to remember I had to use that crab apple on a boy from back home. I was coming down Beale Street. I heard this music coming from a booth. Sure enough, it was Henry. He and another boy had killed a boy named Hunter, and they balled the jack leaving town." (Glover chuckles and makes quick little movements with his fists, as if sprinting.) "Henry had lost one eye and had a scar running down his face." Like a magician, Harry traces a line with his finger down from his forehead to his jaw, transforming his half-closed eye into what looks like an empty socket and speaking in a husky, hypnotic voice. "They went up to this girl's room and got to drinking that corn liquor." Linda becomes uneasy, turning her head away and looking down. Harry continues: "The girl turned out the lights! Man!" Babe Brother, in a trance, clings to every word. Harry breaks the spell by grasping him by the shoulder and giving him advice: "A man that drinks keeps a knife open in his pocket."

After a beat of silence, Linda, feeling excluded, picks up one of the cards on the table, which is illustrated on the back with a painting of a nude woman being approached from behind by an eerie, skeletal figure. Babe Brother reacts angrily: "Don't pick up the cards! You're not in the game!" The three exchange glances, silently aware that Harry has acquired all the power at the table and that Linda will no longer have influence in any game involving her husband. Babe Brother, looking a bit guilty about his outburst, asks Harry, "So did you use the knife?" Harry quietly boasts, "I protected myself and I always will." Leaning back, he puts an arm around Linda and rubs her shoulder. She looks a bit frightened, head down and arms crossed over her breasts. Harry keeps rubbing her shoulder and almost licks his lips. "I like the blues," he says.

As the film proceeds, Harry grows increasingly disturbing. In Burnett's original screenplay there were more sympathetic aspects of the character, including the fact that he had two sons who died. "I made Harry more real," Burnett told an interviewer in *Scenario*, "more a person you could identify with. You could understand his tragedy, and I think, toward the end, in his conversation with Susie, that becomes important" (1996, 99). The only evidence of this tragedy in the final version of the film is a child's photo Harry keeps in his wallet. In one scene, he briefly places it among the family pictures on Susie's bedroom mirror. (A younger version of this child might already be on the mirror and might be the photo Harry covers with his hand in an earlier scene.) Soon after this, however, he attempts to sow discord between Pat and Junior. First he approaches Pat, praising her for the volunteer work she does feeding the poor but giving her advice: "You can't feed everybody. You have to take one in and fatten him up. If you save one, life goes on." Then he approaches Junior and alludes to Pat when he remarks: "Some people are attracted to pain and suffering. They like to be near the dying. But you never can tell what's in your heart."

The longer Harry stays with Gideon and Susie, the more openly sexual and party-loving he becomes and the more we can appreciate Burnett's mastery of a pungent, homely, suggestive dialogue that never resorts to the four-letter words that are commonplace in today's cinema. This is especially true when one day Susie calls for Harry to come down to the kitchen. He arrives wearing a somewhat flashy suit. The camera takes his point of view as Susie smiles, announces "Sur-pri-ize," and steps aside, creating an almost eerie reveal and an impressive entrance for the figure behind her: Harry's old friend Hattie, an attractive older woman with a nimbus of white hair, a naturally provocative smile, and a shyly bowed head (Ethel Ayler, who began her career as a stage understudy for Lena Horne). Harry gazes at Hattie with admiration and crosses the room, pulling out a chair for her at the kitchen table. He touches her shoulders, leans down, and softly asks, "Girl, you still sing and dance?" Uncomfortable, she tells him she's "a different person now." Standing in the background, Gideon observes that the years have been good to Hattie. "Hasn't been the years," Harry says. "Been the men in her life." This makes Hattie even more uncomfortable: "That's not nice. I'm in church now." Harry circles her, looking her in the eye: "Why close the barn door when the horse is gone? I remember you when you weren't saved . . . way back when the Natchez Trace was just a dirt road. . . . I know your mother ain't still operating that house of hers." Very quietly, almost to herself, Hattie says, "My mother passed on."

Harry turns to Susie and slyly tells her, "By the way, I came across Okra, your old childhood sweetheart." Susie looks puzzled: "Okra? Shoot!" Then Harry turns to Hattie and flirtatiously quotes poetry: "'Out of weariness, I spoke to my own heart.'" Hattie looks at him with skeptical amusement: "Harry, you know you remind me of so much that went wrong in my life." He keeps circling her, invading her space. "That's Pushkin," he tells her. "You don't know him." She counters with a couple of folk sayings. "'An empty wagon makes a lot of noise,'" she observes. Then she laughs: "'You tappy head, you ain't worth the salt they put on greens!'"

The laughter she generates inspires Harry to suggest a fish fry, which leads to a party and one of the film's high points. Burnett originally planned to show a good deal of dancing, but he dropped the idea because he had only one day to shoot the event. Despite time constraints, he vividly establishes a gallery of minor characters and creates the feeling of a festive, convivial, musical occasion that has pockets of conflict and a potential for violence. At the start of the evening Susie, with a new hairdo and a pretty necklace, puts snacks on the coffee table (cheese with toothpicks) as the doorbell rings and dressed-up guests begin arriving. Burnett positions the camera near the door-way, giving us a montage of character types as they enter and are greeted by Susie. Some are old friends, such as Hattie and her brother Marsh (Sy Richardson), who gives Harry a dirty glance. Others are relative strangers, such as a bald old man with a sexy, henna-haired young wife or girlfriend who causes Gideon and Susie to exchange looks with raised eyebrows. Still others are old pals of Harry, who hovers near the door, looking on with the amused air of a slightly devilish impresario. Among these is Okra (Davis Roberts), a name worthy of Faulkner or Elmore Leonard, who steps in wearing a plaid

sport coat and a camera strung over his shoulder. A skinny old fellow with grey hair and a natty mustache, he kisses Susie's hand and tells her, "I'm still in love, and not too old to get in a fight." Harry looks on with amusement and gives him a salute.

Babe Brother and Linda arrive, followed by Junior and his family. Babe Brother immediately leaves Linda and goes to Harry, who is relaxing in a chair, ready for mischief. At Harry's bidding, Okra brings something wrapped in a towel into the kitchen (as I've indicated, in this and other Burnett films, the kitchen is a place where significant events happen and hidden things show themselves). Harry removes the towel and reveals a large bottle. "This is the *real* South," he declares. Various men gather around. "Is this the *real* corn liquor?" one asks. "It ain't Geritol," says another. Tea cups are handed out, and Harry eagerly pours drinks.

In the front room, the guests listen to the first of two songs that grace the evening: "See, See Rider," featuring a cameo appearance by jazz and blues artist Jimmy Witherspoon, who plays a character named Percy. As always, Burnett's musical choices are meaningful. "See, See Rider," which was first recorded by Ma Rainey in 1924, is arguably the definitive blues song, and in this context might be described as Harry's theme, telling a story of sex, jealousy, and violence. A montage accompanies the performance: Susie and

Gideon dance and Okra follows them around, taking pictures of Susie; Linda has no one for company; Harry puts his arm around Babe Brother, who drinks from a tea cup ("Buy me a pistol," Witherspoon sings, "just as long as I am tall"); Linda, still alone, looks increasingly sad.

At the end of the song, Harry bursts into the living room, applauds gleefully, and says, "Let's get Hattie to sing a song from the old days!" She gives him a disapproving look. "Harry always tries to be the Kingfish," she announces. "I've told him I'm a different person now. I'm saved." Harry returns to the kitchen and resumes drinking with Babe Brother, but Hattie's brother Marsh interrupts, taking Babe Brother's place at the table. Quietly but angrily, he suggests that Harry may have had something to do with the deaths down South of Marsh's cousin Henry and his best friend (the same people Harry may have been talking about in the story he earlier told Babe Brother and Linda), whose murder by a gang of whites nearly caused a race riot. Harry shrugs, remarking that Marsh's cousin "always had a big mouth," and "sometimes the right action comes from the wrong reason."

As tension rises in the kitchen, Burnett returns to the living room, where Hattie sings the second of the evening's songs: "Stand by Me," a popular R & B number by Ben E. King and legendary rock-and-roll writers Jerry Leiber and Mike Stoller. First recorded by King and afterward covered by hundreds of artists, the song has distant roots in black spirituals and serves as a counterpoint to "See, See Ryder," as if the carnal and spiritual elements that were blended in "Precious Memories" were now split apart. Hattie sings a prayer asking God to "stand by me" during "trials and tribulation," and her song is intercut with two quarrels: the confrontation between Marsh and Harry and a scene in which Gideon goes out to the front yard and berates the departing Babe Brother and Linda for leaving their child with his grandparents and never going to church. As usual, Gideon compares Babe Brother unfavorably with Junior, and this sets Babe Brother aflame. Susie joins the group and tries to calm Gideon, warning that he might have a stroke. "I don't care if I drop dead as long as he learns something," he shouts. Babe Brother asks his mother, "Why is he always comparing me?" He turns to Gideon and shouts, "I'm getting tired of you always reminding me that Big Mamma was born in slavery! If you care about me just show me how to make money!" Gideon starts to leave in disgust, but Susie stops him. Standing between the two men, as she did earlier, she makes them shake hands and tries to prevent them from sleeping in anger.

On the next day trouble deepens, and Harry seems to be the cause, producing a series of uncanny events similar to the ones that accompanied his first appearance. First, he and Gideon go for a walk along the LA rail tracks, reminiscing about their days as laborers. Gideon is exhausted, breathing heavily, struggling to keep pace. "We laid enough of them, didn't we?" Harry asks, and as they gaze down the empty tracks a dream vision appears: a group of young black men with picks and sledgehammers, bathed in a hazy orange light, driving spikes into rails with rhythmic blows. "We'll go a little further," Harry says. "Walking will do you good." But Gideon is obviously on the verge of collapse.

A direct cut takes us to the evening and to an ordinary but eerily portentous image: in close-up, a moth struggles inside the bowl of a ceiling lamp. Susie, in her nightgown, turns out the light. As she goes upstairs, a light from a passing car sweeps across the room, revealing Harry standing in the shadows. Red light from another car flashes past, giving his face a demonic aspect. Another direct cut takes us to the next morning and to a close-up of a whistling teapot. Gideon, in severe pain, tries to get out of bed and calls for Susie to come up from the kitchen. In close-up, viewed from behind, Harry sits quietly in the next bedroom; the camera rises over his head and looks down to reveal that he's peeling an apple with his big knife.

Gideon feels an urgent need to feed the chickens, but Susie calms him while Harry stands behind her, licking apple juice off his blade. A moment later, he emerges from the backyard chicken coop with a struggling chicken in each hand. Susie calls out to him, asking if he can watch over Gideon while she attends to a woman who has just gone into labor. "You go on," Harry chuckles. "I'll fix him some soup. He'll be all right." In the next shot, he comes into the room where Gideon is sleeping and puts a small bowl of unappetizing chicken soup on a night table. Then he opens a bottle of Gideon's pills, studies them, and begins exploring the bedroom drawers. He also sits down and reads the family Bible, nodding at something he finds there.

Most of the succeeding sequences are neatly rounded episodes with ironic, troubling, or amusing endings. After spending time in the hospital, Gideon, still in great pain, is brought home by the family and gently placed on the living room couch. Harry, who has been upstairs bathing, comes down in his house robe to view the patient. "Boy! I thought you about to cross the river," he chuckles, "You look good!" Grinning, king of all he surveys, he reclines in an easy chair and calls out to Babe Brother: "Hey, daddy-o, can you just turn off that tap in the bathroom? My hand's too weak." Babe Brother starts to rush off, but Harry holds him back for a moment: "Say, can you do me another favor? My back kinda hurts. I need some pills." Then he turns to Susie and asks her to bring him coffee. Turning to Junior, he asks for an old newspaper.

Junior reluctantly brings the paper, which Harry spreads on the floor under his big, bare feet. As he begins clipping his toenails, he beckons for Junior to lean down to him. "I will leave you something in my will," he whispers.

Soon Harry's pals become regular visitors. On a sunny afternoon, Harry lolls in a backyard chair near Susie's dying garden, wearing a sport coat and a loud tie, while Okra and the lame Herman (Julius Harris) chase down Gideon's rooster. Eagerly anticipating the possibility that Susie might soon become a widow, Okra asks, "You think Gideon's going to live to see the month out?" In a scholarly/philosophical tone, Harry quotes from Ezekiel 37, in which Satan speaks to Christ: "'I came upon the valley of bones. . . . Heaven is lost to thee.'" Then he adds, "We all got to make away." Never a friend to farm animals, he hypnotizes the captured rooster by drawing a line in the dirt in front its beak, but just when he picks up an ax to chop off the bird's head, the boy next door blatts his horn and the rooster escapes. Okra sits down wearily in the shade. "You gotta catch the next one," he says, "'cause I'm outta breath."

Gideon's condition becomes so serious that the preacher from the family's church (Wonderful Smith) arrives at Susie's door accompanied by several choir ladies garbed in black robes and asks to pray over the sick man. Standing at the foot of the bed, he notices a small mound of dry leaves, known in the South as Plummer Christian leaves, beneath Gideon's feet. Sheepishly, Susie admits to using the leaves along with "cold oil" to abate fever. The preacher sternly disapproves of these vestiges of conjuring: "Sister, I would think you would rely on prayer rather than these old-fashioned remedies." As he reads from the Bible and the choir ladies sing, the camera moves down to a close-up of Gideon's ear. Burnett's original plan for the film was to introduce a second dream sequence at this point, involving the woman in the photograph we saw at the beginning. The setting is a photography shop in the 1930s, and the woman is posing for a picture:

PHOTOGRAPHER (O.S.): What scene would you like in the background?

WOMAN: Something pleasant.

PHOTOGRAPHER (O.S.): We have plantations.

The woman shakes her head.

PHOTOGRAPHER (O.S.): Natchez, cotton fields, Harlem, sunflowers, the Mississippi river.

WOMAN: Put the river behind me. (Burnett 1996, 80)

A still picture of the Mississippi appears on the screen behind the woman and then transforms into a moving picture. A storm builds in the distant sky beyond the river, and thunder is heard. A shirtless boy is riding a grey mule in the rain, and Gideon walks toward him along a picket fence. Gideon encounters a large puddle, which turns into a black abyss, and he falls into darkness.

Neither the preacher's magic nor Susie's can overcome Harry's apparent spell. While the visitors pray, Harry is ensconced in the kitchen, giving Babe Brother a lesson in how to cheat at cards. Nearby, Okra cleans a pistol (later we learn that he's a security guard), and Herman covers his head with a towel and inhales steam from a bowl to relieve sinus pain. Out in the dining room, Junior tries to fix a broken ceiling light while talking with Pat about the problem of Harry's continued presence. "He's the kind of guy you'd like to take out in the woods and leave under a rock," Junior says. Pat wonders where Harry "gets the power to summon up all his raffish friends," who "smell like moth balls." At that moment, as if Harry had somehow caused it, the wires in Junior's hands cross and an electric shock knocks him off his stepladder.

Soon Harry takes complete control of Babe Brother, who treats Linda as his slave. The feisty modern woman who was critical of her husband is reduced to cooking dinner for him and all of Harry's friends (among the large group there is only one woman). When she tries to help Babe Brother carve turkey, he slaps her. Silently and tearfully, she threatens him with a carving fork. In the dining room, party music plays and Harry regales a crowd with stories of the old days. As Linda serves food to everyone, she notices a man at the table slipping a fork in his pocket and a woman putting a cigarette out in her plate. Unable to tolerate the humiliation any longer, she drops a slice of cake on Harry, sticks Okra with a fork, and leaves, taking Sunny with her to Junior's house.

From this point onward, the professional woman becomes increasingly maternal and a full member of a family that she previously disdained and that Babe Brother wants to escape. One peculiarity of the film, as Valerie Smith has remarked, is that in somewhat domesticating Linda by putting her in company with Susie and Junior's wife Pat, it tends to "relegate women to the conventional roles of maintaining culture and tradition" (2003, 879). But one could argue that men in the film have similar roles. When Babe Brother ultimately rids himself of Harry's influence and reconciles with his wife and family, he makes peace with culture and tradition without abandoning his profession. The whole purpose of the film, which perhaps could be described as paradoxically conservative, is to acknowledge the need for progress while also paying respect to the black southern values that enabled certain working-class families to survive.

Soon after his wife leaves home, Babe Brother goes for a walk in the woods with Harry, and the walk has the same mysterious, sinister quality as the one Gideon took earlier in the rail yard. Harry leads the dazed-looking young man across a stream filled with boulders, while on the sound track we hear strange nondiegetic music. Babe Brother finds a huge dead bird and lifts it from the ground. "I could swear I heard my son calling me," he says to Harry. "Maybe I better get back. Maybe something's wrong." Cut to Linda, who tells Junior and Pat that Babe Brother unintentionally bruised her eye. She announces a plan to take Sunny and leave for good if Harry again sets foot in her house. "I want my daddy," Sunny says.

As the family crisis deepens, Harry begins to wear out his welcome. That evening he goes to the bedroom where Susie is watching over Gideon, touches her shoulder in a comforting gesture, and offers to take her place while she has a cup of coffee down in the kitchen. His real purpose is to give his pal Okra an opportunity to offer a tentative proposal of marriage. Clad in a security-guard uniform and bearing gifts, Okra has entered the house and taken a seat at the kitchen table. "I brought you these greens," he tells Susie, "and some salt meat." His outrageous but comic courtship is intercut with shots of Harry pacing the bedroom and gazing at Gideon's body, which stirs slightly. It's almost as if a couple of vultures were sensing potential death. Okra sits across from Susie, smiles, and explains in polite fashion that he has come on a mission of mercy: "You know, Gideon and I are Lodge brothers, and it's always been policy to take care of the wives. If something happened . . . consider this a conditional proposal to be first in line." Susie, her eyes tearing up, stands with great dignity and softly but strongly delivers a superb put-down. "Excuse me," she says, "I have to go feed my dog."

On the next day, things fall apart. The chickens in Susie and Gideon's backyard wander from their coop, and the garden looks dead. Babe Brother drives up outside Junior's house but remains in the closed car, frowning and sulking, unwilling to humble himself by trying to reunite with his wife and child in Junior's presence. Back at Susie's house, Hattie, who is helping wash dishes, gives Susie advice: "I'm telling you, Harry is *evil*! I'm warning you, you can't keep a wild animal around children." Upstairs in his bedroom, Harry studies himself in a mirror. He opens his door to leave but cautiously sneaks out when he spies Sunny sweeping the floor. Hattie wryly suggests poisoning Harry to get rid of him, and when he enters the kitchen she makes a haughty exit. "As God is my witness," Harry says, "I have never done anything to that woman." Susie quietly confronts him: "I have to know who's in my house. . . . Are you a friend, Harry?" The confrontation has a poignant quality because of Susie's air of regret and Harry's quiet acceptance of the situation; one can almost feel for him when he says he isn't all bad. Burnett had wanted to show more sympathetic aspects of the character in these late scenes, in which Hattie would have begun to seem a bit self-righteous after discovering some of Harry's letters to one of his wives. As the film stands, Harry simply compares himself to the boy next door with the trumpet. "If he was a friend he'd stop irritating people," Harry says, "but if he stopped practicing he wouldn't be perfect at what he does." Repressing tears, Susie announces, "I want you to go." Harry tells her he'll be back later that night to collect his things and asks her to put a baby picture that has been gathering dust in his wallet with the other baby photos on her mirror. Patting her on the shoulder, he says he truly hopes Gideon will regain health.

The climactic portion of the film opens with a melodramatic gesture perfectly appropriate to the subtle atmosphere of magic realism Burnett has maintained throughout. Clouds race through the night sky, sweeping past a full moon, and a storm breaks out. Harry, surrounded by "raffish friends," is playing poker with Babe Brother. "Come on and go with us, boy," he says (Babe Brother is "boy" even to the man he's chosen as a model), and breaks into homely, misogynistic poetry: "I know your mind is on your wife, but you should never treat a woman as an equal. Get another woman . . . you ever heard of a real man having only one woman? One woman put you out you have to have another woman put you in. You don't drive around without a spare tire, do you? The more mules you got, the easier it is to plow." With a devilish laugh, he takes Babe Brother's hand. "Come on with us, son," he says. "We'll show you some *steamin'* hot juke joints!" A knife has fallen onto the floor beside the table and Harry picks it up, giving it to Babe Brother with a wink.

Rushing into the storm, Babe Brother goes to Susie's house and tries to get one of his suitcases out of her garage. "Have you lost your mind?" she asks him sweetly, reminding him that his son and sick father are in the house. The roof is leaking and she needs his help, but all he can say is, "I've been busy." Soon Junior, Pat, Ronda, and Linda arrive as a group and go upstairs to move Gideon's bed away from the leak in the roof. Downstairs in the kitchen, Babe Brother sharpens his knife while Sunny watches from beneath the kitchen table. Junior comes downstairs in a rage, ready for a fight. "I bet if your *master* asked you to fix the roof," he yells at Babe Brother, "you'd have re-built the whole damn house!" Long-festering conflict breaks into the open. "I'm so sick of people telling me to do this and that!" Babe Brother shouts, and asks' What's my name?" Junior looks puzzled. "You dumbass," he replies, "it's Babe Brother!" "My name is *Samuel*!" Babe Brother cries. "*Samuel*!" When Junior shoves him, Babe Brother throws a punch. The women upstairs hear crashing sounds and rush down to the kitchen, where they find Junior choking Babe Brother, pinning him to the table. Babe Brother grabs his knife. Pat eventually calms Junior, but when he releases Babe Brother's throat we see that Susie has stepped between the two men—her third intervention—and is holding the blade of Babe Brother's knife in her bleeding hand.

In the shocked aftermath, Ronny holds Babe Brother's son protectively in her arms and the pregnant Pat fears for a moment that her water is breaking. The two brothers rush off with their mother to the emergency room. Burnett originally intended to show a receptionist discussing payment with Susie, who explains that she has Medicare. In the completed film the scenes at the hospital have almost no dialogue and show the resolution of conflict through glances, gestures, and facial expressions. They also bring the family out of their increasingly closed-in domestic world and into a larger community. In the waiting room, Junior and Babe Brother sit on either side of their mother, and a white girl across from them smiles in companionship, showing her bandaged hand to Susie. Time passes in a series of dissolves as patients enter and exit and as an injury victim accompanied by police is brought in on a stretcher. Junior wanders over to the receptionist and asks why the place is so crowded. "Well," the receptionist answers, "it's Friday night. There's a full moon." Burnett has remarked that he intended this to be true to life, but that viewers often take it as another of the film's magical effects. Big city emergency rooms do in fact get more crowded on moonlit Friday nights, but one of the interesting things about *To Sleep with Anger* is the way it repeatedly makes it difficult for us to distinguish between the realistic and the magical.

As more time passes, Junior and Babe Brother have a friendly talk and smile at one another. Susie notices this and visibly relaxes. Glancing at a nearby row of seats, she sees a mother and child and smiles at the child. Blues music rises on the sound track as Burnett transitions to the next morning and to the beginning of the end. The cornstalks in Susie's back garden are nearly dead, and the neighboring boy is feeding his pigeons. Together, Junior and Babe Brother bring Susie home, only to find Harry, who had told Susie he was leaving, standing in the doorway. With her bandaged hand, Susie reaches out to touch Babe Brother, as if protecting him. "I can't believe what I heard happened," Harry says. Linda rushes downstairs to meet the returning family and accidentally kicks over a coffee can full of Sunny's marbles, which spill on the floor. "I just came to get my things," Harry explains. Everybody gives him an unfriendly look and Babe Brother, Linda, and Sunny pointedly stand close together. When Susie goes up to see Gideon, Harry takes a seat, sipping from a teacup. As if hypnotized, Babe Brother walks over to him, but Linda, whose influence is now greater than Harry's, steps between them. "I think you should go see how your daddy is," she says to her husband, and advises him to change out of his bloody shirt. After she and her husband leave to visit Gideon, Harry, looking more aged, gets up from his seat and we see a close-up of his feet as he walks into the area of Sunny's spilled marbles and broom. Upstairs, the family around Gideon's bed hear a crash. On the floor of the kitchen is a broken teacup. Harry has slipped on a marble and fallen, and as he tries to get up he grabs his arm from the pain of a heart attack. He falls back, dead.

The film is almost musical in its "movements" or variation of moods. After Harry's death peace arrives, and gentle comedy is mixed with absurdist humor. Medics are called in to examine Harry but leave the body where it is, explaining that it's the county's job to collect the corpse. As a result, Harry lies flat on his back in the middle of the floor for the rest of the film, blocking a doorway and covered with his pallet. "Honey," Linda says to Sunny in a sweet tone, "I've told you over and over again, pick up the marbles." Hattie and her brother Marsh arrive, and Marsh, obviously pleased, gives money to Ronda, asking her to go on a long walk with Sunny. ("Take your time," he tells her.) Harry's pals show up, and together with Hattie they gather around the body. The camera looks up at them from the perspective of the dead man. "Anybody mind if I take a look at him?" Hattie asks as she lifts the pallet to make sure he's really expired.

Not long afterward, as if by magic, Gideon regains consciousness and slowly gets out of bed. When he makes his way downstairs, he finds almost every character in the film gathered around the dining room table, not far from the body, eating Kentucky Fried Chicken off paper plates and discussing the situation. Babe Brother argues with the authorities on the telephone. ("If he was white," one character says, "they'd have him on his feet and out of here.") "You've been out for almost three weeks," Junior explains to his father. The local preacher adds, "We've had some long conversations with the Lord about you." Gideon sits down at the table. "Who's that?" he asks, gesturing toward Harry with a chicken wing. Hattie smiles: "He dropped dead." Gideon looks at Susie's bandaged hand and asks what happened.

"Oh, I cut it on an old rusty knife," she says. The two brothers silently exchange glances.

That evening Harry is still on the floor, and the gathering in the house has become a combination sleep-in and involuntary wake. Across the street, a small crowd of curious neighbors gathers to witness the strange goings-on. Inside, all is well. Junior reads a magazine as Pat and his children huddle on a couch beside him. Babe Brother embraces Linda and sits at her feet while Sunny sleeps nearby. "It was like I was swimming in muddy water," Babe Brother says, and for the first time he seems to acknowledge the wisdom of his forebears: "You know how country people try to tell you what Hell is like? It was like an internal struggle." Linda nuzzles him and calls him Samuel. Gideon asks when his two boys are going to fix the roof. Babe Brother says he needs to rest a bit, but then checks himself: "Anytime." Gideon shakes his head and considers his old friend Harry. "Here I am worried about myself, and poor old Harry resting on the kitchen floor."

The next morning Harry is still resting on the kitchen floor—even in death, he's a guest who won't leave. Gideon and Susie sit at the dining table with the preacher, who has fallen asleep in his chair. As Susie tends to a cutting of a plant for her garden, Gideon, very quietly, not wanting to wake the preacher, tells another of his naughty stories, which in some ways is a comment on the film we've been watching. "A man wants to make up his own mind about Heaven and Hell," Gideon whispers. "He gets a round-trip ticket to heaven. Finds everybody working in the fields because idleness is the Devil's workshop. Gets an express trip to Hell and finds everybody kicking back and taking it easy. 'What are you doin'?' he asks. 'Sinnin.' Just then the Devil walks by and . . .'"

Susie cuts him off. "I don't want to hear any jokes about black people in Hell." Frustrated, Gideon explains that race isn't central to the story: "White people, anybody!" She shows him her wounded hand. He smiles and shakes his head. "It's just a tale," he says sweetly.

The ending is unexpected, charming, and graceful. Suddenly, briefly, as if nature were reminding us of its arbitrary magic, Gideon's entire house trembles from a light earthquake. In a long shot, we see a bunch of curious kids gathered across the street, one of whom shouts, "You still have that dead body?" A kindly neighbor lady knocks on the door and offers help for all the folks in the house who have been waiting so long for the morgue truck to arrive. She's set up a picnic table and invites everyone over for food. In a wide shot from outside the front door of Gideon and Susie's house, she leads them out, and the large cast of actors exits one by one or two by two, as if for a curtain call at a play. On the sound track, a bit of nondiegetic music is mixed with the kid next door practicing his trumpet. Babe Brother, last to exit, turns to look back into the house before closing the door. Inside, we see Harry's body—the lead actor taking his final bow.

The next shot is our first view of the kid in his room practicing his trumpet. Burnett had originally wanted him to get slightly better as the film went along and planned to end the film with shots of Susie's plants taking root. For me, the ending we have is much better, partly because it's another instance of magic and the miraculous. The boy suddenly hits a perfect note and begins to take command of the instrument. As the final credits roll, his playing leads into the nondiegetic sound of a beautiful jazz tune featuring a trumpet solo. *To Sleep with Anger* is in some sense a comedy, and the closing moments are charming because of their relative decenteredness, their focus on a minor character. They bring harmony to an entire neighborhood and are perfectly in keeping with the film's overarching spirit of humane sociality.

SIX

The Glass Shield *(1994)*

CHARLES BURNETT HAD FIRSTHAND KNOWLEDGE of how police treated the black population in Watts and was strongly opposed to the movie industry's growing tendency to portray blacks as criminal types. *The Glass Shield,* his only film to deal with cops and crime, is a disturbing story of racism, brutality, and criminal behavior *within* the justice system. The picture was suggested by Ned Welsh's unproduced screenplay "One of Us," which tells the true story of John Eddie Johnson, the first black officer at the sheriff's department in Signal Hill, a small municipality located within the larger city of Long Beach, California. Johnson served there in 1981, when Ron Settles, a black football player at California State Long Beach, was arrested and found severely beaten and hanging dead in his jail cell. Signal Hill claimed the death was a suicide. No charges were filed against officers at the station, but lawyer Johnnie Cochran succeeded in forcing the city to pay a settlement to the Settles family.

The Glass Shield's executive producer, Chet Walker, brought the Welsh screenplay to Burnett's attention, but because of the arrangement Cochran had made with Signal Hill, any film that dealt directly with events surrounding Settles's death was subject to a lawsuit. Burnett employed John Eddie Johnson as a security officer and adviser, but his screenplay, which has a protagonist named "J. J. Johnson," is very different from "One of Us." It involves a fictional Long Beach sheriff's station called Edgemar, where a militaristic band of white officers have an off-duty bowling team called Rough Riders and where a black prisoner has died under circumstances like those in the Settles case; its scope, however, is broad, encompassing the deaths of several other black prisoners, the blackmail of white suspects, and a conspiracy between the sheriff's department and district attorney's office to frame a black man for murder. Much of the action is viewed from the point of view of a callow black officer whose idealistic commitment to a police career causes him, at least at first, to repress his identity and betray his community.

The film was financed with money from the French company CiBy2000 and was initially budgeted at $3 million. According to producer Carolyn Schroder, who negotiated with the French and supported Burnett when CiBy2000 tried to change the film into something uncharacteristic of him, the final production came in at $3.3 million. This was a very modest sum in a period when Hollywood budgets were becoming stratospheric, but Burnett's reputation enabled him to assemble an excellent cast of both black and white actors who worked for less than usual, among them Michael Boatman as J.J. Johnson, the officer who hopes to succeed at Edgemar; Lori Petty as Deputy Fields, a Jewish female who, like Johnson, provides Edgemar with token diversity; Richard Anderson as Commander Massey, the patriarchal enabler of Edgemar's clubby, aggressively violent culture; M. Emmet Walsh and Michael Ironside, two specialists in creepy roles, as corrupt detectives Hall and Baker; Elliott Gould as Mr. Greenspan, who claims that a black man killed his wife; and Ice Cube as Teddy Woods, the black who is framed for the Greenspan killing. (The Deputy Fields and Teddy Woods characters are loosely based on the experiences of a male Jewish officer at Signal Hill and a black man who served seventeen years in jail for a crime that prosecutors and police knew he didn't commit.)

Given its subject matter, cast, and production values, *The Glass Shield* had a reasonable chance to achieve good box office. It got favorable reviews from Caryn James in the *New York Times* and Terence Rafferty in the *New Yorker*, but once again Burnett's distributor failed him. Miramax purchased the theatrical and video rights, produced cheap press kits, and marketed the picture as a fast-action cop movie for young black males. "All of the action is in the [Miramax] trailer," Carolyn Schroder told *LA Weekly* at the film's initial release. "The trailer makes it look boom-boom-boom, but it's not" (quoted in Kapsis 2011, 103). Burnett concurred: "They try to . . . appeal to the visceral" (Kapsis 2011, 103). Prior to release, Miramax test-marketed *The Glass Shield* in New York's South Bronx, where, as Wolf Schneider wrote in *LA Weekly*, "a low-income, fifteen to twenty-five-year old audience screamed in protest at the hero's emotionalism in the original downbeat ending" (quoted in Kapsis 2011, 104). Burnett told Schneider that the Bronx viewers were "'more or less rap-oriented kinds of kids who lived with people getting beat up and wanting the good guys to get justice'" (Kapsis 2011, 104). Undoubtedly they expected to see more of Ice Cube, whose image at the time was associated with gang-ster rap. In the Chicago *Reader*, Jonathan Rosenbaum, who admired *The Glass Shield*, reported that Miramax "blocked the film's release for a full year, forced Burnett to substitute a less blunt and despairing ending, refused to let the original version be shown at a Burnett retrospective in New York, and, finally, after sending Burnett on a few interviews, shoved the picture out. . . . [T]his art movie's bookings have been exclusively at drive-ins and theaters like Ford City and Chestnut Station [south-side Chicago entertainment venues catering to black teenagers]" (1997, 161). Even today, Miramax's DVD edition seems aimed at a young audience, with a cover that shows a speeding police car and a large, scowling close-up of Ice Cube, who has a relatively minor role.

The problem of finding an audience was exacerbated by some reviewers who, although they expressed qualified praise, didn't seem to recognize what they were seeing. Todd McCarthy, in a favorable *Variety* review, remarked that "Burnett throws more weighty social and political issues on the table than he can possibly dramatize in two hours" (1994); Chris Kridler in the *Baltimore Sun* claimed that "drama" overtakes the film's "sense of realism" (1995); Peter Raines in the *Los Angeles Times* gave a favorable review but argued that Burnett "works in such large, broad strokes that the film becomes melodramatic" (1995); and *Time Out London* described the picture as a "Lumet-style *policier*" that "feels sketchy" ("The Glass Shield" 1995). All these descriptions are wrong to one degree or another. Although *The Glass Shield* deals with an array of social agents (police, lawyers, judges, accused criminals, activists, and ordinary families), it focuses on only two weighty but interre-lated social issues: a history of white male privilege that permeates the city's criminal justice system and an us-versus-them psychology of law enforcement that turns cops into criminals. Realistic in its treatment of these issues, the film nevertheless abandons the neorealist style of Burnett's early work, opting for an expressionist color photography that generates subtly oneiric, night-marish moods. One of the least melodramatic of cop movies, it provides a degree of humanity to some of its worst characters and avoids a neat system of reward and punishment; indeed, its whole purpose is to show that justice is *not* served. Besides all this, it differs from virtually every Hollywood pic-ture about LA crime since the 1970s in having no nudity, no spectacular action scenes, and not a single expletive in its dialogue. (For a truly melodra-matic, obsessively sexual, spectacularly violent film about a corrupt, racist police force, see Curtis Hanson's *L.A. Confidential* [1997].) Stylistically and dramatically, it also differs considerably from Sydney Lumet's *Serpico* (1973). The Lumet film, more directly based on a true story, concerns a white undercover cop who discovers bribery and corruption in the New York police force; after being shot in the face by his colleagues, he testifies before a government investigating committee, receives a departmental Medal of Honor, and leaves New York to live in Switzerland. The Burnett film, avoiding Method-style actors and realist photography, concerns a raw young officer who, convincing himself that he's doing the right thing and wanting to support his colleagues, suspends his better judgment and lies in court. After discovering that he has helped to frame an innocent man, he recants his testimony and is found guilty of perjury. Because of the ironies of the legal system, he loses his career, and the more deeply responsible parties go free.

In his DVD commentary for *The Glass Shield,* Burnett says that he has often wondered if the film should have been photographed in black and white. That might have pleased critics who expected something in keeping with the gritty look of *Killer of Sheep,* but it would have deprived the film of Eliot Davis's fine color photography and several moments of eerie color-coded menace. It might also have reduced the impact of the opening sequences. Burnett's deliberate stylization, his eschewal of handheld cameras and dislike of cop-movie formulas, is laid bare at the beginning, when a comic-strip fantasy of police action is juxtaposed with the sound of police sirens, screeching tires, a train engine, and a series of gunshots. Brightly colored drawings show a car chase in which Johnson and his partner Fields go after white thugs who have captured a beautiful, blonde young woman. Dialogue is rendered in bold, pop-art lettering. When Johnson and Fields halt their car at the mouth of an alley, she tells him, "Don't try to be a hero!" Johnson ignores the warning, runs toward the villains, and fires at them. Just as he rescues the young woman, one of the bad guys shoots him in the shoulder: "Kapow!" He falls, bleeding from his wound. As his colleagues arrest the thugs and praise his valor, Deputy Fields bends down, holds him in her arms, and says, "You proved yourself. Your shield is made of GOLD!"

Dissolve to a live-action shot of the last panel of the comic strip taped to an open sheriff's academy locker alongside a photo of a lovely young black woman (Victoria Dillard). The camera pans to reveal Johnson's uplifted, ecstatic face as a loudspeaker announces that he has graduated from the academy and will be sent to Edgemar station: "Lucky you," the announcer says, "you're about to make history." The shot has an ambiguous status and might be a continuation of Johnson's fantasy; it's filmed in slow motion, and beyond

Johnson we see a young blond officer dreamily juggling nightsticks. At this point, Johnson has yet to meet Fields; hence his comic-book daydream has less to do with actual thoughts than with the ambience of an immature consciousness. The highly saturated comic-book colors of the daydream will recur in some later scenes that are dominated by red, yellow, and orange lighting, but in the later scenes, color becomes frightening.

Johnson's education in real-life policing begins soon after he arrives at Edgemar on the following day. As he parks his aging car in front of the station and emerges in civilian clothes, an officer mistakes him for a black "trustee" and rebukes him for using the wrong parking space. Smiling, he tosses a bag containing his uniform over his shoulder and flashes his sheriff's badge. When he enters the squad room wearing the uniform, he looks thrilled but nervous. This scene, which identifies several characters and provides important information, is staged largely in a single telephoto shot looking across the room at a group of seated white officers, with Johnson standing behind them at the threshold. A squad leader who is giving the day's orders ends his speech with an admonition that tells us much of what we need to know about the station's core values and attitude toward the community: "Your primary obligation is to protect yourself and your fellow officers." Burnett's film will emphasize this ethos, showing how the dangers of police work breed a kind of herd psychology; where Edgemar is concerned, neither civilians nor the legal system are to be trusted, and the cops bond more strongly with each other than with their own families.

Johnson responds by taking a deep breath and smiling with excitement. Commander Massey enters and introduces Johnson to the seated group, only one of whom rises and shakes his hand, a gesture Johnson eagerly accepts. Deputy Bono (Don Harvey), who later plays a key role, turns his back, ignores Johnson, and joins the other officers in slyly chuckling and smirking at the idea of a black man in their midst. Massey then introduces two other figures: Detective Gene Baker ("my right arm"), who perfunctorily shakes Johnson's hand and exits, and jail guard Foster (Linden Chiles), who offers a friendly welcome. Foster is in the process of bringing a problem to Massey's attention, but Massey treats him dismissively. Deputy Fields, completely ignored by Massey, approaches and introduces herself.

Sergeant Chuck Gilmore (Gary Woods), a mustachioed veteran who looks a bit like a Marine drill instructor, is assigned as Johnson's mentor. (In real life Woods was a friend of police and knew their culture.) Not long afterward, Johnson suffers the first of a series of humiliating incidents staged in

increasingly darkened environments; they teach him Edgemar's methods and ironically determine his subsequent behavior.

The first occurs on a sunny morning when he and Gilmore pull over an attractive black woman in a speeding red convertible (Burnett's wife, Gaye Shannon Burnett, who, as before, oversaw costumes for the film). She explains that she's late for work and her speedometer has broken. When she openly flirts with Johnson ("What's a handsome man like you doing hiding in the bushes trying to trap single women?"), he lets her go with a smile and warning. Enraged, Gilmore orders him into the police car, turns on the siren, chases the woman down, and treats her as a potentially dangerous suspect. "Back me up!" he shouts to Johnson. "Now she *will* be late for work." Burnett photographs Gilmore from behind, at waist level, as he gets out of the car, hitches a night stick to his belt, grips the butt of his holstered gun, and tells the woman to keep her hands on the wheel. (The night stick has two handles that form an L shape; it was regarded as a notorious instrument in the LA black community because it was often used to choke black prisoners in the angle of the two handles, and it caused several deaths.) On the sound track we hear a bit of Stephen James Taylor's haunting score, which in this scene establishes a musical motif associated with Johnson, influenced by black spirituals and jazz. (Taylor was to become Burnett's most frequent collaborator and is to Burnett what Herrmann was to Hitchcock.) Johnson stands by helplessly and exchanges glances with the woman, who looks at him accusingly through her rearview mirror. Gilmore takes her license and registration, gets into his car, and calmly lights a cigarette. When the woman opens her door, he barks an order through his loudspeaker: "Stay in your car, lady!" Eventually he returns the license and registration, along with a ticket. As the woman drives off, he tells Johnson, "They can be ugly as sin or look like Miss America. In the Station, once you stop 'em, you write 'em or you cuff 'em!" Pointing a finger as if firing a gun at Johnson's head, he voices an Edgemar motto: "Don't trust *anybody*!"

Johnson's second humiliation is staged in a moody, slightly darkened interior. He's at his desk in the station, where the walls are blue and the lighting noirish, trying to commit a code book to memory. Viewed from an extreme low angle, Commander Massey walks into an empty frame and becomes a giant close-up. Looking down on Johnson, he speaks loudly enough for others to hear: "One would think you're reading *Gone with the Wind*" (a racist book he no doubt admires). Returning one of Johnson's reports, he announces, "I've seen three-year-olds that spell and use grammar better than that." Johnson has misspelled "Sepulveda" (I had to check to make sure I spelled it correctly here) and made an error in verb agreement, writing "group are" rather than "group is." Massey explains that "intelligent people will be looking at that report somewhere down the line," and it could cause problems if exhibited in court. The chastened Johnson replies, "Yes, sir," and looks shaken.

Turning to exit, Massey encounters Deputy Fields and informs her in passing, "Some of the men are complaining about your heavy use of perfume." A petite young woman with an extremely short haircut, she offers to lower her voice and use Old Spice if it would satisfy the men. Massey isn't amused. "It's not a question of a leopard changing its spots," he says. Stepping close and twining the fingers of his two hands in a somewhat threatening gesture, he slowly and emphatically declares, "People have to fit in." Johnson overhears this but doesn't agree with Fields when she sits nearby and explicitly says what Burnett has already made clear: the Jewish woman and the black man have been given jobs only because Edgemar needs political window dressing.

Burnett's creation of the Fields character and Lori Petty's performance of it are especially interesting aspects of the film. Her initial interactions with Johnson serve to bring out his macho assumptions about women and help to explain his increasingly tense relationship with his girlfriend, Barbara, who is uneasy about his work at Edgemar. We also gradually discover that as a woman Fields suffers as much or more discrimination than Johnson, who can at least superficially fit into the tough male ethos of the station. Ultimately, she will receive extremely violent treatment from other police officers.

Johnson's third humiliation, the setting for which is completely nocturnal, leaves him increasingly insecure and uncertain. On night patrol, he and Gilmore, photographed with orange- and blue-tinted lighting, receive a radio report of a robbery in progress. "Here we go, kid," Gilmore says, and Johnson prepares himself by taking deep breaths, flexing his neck muscles, and pounding on the dashboard with the heels of his hands. He's like a soldier pumping up for battle, and Gilmore gives him a skeptical, eye-rolling look. Here it's worth noting that in preparation for the film Burnett went on some frightening patrols with LA police officers. When I asked producer Carolyn Schroder if the LAPD caused problems in the making of the film, she told me in an e-mail that they "could not have been more cooperative. They participated as background talent in several scenes and hung out on the set frequently just to observe. I never heard one negative thing about the critical nature of the film nor that we used the Federation of Islam for security on the set." On his DVD commentary, Burnett speaks about his adrenaline spikes during the ride-alongs with police. For all his criticism of police, he understands the dangers of their work and on the DVD has wise things to say about how it engenders a warrior mentality and a tendency to close ranks against the outside world.

Gilmore pulls up to the back of a deserted warehouse on an empty, weirdly antiseptic street, where the night-for-night photography is again lit with orange and blue light. Left alone as a guard, Johnson looks through the bars of a rear window into an empty interior lit entirely in blue. The microtonal, nondiegetic music has the rhythm of a muffled, anxious heartbeat, and out of nowhere a swarm of sheriff's cars skids to a halt behind the building. A crowd of deputies leading a German shepherd rushes to the entrance. Johnson looks through the window again and sees a long-haired, bearded, unarmed man in tattered clothes screaming in terror as cops with nightsticks surround him and watch their dog attack him. The brief image echoes historic photographs of Bull Connor's police dogs attacking civil rights marchers in Alabama, but the color lighting also gives it a Kafkaesque quality, as if Johnson were peering into a forbidden room. Confused and horrified, he begins running toward the entrance of the building, only to be stopped by the same deputy who tried to block his entry to the station on the day he arrived. The deputy points a gun, orders him to freeze, and with some difficulty, resists shooting him.

Later that evening Johnson is called to Massey's darkened office, where he finds the commander holding a whispered, conspiratorial conference with Detectives Hall and Baker. Johnson stands at attention in the open doorway while Massey gives him a loud dressing-down that everyone in the station can hear. By leaving his post without considering whether there might have been an armed suspect nearby, he presumably endangered the lives of his fellow officers. Massey's anger builds to the point where he sounds almost deranged. Rising from his chair, he shouts, "If criminals don't fear God they will fear this badge and this Division! Your job won't make you soft! It will harden you to the facts of our time!" Dismissed, Johnson exits in shame, witnessed by the office staff. Once again, he crosses paths with Deputy Fields, who smiles and asks if he still wants to be a peace officer. "They're going to name the Station after me," he says, and when she laughs he resorts to sexism. "You can't be married," he jeers. Fields parries: "Look who's calling the kettle black." Turning and walking away down a hallway shadowed by venetian blinds, Johnson pats his rump and tells Fields, "You better lay off the steak and donuts, honey."

Johnson's three humiliating episodes have taught him six rules: (1) Always back up your partner; (2) Trust no civilian, not even a middle-class black female; (3) If you stop somebody, either ticket the person or bring him or her to the station in handcuffs; (4) Be precisely correct when you write an arrest report; (5) "Fit in"; and (6) Never leave the post you've been assigned. As the film proceeds, he follows these rules, but they have ironic effects; they expose to him the evils of the system, open his eyes to the corruption at Edgemar, and leave him bitterly angry and isolated.

During Johnson's initiation, Burnett briefly cuts away to give evidence of how Edgemar's law enforcement impacts the local black community. A protest group led by a Baptist minister named Banks (Tommy Hicks, who will regularly act for Burnett) holds an interview with news reporters to express anger over the fact that several young black men with no prior criminal records have been arrested and found dead in their prison cells. The minister introduces Mr. and Mrs. Ernie Marshall, the parents of the latest victim, who died while in custody at Edgemar. Law officers have claimed his death was suicide, but a coroner's report has concluded that he died "at the hands of another." The city council and higher legal authorities have apparently done nothing about the matter. Later, we see Banks and Mr. and Mrs. Marshall discussing this case with attorney James Locket (Bernie Casey, an ex-football player with a commanding presence). The Marshalls reveal that the Edgemar Sheriff's Department is following their movements and silently but openly harassing them.

From this point on, the film only intermittently returns to Johnson's point of view and begins focusing on events leading up to a murder trial. We

see Detectives Hall and Baker huddled face to face in the station, drinking coffee and quietly talking. Hall speaks with a gravelly voice and labored breathing, and Baker has a sinister grin. Burnett's tight, profile-to-profile framing of the conversation indicates that the two men are old partners, and it humanizes them to some degree. Aged, pale, and weak, Hall informs Baker that his cancer has returned and his condition is hopeless: "This time the cancer's in my liver, my back—it's everywhere." He wants to keep working as long as possible, because, "I need to leave the wife and kids something."

That evening Fields is parked alone in her patrol car, trying to ignore a couple of drunken young men on the sidewalk who shout lewd jokes at her, when a report of a homicide comes in on her radio. Arriving at the scene—an eerily quiet street, again lit in shades of blue, yellow, and orange—she finds a middle-aged, dead woman slumped against a car's passenger window. Another deputy (the same one who almost shot Johnson) explains that a Mr. Greenspan has been robbed and his wife shot through the driver's side window by two black men. Burnett's camera tracks slowly in on the dead woman's head and then cuts to Greenspan, sitting zombie-like in the other deputy's car; throughout, Elliott Gould plays this character with a stiff, uncomfortable, almost blank face, as if he were a man in shock. Soon Detectives Hall and Baker arrive. Fields reports that no shell casings have been found from the murder weapon and the angle of the shooting seems to contradict Greenspan's account. "I'm sure you'll notice," she says, "that the shot came from down below." Baker looks at her with his satanic grin and orders her to control traffic at the scene: "We don't need a Jewish mother telling us how to do our job."

The next day we learn about lawsuits filed against Edgemar. (In his DVD commentary, Burnett observes that a good deal of the annual budget for policing in Los Angeles is devoted to funds for settling such lawsuits.) Commander Massey announces that the state attorney general will not press charges against four of the station's officers. Everyone but Fields applauds. Massey then announces that two officers, one of them from Edgemar, are being sued for $7 million in the wrongful death case involving Ernie Marshall, and that several deputies in the room will be asked to testify in court. The camera tracks forward, and Stephen James Taylor's microtonal music is heard as Massey says, "Now remember, [pregnant pause], he's one of us. So. Talk to no one." Burnett cuts to a large close-up of a blond, wavy-haired, tanned deputy who turns to Johnson: "Remember that, J.J. You're one of us, not a *brotha*. So, learn to surf. Know what I mean?" Johnson gives him an angry look and says, "I got your surf board."

At a wedding party where Johnson serves as his younger brother's best man (he's clearly more responsible than Pierce Mundy in *My Brother's Wedding*), we get a sense of the divided personality his work has created. He confesses to his mother that the racist atmosphere at Edgemar has made him unsure if he belongs. His parents are in unspoken agreement that he shouldn't be there, but withhold judgment because he always wanted to be a cop. Barbara, whose picture he keeps in his locker but whom he has avoided marrying, tells him he should quit the force. When Reverend Banks joins the group, Johnson withdraws into a defensive shell. "I'm sure Mr. Massey told you not to talk to me," Banks says. "Did you ever ask why? There's no evidence that Ernie Marshall was killed in his cell." Johnson sullenly replies, "I'm not supposed to talk about that." Asked where he stands, he angrily but naively declares "on my own two feet."

The consequences of Johnson's decision to prove his worthiness in an all-white world become apparent in the next sequence, one of the most memorable in the film. It begins with a wide-angle, nighttime shot of a brightly lit gas station on a street empty of traffic. A shiny red convertible Volkswagen bug is parked at the gas pump, with rap music coming from its radio. From across the street in his parked patrol car, Johnson observes a black man in a dashiki exiting the Volkswagen and walking to the station entrance. Suddenly another sheriff's car drives past, comes to a squealing halt, makes a U-turn, and pulls up behind the Volkswagen. Loyal to one of the rules he's been taught (always back up your fellow officer), Johnson drives across the street and parks to the side of the Volkswagen. Officer Bono—a blond,

muscular type with the attitude of a fascist thug—confronts the black man, who identifies himself as Teddy Woods and responds to questioning with a resentful scowl. "Put your hands on your head," Bono orders. "I'm going to take your driver's license." On the opposite side of the Volkswagen, Johnson looks down at a young black woman in the passenger seat (Mkeba W. Dunn) and politely asks, "How you doin' tonight, ma'am?" She gives him an outraged frown and says nothing. The shot/reverse between him and her echoes an earlier shot/reverse, when Johnson exchanged looks with a black woman in a red convertible as a white officer gave her a ticket. As before, he's uneasy but determined to follow another of the rules he's been taught (don't trust anybody). He asks the woman to turn the car stereo down.

Bono uses his handheld radio to call headquarters for a check on a driver's license, and asks Woods, "Where you headed?" Woods replies, "Movies." Bono ignores this, asking, "You going to a party?" Burnett again cuts to the young woman in the car, who gives Johnson a long, hard look tinged with contempt. We can sense Johnson's unease, which he's determined to hide. Bono keeps asking racist questions and getting surly answers: "What do you do for a living, Teddy?" "I work, like you." "How do you afford that car, sell drugs?" "If you do." At this point, Bono gets a radio report that Woods's license has outstanding traffic violations and demands to search the Volkswagen. When Woods points out that no search warrant has been issued, Bono drops his thin mask of officialdom and becomes an overt bully: "If I arrest you that car is *mine!* I can rip it apart, *brotha!*" Cut to Johnson, who has recently been called *brotha* by a

white officer, and then to the woman in the car, who continues to look daggers at Johnson. Woods relents: "My girlfriend's father's gun is under the seat." Triumphant, Bono turns to Johnson and shouts, "Partner, we've got a gun in the car!" Johnson asks the woman to get out and proceeds to look under the seat. Bono puts cuffs on Woods, following a third rule. ("At this station, once you stop 'em, you write 'em or you cuff 'em!") As Johnson slowly brings out a pistol, the car radio can be heard playing "Wade in the Water" by Stephen James Taylor, which alludes to an old black spiritual about slaves escaping their captors. (This song is blended with rap verses over the closing credits of the film.) Johnson echoes Bono: "Partner, we've got a gun in the car!"

That evening Johnson works late, observing still another rule (be precisely correct when you write an arrest report). He carefully enters the serial number of the 9mm handgun he took from Woods. Dissolve to Detectives Baker and Hall, who read the report and almost gloat over their good luck: the weapon in the Greenspan murder was a 9mm, and under their noses is a newly arrested black man they can charge with the crime. On their orders, Johnson brings Woods to an interrogation room. "Thank-you, officer," Baker says, closing the door in Johnson's face. Burnett treats the detectives' conversation with Woods in film noir style: the dark blue room is shadowed by venetian blinds, the camera is set low and pointed toward the ceiling, and a wide-angle lens elongates space so that Hall and Baker seem to tower over the accused man. Baker announces that the gun from Woods's car was used in a murder. "Nobody wants to drag it out," Hall says, and offers a reduction in sentencing if Woods confesses. Woods's only reply is, "My skin is my sin."

Two brief episodes joined by an unusual match-cut emphasize Johnson's continuing refusal to deviate from the path he has chosen. At a dinner with his parents, brother, sister-in-law, and girlfriend Barbara, he smiles and takes pride in having captured Teddy Woods. His father asks when he's going to get married, and his awkward refusal to commit himself leads to a confrontation with Barbara as they exit the house. Flustered, he walks away from her, exiting into the darkness at the left foreground. Cut to a reverse-angle shot of a bright, empty field lit by the late afternoon sun; now in uniform rather than the flowered shirt he was wearing in the previous scene, Johnson enters from the right foreground and continues walking, as if he has stepped straight from one scene into another. In the field, he sees a bullet-riddled car, a group of deputies, and a dead black man on the ground with his hands tied behind his back. He kneels to look at the body while Deputy Fields examines the shot-up car. We never learn exactly who killed the man. A group of Rough Riders, seen from Johnson's point of view and silhouetted against the sun, stand over the body and joke with one another. "Drug deal gone bad," one of them explains to Johnson, and asks, "Know him?" Johnson continues to look at the body, shakes his head, and says he's only thinking about "the choices a man makes in his life." His words will return to haunt him.

The case against Woods becomes stronger when Greenspan positively identifies him as the killer. Attorney Locket agrees to defend Woods and questions him in jail, but Woods can't remember where he was on the night of the killing or whether the arresting officers read him his rights; rebellious and surly, he mutters, "I should have got a white lawyer." His arraignment takes place in a courtroom filled with poor defendants, some of whom can hardly speak English, and presided over by an overworked, impatient, racist judge. Meanwhile Officer Bono is in the office of District Attorney Ira Korn (Eric Anderson), being coached on how to testify at the Woods trial. Slow-witted, almost slack-jawed, Bono nevertheless has a low cunning. Korn asks him why he stopped Woods: "You didn't stop him because he's black?" "Well, yeah!" Bono replies, smiling as if the answer were obvious. "Wait a minute," Korn orders. "There can be no racial motive. Now what reason did you have?" Bono looks around like a dumb kid in a classroom. "Uh, traffic violations?"

A direct cut takes us to the next day. Bono approaches Johnson outside the station, where Burnett frames the two in a shared, conspiratorial close-up. "The prosecutor says I had no reason to stop Teddy," Bono says. "I told them he made an illegal turn." After a pause, Johnson offers help: "Yeah, well I got no sympathy for low-life scum. I'll tell them he ran four or five lights." Visibly relieved, Bono gives Johnson a soul-brother handshake. "Hey man, that's great," he says. "Listen, man, if you ever need anyone to back you up, I'll be there, man!" Johnson is wide-eyed, happy to be admitted to the club. "Okay!" he says. "Great!"

Burnett covers the Woods trial largely with tight close-ups and ever-changing camera angles that capture the to-and-fro of legal maneuvers. On the first day, Bono and Johnson lie under oath about the arrest, Johnson claiming that Woods told him the 9mm handgun was stolen. When called to the stand, Greenspan looks pale and uneasy. Locket moves close to him and in a booming baritone reenacts Greenspan's version of the shooting, pointing two long fingers at him as if they were the barrel of a gun. If the killer fired from a position so near to Greenspan's head, Locket suggests, there should be damage to Greenspan's ear or powder burns on his clothing. How can Greenspan explain why neither of these things happened, and how can he account for the fact that the bullet was fired at an upward angle, not in a straight line from the driver's-side window? Burnett's camera moves slowly forward to a giant, low-angle close-up of Greenspan's pained and bewildered eyes. The DA objects that the witness is being badgered, and the blonde-haired judge, Helen Lewis (Natalija Nogulich), agrees.

On the next day, Massey reviews his troops. Burnett shoots the scene with a telephoto aimed down a line of deputies as Massey confronts each of them and judges his or her work. Fields is using "too many words" in her reports; Bono is "looking good" but needs to hold in his stomach; and Johnson, who has proved his loyalty, is showing great improvement. "Your problems will soon be over," Massey loudly says, and quietly adds, "I'm proud of you." Up until this point Johnson has been in denial where Edgemar is concerned, but very soon after Massey validates him as what amounts to the departmental Uncle Tom, he discovers that he's being used. That evening as he works late going over reports, he finds that the serial number of the gun he took from Woods has been altered. He checks his notes on the arrest and confirms that the number he originally entered was correct. Becoming paranoid (as William Burroughs once said, a paranoid is somebody who just figured out what's going on), he goes to Fields and asks why anybody would change his report. She explains the obvious: Teddy Woods is "a perfect suspect and nobody will care if he gets death." Later, Johnson visits the departmental lockup, which is lit with the same eerie orange, blue, and yellow of the film's earlier crime scenes, and looks at Ernie Marshall's old cell. "How could anybody hang himself in one of these cells?" he asks the desk man, Foster, who advises him to forget it: "There are some decent officers here, but don't go looking into a loaded gun." The shocked Johnson wants to report his discoveries to higher authorities, but Foster explains that the authorities are complicit and there's no one to tell. The department has blackmailed prominent local whites who committed crimes, including relatives of city council members: "People who can afford it pay to get off."

At this juncture, Burnett gives us our only glimpse into the domestic life of one of the white officers from Edgemar. The brief scene (shot at the home of Alilie Sharon Larkin) could easily be cut without affecting the plot, but it establishes something important about the world of the little group in charge of the sheriff's station and slightly humanizes a character to whom ordinary melodrama would never give special attention. Detective Baker, the opposite of Johnson but a no less divided personality, is spending an afternoon with his wife and infant child. When the baby wets her diaper, he hands her to his wife, and the two have an argument about a vacation cruise they've been invited to join. Baker doesn't like the idea because it involves spending money to "wind up on a boat with a lot of people you don't even like." His wife is mildly offended and reminds him, "It's not lots of people—it's family." She goes into the backyard to change the diaper, and he goes to a desk where he's working on a different kind of nautical escape—an elaborate model of a sailing ship in a bottle. The only time we see him enjoying any kind of social interaction is in the Edgemar office or with the Rough Riders' bowling team.

In the final third of the film events rapidly accumulate as the case against Woods begins to unravel and Johnson and Fields form a bond that puts them in jeopardy. Attorney Locket visits Mr. Taylor (Sy Richardson, a veteran of *My Brother's Wedding* and *To Sleep with Anger*), who owns the gun supposedly found on Woods, and discovers that the number on the registration doesn't match the one Johnson seems to have written on his arrest report. Locket then learns that Greenspan is the sole beneficiary of his wife's life insurance. In conference with his partner (Wanda de Jesus) and Reverend Banks, he discusses putting Johnson back on the stand. The problem, as everyone in the room knows, is that it will put Johnson's life in danger from the cabal at Edgemar. "So be it," Locket's partner says, and the preacher adds, in an ironic echo of an earlier remark by Johnson: "Life is about making hard choices."

On their own, Johnson and Fields begin investigating Edgemar's fake reports and blackmailing schemes; the Rough Riders notice their frequent association. One of the deputies asks another, "What do you think the deal is between Johnson and Fields?" His pal answers, "Hanky panky. I caught 'em back there acting pretty suspicious." Sergeant Gilmore remarks, "I better not catch 'em." All this is overheard by Detectives Baker and Hall, who exchange significant glances.

Some viewers of the film have also wondered about the Johnson-Fields relationship. Is Deputy Fields a lesbian? (She has a very short, butch haircut.) Is there something sexual about her growing partnership with Johnson? Spanish interviewers raised these questions with Burnett, and while there's no reason we need to take the author's intentions into account, his response strikes me as useful and true to the evidence in the film. He was trying, he said, "to make [Fields's] relationship with J.J. more dynamic and complex." Johnson and Fields are both outsiders, but their growing bond ironically echoes the intense connections that Edgemar's white male cops have with one another. "There was no love interest," Burnett said, "only a true friendship" (Miguez and Paz 2016, 63). The friendship, however, endangers Johnson's relationship with his girlfriend Barbara, who becomes jealous of Fields. Burnett wanted to make Fields a woman for all these reasons, and his choice also enables him to show how female police officers face more stress than males. Any perception of "weakness" in an officer is resented by men, who expect their colleagues to protect them in violent situations. The Edgemar department has an inherent suspicion of any woman who doesn't have a desk job and treats Fields with obvious contempt.

In court, meanwhile, Locket calls Greenspan back to the stand and asks if he had met Baker or Hall at any time before his wife's death. Greenspan looks as bewildered as usual and says no. When he exits the courtroom, however, two insurance investigators approach him and he angrily refuses to talk to them without his lawyer. That evening at the bowling alley, Massey, Baker, and Hall are served a subpoena to appear in court. The enraged Massey says that Hall, who seems both ill and drunk, "can't be in court looking like that" and orders Baker to "fix it." Several things happen as an apparent consequence of the order. While Johnson is on night patrol, a car with darkened windows speeds past a stop sign and leads him on a chase. Johnson stops the car on a lonely street and calls for assistance, but the driver fires several shots, hitting Johnson, who falls and empties his gun at the escaping vehicle. (This is the only time in the film when we see gunfire.) Luckily, Johnson is wearing a life vest, on the advice of Barbara. He's in considerable pain and is driven off in an ambulance while his fellow officers stand around and smirk. Next, a group of cyclists finds a body tossed off the side of a woodland road; the coroner reports that the body is a white male John Doe in his fifties, severely beaten and acid-burned beyond recognition. Not long afterward, defense attorney Locket discovers that Greenspan is missing. The insurance investigators also discover that Greenspan was having an affair and had hired someone to kill his wife.

In the Edgemar office, Hall has a coughing fit and, while Massey is talking with him and Baker, collapses. Burnett gives us a Hitchcockian, bird's-eye view of the twisted body on the floor as Massey and Baker attempt resuscitation. In a large close-up, Massey looks at the desperate Baker and grimly announces, "Gene, he's gone." Teary-eyed, Massey turns and asks, "Will someone go out, lower the flag?" Soon afterward, Johnson arrives at the station with an arrested felon and speaks to the jail guard, Foster:

JOHNSON: Why's the flag at half-mast?

FOSTER: Hall died.

JOHNSON: That's too bad.

FOSTER: It depends.

That week at the gathering of the Rough Riders' bowling team, where several beer-drinking deputies are having rowdy fun, Baker confronts Foster and asks why he wasn't at Hall's funeral. "You guys are turning this place into a blood bath," Foster replies.

When Baker sees Fields and Johnson meeting in secret behind Edgemar, he makes another attempt to "fix it." Massey announces that the station will make a major drug bust, headed by Baker and the Rough Riders. Virtually the entire unit goes out at night and creeps down a dark alleyway, guns drawn, to a dilapidated Pine Street address, where Johnson and Fields are assigned to enter the back door while everyone else crashes through the front. When radio communication becomes confused—a deliberate tactic on the part of Baker—Johnson is wise enough to hold his and Fields's position at the rear of the house (an ironic reversal of the earlier scene when he abandoned his post). He correctly assumes that if they go through the back door they will be "accidentally" shot. Ultimately, the raid is called off because nobody is found at the location. Johnson subsequently discovers that the address has already been raided several times and two people were killed on its front lawn—it's hardly the sort of place where drug dealers would continue to operate.

Burnett moves swiftly through the climactic phase of the Woods trial, in which the prosecution's case virtually falls apart. Fields testifies that on the night of Greenspan's wife's death his behavior was suspicious; when DA Korn tries to make her seem unqualified, we learn for the first time that she was a criminal lawyer for several years in Minnesota and is now studying for the California bar. Officer Foster testifies that Baker and Massey threatened him if he did not go along with their story about the death of Ernie Marshall; he also explains that the Rough Riders are a group of men recruited by Baker and transferred to Edgemar because of their reputation for violence. The DA's only response is to argue that the Rough Riders are a bowling team and to accuse Baker of lying to investigators.

Johnson offers the most damning testimony, in which he declares that the 9mm gun used as evidence in the trial was not the weapon he took from Woods. When Commander Massey is called to the stand, he denies coaching Foster about the Marshall case and claims that Johnson is an incompetent who wouldn't be in the department if the city council hadn't made him a "special case." Asked how the department could have put the wrong gun into evidence, he says "we're looking into trustees." Afterward, Johnson finds "Nigger" written in soap on the mirrors of the courtroom toilet.

While the jury is considering its verdict, the Rough Riders give Massey a surprise birthday party at Edgemar, complete with a cake, a hearty singing of "For He's a Jolly Good Fellow," and the gift of a fancy fishing rod. Genuinely moved by his men's affection and probably anticipating retirement, Massey reacts humbly, fighting off tears and promising to catch a "big Marlin." As Fields and Johnson watch the celebration from another room, she turns and asks, "So, what did you get him?"

Despite the weak case against Woods, the trial results in a hung jury. Massey urgently meets with Baker to tell him that the department can't risk going to trial again, but their conversation is interrupted when a fight breaks out in the squad room. Johnson, having betrayed the station in court, has become an object of abuse and has struck back at an openly racist deputy. In another bird's-eye shot, Burnett shows Massey calling Johnson into his office, loudly rebuking him, and assigning him to a desk job. No longer compliant, Johnson angrily stalks out, bent on filing a legal complaint. In Judge Lewis's office, meanwhile, the handsome DA Korn (nicely played by Erich Anderson with a touch of smarmy condescension), fearing that Edgemar's and the prosecution's machinations might become known, wants to drop the case against Woods. Attorney Locket disagrees. The judge turns to Locket and asks if he happens to belong to a high-end social club where Korn and many of the city's lawyers congregate. He smilingly replies that the club doesn't have black members. The judge is aware of this. On her desk, we see a photograph of a smiling black boy. She recalls an occasion when she and her late husband went to the club with their adopted son and experienced a racist response. She rules that Woods should be tried again and plans to be the judge.

Woods and his defenders are on the verge of victory, but Johnson and Fields, who have developed a trusting partnership and platonic affection, put themselves in danger from vengeful forces at Edgemar by secretly trying to expose the station's crimes. The action of the film accelerates as their investigation unleashes all the brutal forces Edgemar has at its command. Johnson has already learned from Foster that the head of business affairs on the city council is a child molester whose name was changed on the Edgemar arrest record. Fields, subjected to a kind of frat-boy abuse (when she tickets an over-parked car and calls to the station for a tow truck, she gets sexist and racist jokes in response), finds herself in a much worse situation when she steals a file showing that the son of a city councilman had his identity concealed after arrests for drugs and a hit-and-run accident. Her actions are noticed by Sergeant Gilmore, and by the time she can arrange a late-night meeting with Johnson to give him the stolen file, her nerves are frayed. The meeting takes place on an empty street, where Eliot Davis once again creates the eerie mix of cold and warm lighting effects we've seen in sequences involving death or violence. Fields is so frightened that she almost shoots Johnson as he approaches her car. When she explains that her phone is being tapped, he offers to escort her home, but she brandishes her large handgun and insists she can take care of herself. Johnson gives her a hug, tells her to "be safe," and goes on his way.

In Locket's office the next day, where the actors are silhouetted against bright light from a window, Johnson gives Locket the incriminating files, which suggest that Massey has been blackmailing members of the city council and pulling strings in various cases, including the one involving Ernie Marshall. Just then a call comes in announcing that Fields has been injured. Johnson rushes to the hospital and finds her unconscious and on life support after a severe beating. Enraged, he goes straight to the Edgemar office and confronts Baker, who pulls a gun and looks as if he would take pleasure in shooting him. The unarmed Johnson tears open his shirt, yelling insults at Baker and offering him the chance to pull the trigger. Massey tries to defuse

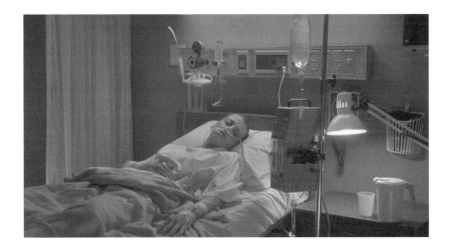

the situation but also says that if Johnson is killed he will testify it was self-defense. Just then Bono intervenes by patting Johnson on the arm, quietly advising, "Chill out, man." This gesture from a man he's grown to hate sends Johnson over the edge; he leaps on Bono and two deputies must pull him off. They spread-eagle him on a desk, and Baker inserts the barrel of his gun into Johnson's mouth. In a tight close-up, Johnson gives a prolonged cry of fear, rage, and defiance, expecting to die. Massey pulls Baker away, telling him not to be a fool, and orders the Rough Riders to put Johnson in a cell. "I have a right to make a phone call," Johnson says as he steps behind bars. "You're not under arrest," a deputy replies. "Then let me out of here."

Luckily, Foster arrives and is witness to the imprisonment. Massey realizes that the department can't keep Johnson locked up forever and ponders the situation. Without revealing his intention, he orders a deputy to "Get Jack Bono" and releases Johnson.

Across town in a darkened office, Locket shows the incriminating files to City Councilman Ross (Joseph Walsh), threatening to inform the newspapers; Ross then calls the state attorney general, and soon afterward U.S. marshals enter the Edgemar office and seize all records. Massey and Baker, joking with one another at the bowling alley, are surprised by an officer bearing a subpoena.

It's an apparent triumph for Johnson. He and Barbara visit Fields in the hospital, where she has recovered consciousness. (Burnett says that Miramax cut parts of this scene.) Johnson embraces Fields in an ironic reversal of the comic-book dream at the opening of the film, in which he lies wounded and she embraces him. At his parents' home, he opens a bottle of champagne and announces that he's out of a job. The good news is that he and Barbara are engaged; the tension resulting from his past loyalty to racists at Edgemar is banished, and the two are reconciled. In a sense, he has become the hero he aspired to be. Courageously risking his life, he has uncovered crimes and helped bring evil doers to justice. He's matured, able to enter a married relationship and no longer forced to suppress part of his identity. Just then, however, in a major stroke of irony, a knock is heard at the door, and Stephen James Taylor's music rises on the sound track in the form of muffled drums. A uniformed marshal has arrived and asks to speak with Johnson. A canted camera angle expresses a world out of order, in which Johnson is presented with a summons to appear in court. At Locket's office the next day, he and Barbara hear the bad news: in Locket's words, he's been "charged by the government with violating Teddy Woods's civil rights under the cover of authority." Bono has given him up in exchange for immunity. Dumbfounded, Johnson almost laughs at the injustice and pleads an excuse. He was molded by his job: "I was a *cop!* I was thinking like a *cop!*"

We've come to the ending of the film, which was somewhat revised after preview showings. Exiting Locket's office, Johnson puts Barbara in his car, walks to the other side, and bashes his fist through the back window. Uncontrollably distraught, he begins beating against the roof of the car, and when Barbara goes around to him he almost strikes her. In close-up, she asks a question that reminds him of his choices in the Woods case and refers us back to the cartoon at the beginning: "Whatever happened to rescuing innocent people from the bad guy?" Johnson cries, "I was doing my job! I just wish once you could hear something from my point of view! You were supposed to be my woman!" She will have none of this and indirectly explains the title of the film. "I'm not your property," she says. "I'm not going to say you were right just because I love you. I can see through that badge. It doesn't hide the evilness." Softly, Johnson continues to plead: "I thought I was doing the right thing." In the ambient sounds, from somewhere in the far distance, we can hear a police siren. "I really thought I was doing the right thing. Could you just leave me alone right now? I need to be alone." She takes his hand and says, "No, you don't." They embrace one another tightly, and a close-up shows that Johnson is weeping.

The original ending, which kids in the South Bronx test screening had jeered at and which Miramax wanted Burnett to revise, doesn't differ greatly from this one. On his DVD commentary, Burnett says the original was "too long" and needed to give a greater sense of "redemption." (He also wryly notes that an excessively new-looking car had to be used for the reshoot because the original was banged up.) In an e-mail, producer Carolyn Schroder told me that the revision was "tapped down" and made less "dramatic," but was not a loss to the film. The dialogue seems to have remained essentially the same in the two versions, with one important exception that can be glimpsed in the DVD extra involving Stephen James Taylor's music. As Taylor sits at a dubbing console, a bit of the original ending of the film is running on a video screen. In it, we see Johnson shouting "I'm *guilty!* I'm *guilty!*" and breaking into tears of despair. The new ending may be a bit shorter, but I suspect the original was aiming at something closer to the spirit of tragedy.

In a concession to the audience that Burnett has said he feels uneasy about, *The Glass Shield* closes with a faux-documentary series of titles explaining what subsequently happened to several of the characters. Apparently viewers were unhappy with the open-endedness of the film and wanted to know if justice triumphed. We're told that Johnson left the department after pleading guilty to perjury, for which he was given a suspended sentence. Teddy Woods was released and filed charges against the department. Baker (probably guilty of murder) was found guilty of perjury in the Ernie Marshall trial and given four years at Mountain View Honor Ranch, where he awaits an appeal. Commander Massey was not convicted and retired from the department, becoming the owner of a one-hour photo shop, which was robbed twice in its first year. The attorney general closed Edgemar, and Bono and his fellow Rough Riders were reassigned to other stations. All this is of course fictional, but ironic as an account of justice.

The film's depiction of life in an LA county sheriff's department and the inadequate punishment of its criminal officers is by no means an exaggeration of historical circumstances. *The Glass Shield* comments on that situation during its closing credits, when we hear Stephen James Taylor's rap song, "Black Man Sings the Blues," performed by Lance Eaton and Ernie Banks. Unfortunately, the beat has gone on. In 1998, four years after *The Glass Shield* was released, Leroy "Lee" Baca was elected to head the County Sheriff's Department, where he served for sixteen years before resigning and pleading guilty to one count of lying to federal investigators. According to the American Civil Liberties Union and the Federal Bureau of Investigation, under his administration the department created a culture of corruption and civil rights violations in which prisoners were routinely beaten and raped in their cells. On February 10, 2016, when tensions between police and black communities were high throughout the United States and the Black Lives Matter movement was gaining strength, the *New York Times* reported that Baca would be given a more lenient sentence than some of his associates because of his guilty plea to a single charge. "I will always love the men and women of the Sheriff's Department," he said to reporters outside the courthouse. In May of that year, Baca was sentenced to three years in federal prison.

SEVEN

Three Films for Young Adults and Families

SELMA, LORD, SELMA (1999), *FINDING BUCK McHENRY* (2000), AND *NIGHTJOHN* (1996)

AMONG BURNETT'S FILMS FOR TELEVISION are three low-budget pictures about black history, intended primarily for an audience of young adults and their families. Burnett didn't write the screenplays for these films and in a sense could be regarded as a director for hire; nevertheless, their subject matter was of great interest to him, and he didn't regard their genre as any less important than his adult theatrical features. They appealed not only to his tendency to see things from the point of view of children or the young, but also to his pedagogical instincts. One of them, by general agreement, is among the finest pictures of his career, and for that reason I've chosen to discuss it last in this chapter rather than in its chronological order. The other two, which are minor by comparison, I describe briefly.

Speaking to interviewers about the three films in 2016, Burnett remarked that young people need to "identify with an image. . . . It helps them to define themselves. . . . it's important that kids have films where they can see themselves and participate in forming their own narratives." In his own childhood there had been a dearth of such things. "[T]here were hardly any books in my school that had proper images of me. Therefore I didn't think I had a future because I had no images of the past or present." Films for the young, he told the interviewers, also have an obligation to "speak the truth," especially where African American history is concerned—a need as great today as it was when he made his films. In the early twenty-first century, he pointed out, high-school textbooks in Texas are required to have the approval of the state board of education, which, by determining which books will be assigned throughout the state, has created the largest market for U.S. educational publishers and the greatest influence over what they print. "Texas has been rewriting history. These text books make the history of slavery just a way of life that did no harm to black people. There is a conservative movement to limit education. There has always been a challenge to teaching black history or Latino history. . . . The Civil War is not being taught in schools. Recent history is erased. There are kids who don't know who Martin Luther King is and for sure don't know who the lesser Civil Rights leaders are" (Miguez and Paz 2016, 64–65). Burnett's three films were an attempt to redress that situation and are still relevant.

SELMA, LORD, SELMA

Coproduced by Walt Disney Television and originally broadcast on the Disney Channel's popular *Wonderful World of Disney, Selma, Lord, Selma* was a remarkably progressive event given Disney's history of making animated films that to one degree or another have been described as racist. (The chief examples are *Dumbo* [1941], *The Jungle Book* [1967], and the most controversial, *Song of the South* [1946], which Disney removed from circulation.) *Selma, Lord, Selma* deals with the 1967 "Bloody Sunday" march from Selma to Montgomery, Alabama, where black protestors campaigning for voting rights planned to confront Alabama governor George Wallace but were met at the start with police attack dogs, billy clubs, and tear gas. The principal characters depicted in the film were real persons, among them Martin Luther King Jr. (Clifton Powell), who came to Selma and helped organize the march; Sheyann Webb (Jurnee Smollet), a twelve-year-old schoolgirl who inspired the marchers and took part in the event; Sheyann's friend Rachel West (Stephanie Zandra Peyton), who also took part; Jimmie Lee Johnson (Zachary Rogers), who was killed by police while trying to register voters in Marion, Alabama, and whose death was an immediate spur to the march; and Jonathan Daniels (Mackenzie Astin), a young white man from the North (dubbed a "white nigger" by Selma racists) who was studying for the Episcopal priesthood and who, like Johnson, became a martyr.

Unfortunately, Burnett encountered problems with the project, only one of which he was able to fix. Because of the production's severe budget limitations and the lack of hotels and technical support in Alabama, the picture was shot on a tight schedule in Georgia. Burnett nevertheless insisted that scenes of the Bloody Sunday march be staged where they actually occurred, at the Edmund Pettis Bridge in Selma; this, he argued, would be true to history and a tribute to those who had shed blood on the bridge. He eventually prevailed and was given a single day to shoot there. Another problem had to do with Disney's more intractable standards of design. Burnett had hoped that the film would show the impoverished conditions of black families in the 1960s. When he began shooting, however, he found that the production company wanted Sheyann Webb's home in a poor housing project to be "played" by a neat red-brick housing unit with a manicured lawn and flower beds. The entire film, which shows the interiors of a black home, school, and church, has a colorful, well-appointed quality, as if the black citizens of Selma had little to complain about except voting rights. (A short documentary included as an extra on the DVD, which contains interviews with Sheyann Webb and Rachel West Nelson, newsreel footage of Selma, and an old photo of Sheyann and Rachel as children, gives a better sense of the real conditions.) In the end, Burnett chose not to fight against Disney's design as he had against the idea of staging Bloody Sunday on a bridge in Georgia. "I can understand Disney's reasons for not wanting to show the ugliness of poverty," he said to interviewers. "Most of us are not used to seeing poverty and when we do that can take you out of the picture. . . . You have to learn to make compromises and to know what battles to fight" (Miguez and Paz 2016, 76–77).

The screenplay for the film, by Cynthia Whitcomb, is based on a book of the same title by Sheyann Webb, Rachel West Nelson, and Frank Sikora, which centers on the two women's memories of the march. The central character and point of identification for young viewers is Sheyann, played in lively style by Journee Smollett, who had recently acted in Kasi Lemmons's *Eve's Bayou* (1997). Sheyann is exhilarated when she learns that Martin Luther King Jr., a man about whom she's written a school essay, will appear at a Monday meeting in Selma's Brown Chapel church, and she risks trouble by skipping school to attend the meeting. When she hears King speak she learns that only 2 percent of Alabama's black population can vote, and when she gets King's autograph she is fired with a spirit of activism. Her parents are disturbed, and her schoolteacher, Miss Bright (played by Martin Luther King's daughter Yolanda), gives her a lecture and keeps her in at recess. But Sheyann persists, taking along her friend Rachel to an evening meeting at the church. She and Rachel, dressed in saddle shoes and bobby socks, walk past a couple of cops on the street, who relish telling them about a recent bombing in Birmingham, in which four little girls were killed; when they enter the church after hearing this, the girls look under some of the pews for bombs. At the start of the meeting, King becomes aware of Sheyann's enthusiasm and discovers that she's a talented singer. Reminding everyone of the biblical prophecy that "a little child shall lead them," he invites her to sing a protest song. Soon she has the entire congregation joining her in a rocking version of "Ain't gonna let nobody turn me round, marching to the freedom land!"

The film devotes almost as much attention to Jonathan Daniels, the young Episcopal activist from New Hampshire, who serves two functions: he helps educate Sheyann, who develops an innocent crush on him, but more important, he becomes a conduit through which the audience learns about certain whites in the community. A fence-sitting woman tells him she doesn't have time to get involved with the protest, and the local Episcopal priest, who has a benign character, says that "nigras" in Selma are satisfied with their lot and need to be treated like children. As the film proceeds, we see that several blacks—Sheyann's parents, her teacher, and a poor laborer who is encouraged to register as a voter—are not so much satisfied as fearful of white reprisal, and with good reason. Soon the Ku Klux Klan burns a cross outside Brown Chapel, and the atmosphere around the protests becomes menacing. The mayor of Selma (Tom Nowicki) seems fairly decent but can't or won't control his overtly racist police. White violence eventually turns murderous, but the courage of Sheyann, Daniels, and the black protesters wins converts. Jimmie Lee Johnson's murder at the hands of a white policeman (shown in gauzy flashback as Daniels's memory image) galvanizes the black community, and more than two thousand mourners attend his funeral. After blacks are attacked on the Edmund Pettis Bridge during their initial attempt to march to Montgomery, and after Daniels is murdered on the street by a local Klansman, Sheyann's parents, her teacher, and the white Episcopal priest who cautioned Daniels all join the movement.

The film's screenplay is obviously keyed to an audience of schoolchildren and for some viewers may feel too much like a straightforward, somewhat spruced-up history lesson. Nearly every speech between characters has the stilted effect of expository information being doled out; people debate, declare their political attitudes, and are represented as one-dimensional types. But this approach can be defended. It isn't far-fetched if we compare *Selma, Lord, Selma* (and in a lesser way *Finding Buck McHenry*) with Berthold Brecht's short *Lehrstücke*, dramatic "teaching pieces" intended to educate audiences politically. Also like some of Brecht's dramas, the film is almost a musical. Journee Smollet, a charming singer, belts out her numbers, and Burnett (aided by the musical score of Stephen James Taylor) puts a good deal of emphasis on the protest songs of the civil rights movement, which can be heard throughout.

Although Disney was inhibited about showing poverty, the film doesn't stint in showing the cruelty of white supremacists. (One thing the film doesn't make clear is that the U.S. Supreme Court had already struck down segregation laws, but places like Selma found ways to ignore them.) When Sheyann tries to help a protester by filling a cup of water from a fountain, a white knocks the cup out of her hand and calls her "tar baby." When blacks gather at the city hall and attempt to register as voters on one of the two days a month when registration is permitted, they're told by the police chief that only three people a day can assemble. When a black woman manages to get inside the office, she must pass a "test" by telling the registrar the number of jelly beans in a giant jar. When she complains, she's arrested along with Martin Luther King Jr. and the other protesters. While King sits in his cell, an officer leads a middle-class white couple on a sightseeing tour; the woman leans forward to glimpse King behind bars, and her husband, as if cautioning a spectator at a zoo, says, "Sweetheart, don't get too close."

Burnett depicts the Bloody Sunday violence in an Eisenstein-like montage (one shot shows a policeman's foot stepping on a child's doll), and, given that he had only one day at the location, does a credible job: horses charge, dogs attack, gas swirls, cops and vigilantes swing truncheons, and many wounded sprawl in the street. As a direct result of Bloody Sunday, President Lyndon Johnson proposes a civil rights bill and announces, "There is no Negro problem; there is no Southern problem; there is an American problem." Out of necessity, King is in Washington when the aborted march occurs, but he returns to Selma with support from activists, and on March 21, backed by a court order, leads a second, successful march, with Sheyann and Rachel near the front of the line. Authorities in Selma try to construct an improvised wall to keep blacks out of downtown, but protesters respond by saying (as they could in the later era of Donald Trump): "Hate is the only thing that constructed that wall." This time national media are present in force and follow along with the marchers, who are met at the bridge with a barricade manned by armed police. The mayor, recognizing defeat, orders the barricade removed; the marchers proceed along the fifty miles to Selma, and several months later, on August 6, LBJ signs the national Voting Rights Act.

Over fifty years after the events shown in the film, the conservative-dominated Supreme Court gutted several key provisions of the Voting Rights Act and opened the way for southern states to enact new rules that discourage the poor and people of color from going to the polls. In this environment it's all the more important for young people to see *Selma, Lord, Selma,* and for everybody to see Ava DuVernay's more elaborately produced *Selma* (2014), which is addressed to an adult audience and gives a complex picture of the various political forces at play in the 1960s among blacks and within the federal government.

The introductory credits describe *Finding Buck McHenry* as "A Charles Burnett Film," but it was a picture on which, to a degree, he was in conflict with the writers. Produced as an after-school movie for Showtime TV, the film's screenplay by Alfred Slote and David Field, adapted from Slote's novel of the same title, tells the story of a baseball-crazy white boy named Jason Ross (Michael Schiffman) who comes to believe that Mac Henry (Ossie Davis), a longtime black janitor at his high school, is in reality a legendary Negro League ballplayer named Buck McHenry. (The character is fictional, but the name is Slote's way of paying tribute to three great Negro League ballplayers: Buck O'Neil, Walter "Buck" Leonard, and Henry McHenry.) Jason is an avid collector of baseball cards and memorabilia but has been cut from his Little League team because he can't take coaching. A backup catcher, he's also a terrible hitter who imitates the unorthodox stance of the celebrated pro Ken Griffey and whiffs at every pitch. Mac Henry happens to see him at bat, takes an interest in him, and in a few hours greatly improves his hitting. This stimulates Jason's curiosity. After consulting with the friendly manager of a baseball card shop, Jason learns something about the history of the Negro League and becomes obsessed with the idea that Buck McHenry is hiding behind an assumed name.

Jason visits Mac Henry's home (which looks a bit too prosperous for a janitor) and meets his grandson Aaron (Duane McLaughlin), a grieving boy who is a gifted pitcher but has recently lost his parents in an accident. After a good deal of pleading for their help, Jason joins forces with Aaron and Kim Axelrod (Megan Bower), the athletically talented daughter of the town's newly arrived TV sports reporter (Kevin Jubinville). The three persuade Mr. Henry to coach them, and as a result their "team"—catcher, pitcher, and fielder—challenges and beats the full team that had cut Jason from its roster. This enables them to recruit a full team of their own under Mac's coaching, with the owner of the baseball card shop as their sponsor. The legend of Buck McHenry grows, but Mac keeps insisting that he isn't who Jason thinks he is. Ignoring Mac's wishes, Jason, with help from Kim's father, persists in trying to out the old man. Jason's parents forbid his efforts because they conflict with Mac's desire for privacy, but the plot reaches a climax when Mac (somewhat like Odysseus) reveals a scar on his leg identical to the one Buck McHenry acquired in a violent game. Eventually, everything works out: Mac admits who he is and explains his history, and in the process we learn more about the history of Negro League baseball and American racism.

Burnett's experience with the film wasn't entirely happy because the original script put too much emphasis on Jason and his family. "I had to change the dynamics," he told interviewers, "and let the black family be adults and not let a 14-year-old white kid dictate to a grown black man how he should live his life. The black couple have a grandson who just lost his father and mother in a car accident. In the screenplay, the Henrys were more concerned about the white 14-year-old boy than about their grandson. There were many things I had to change very slowly, to make a film that wouldn't embarrass anyone. This didn't make me popular but I wasn't going to make a bad movie" (Miguez and Paz 2016, 63–64).

In the completed film Jason remains a central character, but Mac/Buck is a more commanding presence and in greater control of his identity. (Despite this, the cover of the DVD release features the two white kids with the black kid in the background and no sign of Buck.) Ossie Davis, supported by his wife Ruby Dee as Buck's wife, gives a quiet performance tinged with his characteristic deep-voiced gravitas and handles the light comic moments with subtlety. Buck and his wife are intelligent, mature, and concerned about their depressed grandson. Jason's persistence annoys them, but his friendship with Aaron provides a way for Buck to use baseball as therapy.

When Jason becomes increasingly sure that Mac is in reality Buck, he becomes even more annoying; he talks to the TV sports reporter, who undertakes his own investigation and decides that a show about a janitor who was a baseball star will get great ratings. Always a headstrong kid who thinks he's right, Jason throws a tantrum when his parents tell him he can no longer continue to pry into Mac's life. Soon afterward, however, he relents and offers to sell his valuable Ken Griffey baseball card if his father will take him to the Negro League museum in St. Louis so that he can learn the full story of Buck McHenry.

Improbably, the father agrees. He and Jason fly to St. Louis, where the film gives us a history lesson that was no doubt the main reason Burnett wanted to direct it. At the museum, the wide-eyed, awed Jason sees clips from a documentary about the Negro League and begins to appreciate not only the greatness of the players but also the depth of racism and segregation that hampered their careers. (Even before the trip, he has become aware of racism; his Willie Mays rookie baseball card is less valuable than Mickey Mantle's rookie card, even though Mays had a better record than Mantle.) He and his father also meet the gentlemanly historian Ollie Johnson (well played by Ernie Banks, one of the greatest fielders and hitters of the twentieth century, who began his career in the Negro League but spent most of it with the Chicago Cubs, becoming affectionately known in the city as "Mr. Cub"). Johnson's home is itself a kind of baseball museum, and he gives the two visitors a history of a few players who spent all or some of their careers in the Negro League: Satchell Page, Josh Gibson, Hank Aaron, Roy Campanella, and Jackie Robinson. He also takes them to a cemetery and shows them the grave of Buck McHenry. Like all the Negro League players, he explains, Buck and his teammates toured the country and made money by deliberately losing to white semipro teams. During one of these games Buck was savagely spiked in the leg by a white player, and he retaliated by breaking the player's jaw. The local police charged him with assault. Afterward he left baseball, dying in obscurity.

Educated and chastened, Jason returns home and visits the man he's always called "Mr. Henry," who is fishing and resting beside a lake. Jason apologizes, but Mac rolls up his pant leg and reveals a long scar. "Once upon I time I was Buck McHenry," he says, and decides to go on TV because it's "time somebody told history like it really was." During the television interview with Kim's father—who until now has seemed an ambiguous character, a caring single parent but also a reporter eager to boost his career—Buck relaxes and seems happy to talk about "black man's pain." In a long speech beautifully delivered by Ossie Davis (who won a daytime Emmy award for Best Performance in a Children's Special), he recalls barnstorming in the Negro League when black teams were forced to endure racial taunts from the all-white spectators and lose games to the inferior white players, all for the sake of a bit of cash. When his leg was spiked, he lost control and was on the verge of murdering his opponent. It wasn't simply the injury or the trouble with the law that made him quit baseball; he was afraid that if the same thing happened again he might kill somebody. Ollie Johnson agreed to give him a tombstone in St. Louis and swore to keep his identity secret.

In its closing episodes, the film becomes an important history lesson for young people and an engaging, feel-good story. After winning the local championship of the Little League, Buck McHenry and his team are given a party, at which Ollie Johnson and everyone else pays long-overdue tribute to Buck.

NIGHTJOHN

One of Burnett's most impressive films, worthy of discussion alongside any of his theatrical features, is *Nightjohn,* an adaptation of a young adult novella by Gary Paulsen, coproduced by Disney and Hallmark and aimed primarily at a family audience of teens and adults. Although the film was originally shown on TV, it had a strong critical reception. Terence Rafferty of the *New Yorker* named it the best American picture of the year, the National Black Programming Consortium chose it as best drama of the year, and several art cinemas screened it. At one point Disney offered to give away free VHS copies as a public service, but rescinded the offer when the demand became too great.

Gary Paulsen's successful novella and its sequel, entitled *Sarny,* are told from the retrospective, first-person viewpoint of a slave girl named Sarny, whose life is changed by the almost mythical Nightjohn, an escaped slave who returns to the South to teach other slaves how to read and write. This character is indirectly based on men who actually existed, though little is known about them. Early in the novella, he's described as extremely black, and this may be one reason he's called Nightjohn. At one point he identifies himself as "John Niger," which suggests that he's from Niger; his fellow slaves probably think he's saying "Night," and this, too, may account for the name. More significantly, he does his teaching at night. "We all have to read and write," he insists, "so we can write about this—what they doing to us. It has to be written." But most of Nightjohn's potential students don't want such skills, for even the mildest form of literacy is forbidden by their owners and punishable by dismemberment or death. Sarny, however, is an exception to the rule; eager to learn, she escapes punishment and leaves a written account of her teacher's heroism. (It has been estimated that by the end of the Civil War roughly 10 percent of the emancipated slaves were literate.)

A complicated period film shot with a modest budget on a tight schedule, *Nightjohn* takes a "realist" approach to costumed history, in the sense that, like *Selma, Lord, Selma,* it treats the past as if it were unproblematically available for representation in the present. It differs, for example, from

Burnett's later treatment of the same historical period in *Nat Turner: A Troublesome Property,* in which the problem of truthfully representing history is foregrounded. Most history films and novels have a realist form, and there is always a danger, at least theoretically, that their ideological purposes will be concealed by their apparent claims to unmediated truth. Where films about slavery are concerned, the theoretical issue takes on importance because the origins of the Hollywood historical film can be traced back to D. W. Griffith's appalling racism in *Birth of a Nation* (1915). *Nightjohn* belongs to a series of black-written or -directed films—the two TV adaptations of Alex Hayley's *Roots* (1977 and 2016), Gordon Parks's *Solomon Northup's Odyssey* (1984), Steve McQueen's *12 Years a Slave* (2013), and Nate Parker's *Birth of a Nation* (2016)—that give a realist response to Griffith; they are no less ideological, but they have humane, democratic purposes and far greater justification for their truth claims. (For useful commentary on such matters, see Martin and Wall 2013.)

Nightjohn was originally intended to star the black actor Delroy Lindo, who insisted that Burnett should be the director. Disney was hesitant to accept Burnett because of rumors that he was a difficult personality—an absurd notion, probably caused by the fact that he had fought Disney producers for proper representation of black history. In the end he was hired, but Lindo's scheduling conflicts made it impossible for him to accept the role. Burnett nevertheless managed the picture with great skill, shooting it within the allotted twenty-four days in Sumter, South Carolina, which is not to be confused with Fort Sumter, the site of the first battle of the Civil War. Sumter has a picturesque, well-preserved 1858 Gothic Revival plantation house, which from 1896 until 1970 was the home of James McBride Dabbs, a rare white advocate for civil rights. The town also has a large old church from the same era and cotton fields that provide authentic background.

Jesuit priest Bill Cain's screenplay, which makes use of these settings, differs considerably from the novella. This is entirely justified, although Cain (who was also a producer of the film) didn't do quite as much as he might have to retain Paulsen's demotic language. According to a diary he kept during production, his decision to avoid historically accurate dialect in the interest of clarity was a source of arguments on the set: "It would probably be easier if we cared less. But we don't, and passions run high even on small details" (Cain 1996). Photographer Elliot Davis and composer Stephen James Taylor, both of whom had done innovative work on *The Glass Shield,* have the same jobs here. The handsome, muscular, and imposing Carl Lumbly, who played Junior in *To Sleep with Anger,* is cast in the eponymous role (he initially turned down the offer of playing a slave but changed his mind when he read the script and found that Burnett was directing) and is accompanied by a number of equally fine actors, among them Lorraine Toussaint as Dealey, a midwife, field-worker, and house slave; Beau Bridges as Clel Waller, the overbearing plantation owner; and Bill Cobbs as an elderly slave and blacksmith with a missing forefinger and thumb. Most remarkable of all is Allison Jones, an eleven-year-old from a Georgia arts school who had never before acted in a film and who gives an enchanting performance as Sarny.

In interviews, Burnett expressed two reservations about the completed film, both related to conditions imposed on the production. First, television's Office of Standards and Practices prevented him from showing a black overseer whipping slaves; this character, named Joe (Gerald Brown), appears in the film, but only as a slave driver mounted on a horse and carrying a bull whip. Second, Burnett thought the completed film looked a bit too polished. The Paulsen novella is raw and explicit about the horrific conditions of southern slaves and puts far less emphasis on their wealthy masters. In Paulsen, slaves are twice a day fed cornbread, buttermilk, and sometimes bits of pork fat poured into a communal wooden trough, into which they dip gourds and from which slave children lick the remains. At night, exhausted, they sleep piled together in unlighted rooms on corn-shuck pallets. When an innocent, mentally addled slave girl named Alice is found wandering the forbidden grounds of the Waller mansion, the owner takes pleasure in whipping her with a rawhide belt, rubbing salt into her huge wounds, and leaving her chained against a wall for a full day so that maggots can begin feasting on her blood. Sarny recalls that the few slaves who tried to escape were virtually eaten alive by trained dogs and their remains hung in trees.

Waller is the only white character in the novella, although at one point, while working outside the plantation house, Sarny hears white women inside gossiping. When Waller sees Sarny writing numbers in the dust, he savagely punches and kicks her, demanding to know who taught her. Then he seizes an older slave named Mammy (Dealey in the film), strips her naked, puts a horse collar and bridle on her, and has her pull him around in a carriage until she tells him who is teaching reading. When she doesn't say, he starts to whip her. Nightjohn steps forward to confess, and Waller chops off his toes. Nightjohn soon escapes, but later, at the end of the novella, returns secretly to educate Sarny and other slaves at night in a "pit school" he has dug in a hidden spot in the woods.

In the film, on the other hand, Sarny and a relatively small group of slaves live in a primitive shack that has a table, chairs, an oil lamp, and a fireplace. Field slaves are worked to exhaustion each day, but they have enough time for some amount of gossip and sociability. Waller is a boorish and brutal owner, but not an outright sadist. In both the novella and film, however, slaves have value merely as property; like farm animals, they're kept alive only for their labor and ability to reproduce themselves. The film is perhaps appropriately limited in the degree of violence and sordidness it shows to a TV audience that contains children, and as Jonathan Rosenbaum has pointed out, the somewhat Disney-style "fairy-tale feeling" is used well to "focus on real-life issues, not to evade or obfuscate them" (2004, 287). Burnett is good at building a tense atmosphere of repression and terror, particularly when slaves are forced to witness barbaric punishments of anyone who breaks rules. Despite the compromises he had to accept, the film is characteristic of him in its focus on childhood, its emotionally moving emphasis on the emancipatory force of literacy, and its fundamentally educational purpose. For a director who suffered as a child from uncaring teachers and who hoped to make a picture about Frederick Douglass, the theme of reading as a pathway to freedom had special appeal.

The film's emphasis on the plantation era's treatment of slaves as mere property, without personal identity, is evident from the beginning, when we see Sarny's difficult birth. Her mother (Robin McLamb-Vaughn) cries in agony while Dealey manages the delivery in the slave cabin. Waller, viewed from the low-angle perspective of the women, enters and takes the child from its mother; holding it to the light, he puffs his pipe, smiles, and loudly declares that the baby is "black but pretty." He also half jokes to the mother that she has cost him money because he was expecting a boy and "can't give away girls." The mother takes her daughter back for a moment and sings a lullaby. A direct cut takes us to the child Sarny, now a few years older, repeating the lullaby and waving as her mother, sold as a "breeder" slave, is driven off in a carriage to another plantation. From this point on Dealey becomes Sarny's surrogate mother, and Sarny's offscreen narration provides commentary on her personal development.

Although *Nightjohn* is to some extent a bildungsroman concerned with Sarny's growth and education, it has two subsidiary romance plots, neither of them in the Paulsen novella, one involving the slaves and the other their white owners. Significantly, the double plot is centered on powerful and potentially dangerous forms of handwritten letters. Despite southern law, a male slave named Outlaw (Gabriel Casseus) wants to marry a female slave named Egypt (Monica Ford), who works on a neighboring plantation. In order to visit her he needs a written pass signed by Waller, and his struggle for what one might call the letter of transit results in his public whipping. Meanwhile, Waller's beautiful, romantic, insecure, and slightly distracted wife (Kathleen York) begins an affair with the handsome, sophisticated Doctor Chamberlaine, a Harvard-educated newcomer to the South who is Egypt's master and who has literary interests. The affair proceeds through letters passed between the two, arranging for clandestine meetings. Sarny, appointed one of the Wallers' house slaves, becomes a go-between, carrying the letters back and forth along a dirt road to the lovers. Once she begins to study with Nightjohn, she's able to examine the letters during her walks and improve her reading, and when she becomes adept at both reading and writing, she's able to create a forged pass for Egypt.

By expanding Paulsen's story to include white characters, the film has the virtue of giving us a more complete view of plantation-era society and economics and an especially interesting picture of the psychological dynamics of master-slave relations. (Maria Miguez [2016, 121] has pointed out that, significantly, there is no white character who serves as a "Schindler figure" or good-hearted member of the privileged class who intervenes in some way to help the oppressed, as there is, for example, in *12 Years a Slave* and *Django Unchained* [2013].) Sarny's position as a house slave is made possible by Dealey, who, because she already works in the big house, knows that Mrs. Waller is in need of an extra servant to watch over her youngest child, Homer (John Herina). The field slaves are dubious about Sarny's ability to do the job because she's quiet as "still water" and would need to chat with white people, but Sarny's quietness is the sign of an intelligent, spirited girl who keenly observes her surroundings and learns from them. Her growth becomes an excellent illustration of what contemporary economists who specialize in game theory describe as the acquisition of "strategic thinking," a skill often developed by individuals who interact with powerful others. Strategic thinking is rather like a social chess game in which A thinks, "If I do this, B will do that, and if B doesn't do what I expect I'll do something else to counter B's move." When the slave Sarny is brought into direct contact with her white owners, she becomes a master of such thinking.

Sarny's first, almost wordless experience of the world inside the Waller mansion establishes her curiosity and rebellious character. Entering the dining room alone, she gazes at a landscape painting—an art form she's never seen before—and surveys the dining table with its white tablecloth, exquisite china, and silver dining utensils. Above the table is a gold chandelier, which she reaches out and touches. "Delia says it's best not to want what you can't have," her offscreen narration tells us, "and I don't. I don't want nothing." She studies her reflection in the back of a silver spoon, but quickly replaces the spoon when Dealey and Mrs. Waller enter. The plantation's mistress airily waves her hand, asks Dealey to please give her a hairdo, and sashays out. As Delia and Sarny follow, Sarny turns to Dealey. "See, I told you they walk funny," giving a dead-on imitation of her mistress's swaying gait and wavy hand.

Later, she enters the master bedroom and examines its four-poster bed. She sits on the soft mattress and flops across it on her back, extending her arms on either side of her body. Turning her head, she sees a small pile of cloth dolls at the end of the bed. In a wide shot, she continues to luxuriate. Suddenly a tow-headed little white boy who has been hiding emerges from behind the bed and leans forward, looking down at her face. A tight close-up frames the two in profile as Sarny looks back at the boy from an upside-down position. Rushing downstairs to Dealey, she cries, "I can't take care of that child! He's almost grown and he ain't even house broke!"

Sarny is nevertheless assigned as Homer's minder and servant. One of her jobs is to stand next to him in the front row of the Sunday church service. Religion, and especially the Bible, are vastly more important to this film than to Paulsen's novella, in which such things are barely mentioned. In the film they function not only as forces of white deception and control, but also, ironically and more importantly, as potential sources of subversive literacy. (The opening line of the Bible, after all, tells us that in the beginning was the Word.) We see Reverend Rush (Danny Nelson) giving a sermon in which he claims that southern male chivalry is the last bastion of civilization and that, according to Exodus, God Almighty threw escaping slaves into the Red Sea. The sermon both flatters the white patriarchy and lies to the slaves, who are required to stand mute in the church balcony (an area that segregated southern movie theaters, which at least had seats, called the "crow's nest").

Inside the Waller mansion after church, several white characters eat Sunday dinner: Waller, his wife, his younger brother James (Jordan Williams), his oldest son Jeffrey (Joel Thomas Traywick), the Reverend Rush, the local bank president, an English visitor named Fanny Bowen (Shannon Eubanks), and Dr. Chamberlaine. Burnett covers the scene with a restless camera that swings back and forth across the table as the individual characters speak. Their conversation reveals barely repressed hostilities within the white community, which is fraught with sibling rivalry, marital tension, political disagreement, and potential battles over money. Sipping fine wine and chiefly addressing his younger brother, Waller talks boastfully about his riches. Reverend Rush effusively praises him for giving so much to the church, and Waller chuckles, "What I'm raising isn't cotton. It's money. All I need is a few more niggers to go out there and pick it off the stem." Mrs. Waller chides him in a tone of exaggerated sweetness, pointing out that Fanny Bowen and Dr. Chamberlaine "are not accustomed to such language." Fanny declares her disapproval of slavery, an institution the English have abolished, and at this point the underlying tensions begin to be expressed in terms of the themes of books and writing. Chamberlaine turns to Fanny and remarks that "according to your Mr. Dickens," the English only exchanged black slavery for white slavery. "You read, Doctor?" Waller asks. "It's a skill required at Harvard," Chamberlaine faux-modestly replies. "My wife," Waller says, "thinks life's a book—a romance." The wife counters, "You think life's a book, too—a ledger." As the meal ends, Dealey asks for a written pass that would allow Outlaw to visit Egypt. Sarny, intently listening while clearing the table, drops a tray, and Dealey immediately spanks her to keep Waller at bay. But Waller isn't satisfied. In order to punish both Sarny and his wife, he orders the reluctant, embarrassed mistress of the plantation to strike Sarny in the presence of the guests.

Another of Sarny's jobs is to chew tobacco from a pouch and spit on the Waller rose bushes so that insects won't attack them, a job that gives her access to a valuable commodity. One day, as she walks along a dirt road still chewing, she has her first glimpse of Nightjohn, who is part of a chain gang of slaves marching toward the plantation in shackles and iron collars. Viewed from her low-angle perspective, Nightjohn looks down at her as he passes; she contemptuously spits tobacco on the road, but he gives her a knowing smile. The camera then follows him to Waller's house, where, in a crane shot, it looks down on a group: Waller, an armed man on horseback who has a row of slaves to sell, and the group of chained men.

The next two sequences are linked by parallel editing, showing how Sarny and Nightjohn each experiences the economics of slavery. Sarny has been summoned to the library of the bookish Dr. Chamberlaine. Amused, he holds up a book and asks, "Now who do you think Tom Jones might be?" Sarny frowns and asks, "Is he a slave?" Laughing to himself, Chamberlaine explains that Jones is a slave "only to his passions." In pursuit of such things, he gives her a note to carry to her mistress and pays her with a penny. "How much this be?" she asks in astonishment. Cut to Nightjohn, standing in the road. "Five hundred dollars," his owner says, describing him as a "big buck" with perfect teeth. The price makes Waller suspicious because a slave of this quality ought to be worth $3,000. Waller wants to see the slave's back, and when Nightjohn's shirt is removed we see deep scars, signs of rebellion inscribed more vividly than words. Waller offers $50 dollars, at which point the man on horseback orders Nightjohn to remove his pants. "I seen enough," Waller says, but the owner explains that for fifty dollars he isn't going to include the slave's clothing.

Nightjohn's first day on the plantation attracts a good deal of attention, for he's no ordinary newcomer. Wearing nothing but a loincloth, he briskly hoes the fields and leads the other slaves in singing a work song. When the evening dinner bell rings, the slave driver Joe stops him: "Not you, boy," Joe says. "Massa says you got to put in a *full* day's work, heh, heh." As Nightjohn walks back to the fields, Dealey slips him a piece of bread. Late that evening, we find him wearing a shirt and pants obtained from other slaves and digging a garden of his own outside the slave quarters. Inside, he squats by a fire and spies Sarny lying almost atop Dealey on a narrow cot against the wall, stealing glimpses of him while pretending to sleep. Smiling, he tells her that he'll trade for "a lip of tobacco." "You come in naked as the day you was born," Sarny says. "What *you* got to trade?" What he's got, Nightjohn replies, "nobody can take away from me." Sarny thinks that's impossible. He explains that he has the alphabet, from which you can write words. He offers to teach her the first letter that very night if she won't be so stingy with the tobacco.

Nightjohn proves to be a gifted teacher and Sarny an eager, talented student. He proceeds by showing her letters of the alphabet written in the dust with a stick—letters that can be erased if anyone comes near. When she asks why an "A" has no bottom, he tells her it stands on its own two feet. As the secret instructions continue, she realizes that she has things she can use for practice: "Misses give me plenty to read—all her letters to the doctor!" Meanwhile, in one of the film's many ironic parallels, the lack of a letter causes a problem for Outlaw, who, aided by the elderly blacksmith, sneaks away at night and gives a forbidden, handmade engagement ring to Egypt. His momentary exit from the plantation is discovered by Waller, and a public whipping ensues, from which we learn something about the contradictions of black/white relations. Waller wants the old man who aided Outlaw to hold him down while Waller's son Jeffrey administers punishment with a bullwhip. Jeffrey, an innocent looking young man, resists because he and Outlaw have hunted together from boyhood. "Daddy," he pleads, "we're friends!" His father declares (rightly, given the true situation) that friendship between master and slave is impossible. "God made this boy to pick your cotton," he tells Jeffrey. Taking up the bullwhip himself, he sends his son back to the big house.

In her narration, Sarny emphasizes Waller's close watchfulness over the slaves, but notes that he hasn't "watched the one thing he needed watching": the affair between his wife and Chamberlaine. "Penny by penny," she says, the two lovers "were making me a rich woman." It isn't long, however, before slaves watching Sarny come to the realization that she's learning to read. An angry confrontation ensues between Dealey and Nightjohn, who argues, "*You* teaching that girl the wrong thing—to be afraid!" He reveals that he's run away from captivity three times and ultimately gotten all the way to the North and freedom. His astonished auditors can't understand why he isn't still free, but he explains that he came back solely to teach. This causes the tension between Dealey and Nightjohn to subside, and with an exchange of close-ups Burnett suggests an attraction between them. While working in the fields, they have a secret conversation almost like the old Hollywood movies about men or women in prison, in which he tells her that his wife was killed after dealing with an overseer who was going to whip their child. The wife chopped the overseer up with a hoe and killed his horse. "Afterward she felt real bad," Nightjohn says, "about the horse."

The more Sarny works in the Waller house, the more risks she takes. While feeding chocolate pudding to Homer she secretly takes a spoonful for herself; more important, she discovers that Homer has a set of alphabet blocks and determines to have them. At virtually the same moment, her mistress is in a quandary about whether to visit Chamberlaine, who has sent a carriage for her. Sarny offers to watch over Homer during the visit and take the blocks along as playthings. "I can take care of the baby," she tells Mrs. Waller, giving her a wide, beautiful smile. "I *love* your little boy!" Later, when Sarny returns to the slave quarters, she brings a cake Mrs. Waller has given her as a reward. Everyone thinks she's stolen it; she denies this, admitting, however, that she did steal the alphabet blocks.

Another quarrel breaks out over Nightjohn's influence. The old slave who has helped Outlaw visit a neighboring plantation is especially angry. Nightjohn tells him, "Words are *freedom*, old man. Laws, deeds, passes—all they are is words! White folks got all the words and they mean to keep them!" In a

powerfully acted close-up, the old man bitterly and almost tearfully recites the entire alphabet and declares that the whip and the gun, not words, make power. As proof, he holds up his right hand and removes a glove, explaining that his missing thumb and forefinger were lost not in an accident at the blacksmith forge but in punishment for his attempt to learn writing. Even so, Nightjohn intends to go outside and teach anyone who wants to learn. That evening he and Sarny meet under the stars and sit facing one another in a shot that frames them against the background of the universe. Nightjohn, a representative of the night sky and a kind of Promethean bearer of stolen knowledge, writes Sarny's name, which she's never seen, in the dust at their feet. "That's you, girl," he says. "That's who you are." In this context the name functions quite differently from what the once fashionable French theorist Louis Althusser described as a "subject position" or ideological "interpellation" in the service of church, state, and family. Sarny has no family name and barely any identity; she's an unwilling, rebellious subject, and by enabling her to see her name in writing Nightjohn gives her a magical thrill of agency.

On the next day at the Waller mansion, Mrs. Waller teaches Jeffrey to waltz while an expressionless slave stands stiffly against a wall and claps out a rhythm. Sarny leads Homer to an outhouse; another of her jobs is to wipe the boy with an old newspaper after he defecates, but this time she tears off a small piece of the paper and tells Homer he's old enough to start wiping himself. The remaining newspaper she keeps for herself, and at the end of the day she takes it back to the slave quarters. Nightjohn finds her studying it intently, trying to figure out the meaning of the first piece of printing she has been able to inspect. "Read what you got there," Nightjohn says. She pretends to read: "It says all the slaves are free," she tells him, "and nobody got to work for nobody no more." Then she smiles slyly and the two share a laugh.

The film now shifts to the harvest of cotton, chief source of the plantation era's economy and one of the first U.S. commodities with a global market. Waller's intense preoccupation with money derives in part from the fact that he's invested more than he owns in hopes of a very large crop—so large that he doesn't have quite enough "niggers" to pick it. As the harvest begins he announces that this will be the most important moment of his life and that everybody has to help, not only the slaves and Joe the slave driver but also his two oldest sons, his wife, and himself. He promises a big party at the end for everyone in the area, including the slaves. Outlaw is eager to get started because he will see Egypt at the party. There follows a montage of the characters working in the glare of the sun, picking cotton and filling huge bags, pausing only to wipe a brow or drink from a gourd. According to screenwriter Bill Cain, the production lost three precious days because of rain that interrupted the shooting of these scenes. They give us a palpable sense of oppressive heat, and Stephen James Taylor's music provides a mournfully lovely, hymnlike background to the action; nevertheless, probably because of the interrupted shooting schedule, the film doesn't do as much as it might have to show that cotton picking by hand is among the most painful and exhausting forms of agricultural labor. Until machines took over the job, workers spent days and nights bent over the cotton plants, fighting off insects, moving at relentless speed, repeatedly cutting their bare hands and arms on thorns.

The only persons exempt from labor are Sarny and the little boy Homer, who remain at the big house. On the second day of harvest, Sarny tries to entertain Homer with a game of hide-and-seek and in the process finds an opportunity to enter the Waller library. "Now where can that boy be?" she calls as she wanders among the books and notices an open ledger in which Waller keeps his accounts. Turning its pages, she sees a list of names with markings next to them that she doesn't understand. Just then Waller and his son Jeffrey return from the fields and enter the room from behind her. Waller doesn't accept her claim that Homer is hiding. "He's in here," she assures Waller, avoiding his eyes and trying not seem insubordinate, "he's just too scared of you to come out." Waller slaps her viciously, but Jeffrey comes to her defense, and Homer emerges from behind a chair.

Back at the slave quarters that night, in a nicely acted series of close-ups, Sarny tells Dealey and Nightjohn that she's less disturbed by Waller's slap, the marks of which are still visible on her face, than by what she takes to be Nightjohn's betrayal. "You lied," she tells him. "You said you'd teach me all the letters!" She uses a stone to scratch out some of the marks she's seen, and Nightjohn explains that they aren't letters but numbers, which are easy to teach because there are only ten of them, the same as the fingers of her hands. Dealey looks down and clasps her own hands. She tells Nightjohn that she, too, wants to learn numbers, and there is love in their exchange of looks.

Sarny gets a chance to test her newfound knowledge at the Sunday church service, where once again the ironies or contradictory implications of religion—what it signifies for whites versus what it signifies for slaves—become apparent. This suspenseful sequence, which also involves an emotionally moving discovery, is organized by point-of-view shots involving three characters: Sarny, seated with Homer in the front row; the Reverend Rush, about to deliver a sermon; and Nightjohn, standing in the balcony with other slaves. Sarny looks at a sign on the wall indicating page numbers of the day's hymns. In a low-angle close-up, the preacher calls for the congregation to turn to the first number; in a high-angle close-up, Sarny opens the hymnal, finds the page, and as the whites sing the verses of the Lord's Prayer she quietly reads them to herself. The sound mix changes to indicate subjectivity: singing fades into the background and we hear Sarny's voice whispering the verses. Her eyes fill with tears of joy. "I be reading!" she tells herself. She smiles with pride and gratitude and exchanges glances with Nightjohn as he stands in the balcony. Reverend Rush notices her tears, steps to the front row, and looks forbiddingly down. She quickly closes the hymnal, and Nightjohn looks concerned. Rush pauses. "Child," he asks, "are you saved?" In an extreme high-angle close-up Sarny looks back at him, gives him her best beaming smile, and announces, "I *am* saved!"

Her words go to the very heart of the film's complex treatment of religion: she has achieved a kind of salvation, but not the kind Rush propounds. Cut to a baptism scene at a nearby river, where Rush dunks Sarny in the water and shouts hallelujah as the other slaves and the Waller family gather around. Rush seems genuinely happy at having saved another soul for the Lord—a bizarre contradiction of plantation culture, given that Sarny isn't allowed to read the white Bible, can't fully worship in the white church, and presumably wouldn't be admitted to the white heaven. Sarny, Delia, and Nightjohn quietly joke among themselves about the dangers Sarny has avoided, but the mood among the whites is different. Waller approaches his son Jeffrey and is furious because the family Bible, in Jeffrey's keeping for the ceremony, has gone missing. Back at the Waller mansion, he attacks Jeffrey and beats him in front of his mother.

We soon discover that Sarny has taken her most significant and dangerous step toward the liberating effects of knowledge: she has stolen the Bible. She stays up all Sunday night reading it, and before dawn the next morning, as the slaves are heading out to pick cotton, she rushes up to Nightjohn and excitedly announces that the preacher has lied: God let the slaves go; he's on their side. "Not today," Nightjohn says grimly, and marches off to the fields.

Each stage of Sarny's education brings with it thrilling, courageous acts of discovery, along with increasing risks of savage punishment. Late that night, by candlelight, she examines another purloined sheet of newspaper, much to the annoyance of the exhausted old blacksmith, who accuses her of disturbing everyone's sleep by only pretending to read. Defiant, she begins to read aloud, stumbling over the first word, "Gazette," which Nightjohn, rising from slumber, explains is the title of the paper. Then she stumbles over "insurrection." Nightjohn, becoming alert, defines this as "uprising," and he the other slaves anxiously gather around. "Read, girl," the old man says. "Don't keep us waiting!" Slowly, she reads a report of the revolt of Nat Turner and his "army of slaves," who have killed over fifty whites and forced the Virginia militia to retreat when rain damaged their gunpowder. This news gives us the date of the film's plot: 1831, a later period than in Paulsen's story and a crucial moment in black history that several filmmakers, including Burnett, will revisit. Nightjohn slyly apologizes for allowing Sarny to read at night.

Emboldened by her discoveries, Sarny takes another opportunity to play hide-and-seek with Homer and investigate Waller's ledger, in which she finds entries for "old man," "Dealey," and "John" with cash numbers beside their names. At roughly this point the harvest ends, and Waller fulfills his promise of a separate party for the slaves. The happy occasion, shot at the magic hour, gives Outlaw and Egypt the opportunity to defy the southern law against slave marriages and pledge themselves to one another. We see them "jumping the broom," a wedding ritual performed by slaves in lieu of a church ceremony, as their friends gather around (according to Bill Cain's diary, this scene was shot on day eighteen; the cast was in a weary but relaxed mood and at one point Gabriel Casseus, who plays Outlaw, dragged Burnett in front of the camera). The slaves' happiness, however, is short lived; soon afterward Egypt is returned to Chamberlaine's neighboring plantation, where she discovers that she's pregnant.

For Waller, too, the end of harvest results in trouble. In anticipation of big profits from his crop, he and Jeffrey visit the local banker, only to learn that the entire region has vastly overproduced cotton and prices have fallen, leaving Waller with $25,000 in unpaid bank loans. His agonizing discussion with the rather Dickensian banker is shot in a style reminiscent of John Ford in the 1940s: a low-level, wide-angle camera brings the entire room into focus and makes the ceiling look as if it were weighing down on the characters. Waller bitterly complains, "All my life's been like this, and still I never see it coming." The banker smiles primly and announces that he's "taken the liberty" of writing out a new loan to help Waller with next year's crop. Just then Waller's brother James, invited to dinner by the banker, enters and looks pleased with himself. Unlike Waller, he hasn't invested all his money in cotton; a significant amount has gone into banking, which means, although he doesn't say so, that he will profit from his brother's debts. He and the banker exchange brief, smirking looks, and Waller punches James in the face, knocking him out. Late that night, the extremely drunken Waller is helped home by Jeffrey and Outlaw.

On the next day, by means the film doesn't explain, Nightjohn somehow acquires ink and a quill pen and uses blank pages from the stolen Bible to forge passes so that Outlaw and Egypt can make an escape. Before he can complete both passes, however, Jeffrey bursts unannounced into the cabin, and the slaves hasten to conceal the writing material. Jeffrey apologizes for the intrusion and explains that he's come to thank Outlaw for helping him on the previous night. He assures everyone that his father "isn't a bad man" and offers to shake hands in friendship with Outlaw. But Outlaw is holding the forged pass behind his back. This leads to an improvised game with Jeffrey, who laughingly suggests that Outlaw must have stolen a chicken. The incriminating piece of paper is secretly passed from one slave to another, and Nightjohn exits with it while Jeffrey runs about the room and searches everyone. Finding nothing, he sits at the table, smiles, and breathlessly announces, "Now, see? That's the way it should be—friendly!" Then he looks down at the floor and sees his family Bible lying at his feet. Confronting

Outlaw, he says, "I took a licking for this Bible! I thought we were friends!" Outlaw looks back at him somberly and replies, "That's what we about to find out."

The discovery of the stolen Bible leads to a pair of climactic, theatrically public reckonings (shot on the last five days of an increasingly rushed schedule), one ending with the brutal punishment of Nightjohn and the other with Sarny's partial victory over her owners. In an attempt to shield Sarny, Dealey claims to be the Bible thief. Waller doesn't believe her, but he and a couple of armed men gather the slaves outside their quarters to witness her punishment. Holding the Bible in one hand and a bullwhip in another, Waller gives a loud speech, impressively delivered by Beau Bridges in a lawyerly tone of amused contempt. "Now *this* is a Bible!" he shouts to the group. "A preacher's Bible! And whoever stole it can read!" Burnett employs a Steadicam to follow Waller as he circles among the slaves. Reaching the frightened Sarny, who is being guarded by the old man, he bends down and says, "Ain't nothing else to do but read it!" Confronting Outlaw, he announces, "Dealey here says that she stole it, and she's a smart woman. But when it comes to reading, she's as ignorant as dirt." Returning to the front of the gathering, where Dealey is standing, he suddenly whirls and yells, "*So*

who stole this Bible?" In a reverse shot of his silent audience, we see Nightjohn moving from the back row toward the front.

"Well, if that's the way you want it," Waller says, facing Dealey and cracking the bullwhip. In a large close-up, Dealey looks him in the eye and quietly tells him, "I done good work for you all these years. You don't want to do this to me." Waller grins. "You right as always. I gave my son a licking over this Bible, and it's his beating to give." But Jeffrey steps around his father and doesn't take the offered whip. In a pleading voice, he asks, "Dealey, can you read?" Not words, she says, but faces, and his is the face of "a boy I helped raise. Not a bad boy. Just a boy afraid of losing his Daddy or turning out to be like him." It's an exact reading of Jeffrey, as Waller acknowledges when he orders his son to return to the house. But Jeffrey has reached a crisis. Torn between the two fears Dealey described, he tries to assert power over his father and at the same time do his father's will. Pushing Waller aside, he grabs the whip and frantically shouts "Who stole the Bible?" As he begins to beat Dealey, Nightjohn's hand suddenly enters the frame and grabs his wrist. "It was me," Nightjohn says. "It was all me."

For the establishing shot of Nightjohn's punishment, Burnett uses a camera crane looking straight down from a god's-eye view at a flat tree stump that serves as a chopping block. Gathered around the stump are armed men and Waller's two older sons. Nightjohn is forced into a kneeling position, his right hand placed palm down on the stump and held there by Waller and Joe, the black slave driver. From a low angle near the ground, we see Waller holding an axe and loudly pronouncing judgment: "It is against the law for any negro slave to read or write! This is what you learn!" He brings the axe down and chops off Nightjohn's forefinger and thumb—the same injury the old blacksmith suffered. A close-up shows Sarny weeping. As Nightjohn drops forward in agony and tries to staunch the bleeding, Waller towers over him and asks, "You learned your lesson, boy?" Carl Lumbly's performance during this scene is emotionally charged; trembling and trying to suppress pain, speaking in a halting voice, he answers, "Yes sir! I learned my lesson. My lesson got no bottom!" Taking a stick in his left hand, he begins to write letters in the dust. "This is for Joe," he says. "A stands on its own two feet." "B reminds me of my wife." The open-mouthed "C got something to say." He continues to write and looks at Sarny: "When you lose one hand the other gets stronger . . . always be looking for you." Waller seizes a rifle, but Jeffrey intervenes again, saving Nightjohn by knocking him out with the butt of a rifle and ordering that he be taken out and sold to anybody who will buy him. "What did he write?" Sarny quietly asks, and sees "John" written in the dust.

In the wake of Nightjohn's departure, Sarny takes up his role and surpasses him in the cleverness of her revolt. That evening, as Delia sings to her the lullaby we heard when Sarny was born, she forges a pass so that Egypt and Outlaw can escape. On her way to Sunday church the next morning, she delivers a letter from Mrs. Waller to Dr. Chamberlaine, and to his puzzlement returns the pennies he gave, explaining that she can no longer keep his secrets. As he writes a reply to the letter, Sarny deliberately puts one of his books in its proper alphabetical position on the library shelf; Chamberlaine soon discovers what she's done and shouts after her, but she's already gone. As she has planned, he goes after her.

This leads to the second of the two climactic episodes—more theatrical, improbable, and melodramatic than the first, yet undeniably moving and fully appropriate to the positive spirit of the film. When Chamberlaine arrives at the back door of the church, Sarny is standing in the front row with Homer, and the congregation is singing a hymn. Suddenly Waller and an armed search party break into the front of the church and order everyone to sit down. Waller waves the two passes, written by two different hands, which have enabled Outlaw and Egypt to run. Nightjohn obviously wrote the first pass, but who wrote the second? Enraged, he aims his rifle at the slaves in the balcony and threatens to start shooting all of them at the count of three if no one confesses. "One, two," he shouts, but Sarny jumps up and shouts, "three!" In the hushed silence that follows, she gazes up at the balcony and declares that Waller isn't going to shoot anybody. Looking at the old man, she explains, "There's a piece of paper at the house says you worth five hundred dollars." Although Nightjohn was punished and sent away, he was worth only fifty dollars. Delia, on the other hand, is worth a thousand. "You his wealth," she says to all the slaves.

Waller aims the rifle at Sarny and prepares to shoot, but she tells him, "I'm worth more than you know." Turning for a moment, she looks back at Mrs. Waller, who is seated near the front of the church, and says, "Mrs. Waller going to speak for me." Surreptitiously, she draws the edge of Chamberlaine's letter out of her pocket so that Mrs. Waller can see it. Getting no response, she offers to speak instead for Mrs. Waller. The husband looks suspiciously at his wife, who adopts an air of unconcern and says, "Shoot her." But Waller replies, "Not before I hear what the girl has to say." At this crucial moment Dr. Chamberlaine rises from the back row and, left with no choice, improvises a solution by announcing to the astonished congregation that he was responsible for the second pass. New to the area and unfamiliar with its customs, he explains, he made the error of teaching elementary writing skills to the girl Egypt so that she could assist him. He thought it foolish to deprive slaves of education, but he now realizes that he was very much wrong. Approaching Waller, he offers to repay him for what has been lost. Waller says nothing. His eyes indicate that he senses something wrong, but he implicitly accepts

Mrs. Waller tells her husband that she wants Sarny to be sold and marches out of the church with Waller and the other whites. Chamberlaine remains behind with Sarny and gives her a coin in exchange for his letter. When he exits, Sarny is left alone on the ground floor, and the slaves remain standing in the balcony. This moment of relative freedom may or may not be true to the real conditions of southern slavery, but it gives the film and its audience an opportunity to honor Sarny. The slaves, led by the old man, look down on the young girl whose bravery and intelligence has taught them something and break into a hymn in praise of the Lord.

The film ends with Sarny's departure, and in several ways, like most classical narratives, its conclusion returns us to the beginning. Delia gives Sarny a maternal embrace and hopes that Sarny will remember her. "I remember everything," Sarny says with a radiant smile. Dressed in rags, she's brought to the crowded carriage that will take her away, and as she stands waiting she tells one of the new slaves that she'll make a trade for tobacco. When he asks what she has to trade, she writes an "A" in the dust. Loaded onto the back of the carriage in the same position her mother occupied, she smiles and waves back at Delia. As the carriage drives off, she tells us in her offscreen narration that she looked for Nightjohn but never saw him again. Even so, she met many who knew him or who knew those who had met him. "We all got Nightjohn in our family somewhere," she says. The film concludes with the low-angle image of Nightjohn kneeling on the ground and looking up at the starry night sky. He's an emblematic hero and proof of the film's thesis: words, at least in this context, are freedom.

EIGHT

————

The Wedding *(1998)*

A TWO-PART MINISERIES PRODUCED by Oprah Winfrey and broadcast by ABC in February 1998, *The Wedding* is one of Burnett's most expensively mounted films. In a video interview conducted by actor Delroy Lindo when the picture was about to appear, Burnett commented on the difficulties he had encountered in directing what once were called "television movies of the week": everything depended on having a good relationship with the writer and especially the producer, and it greatly helped to have a photographer who could work fast. There was pressure to work quickly, a constant need to make rapid adjustments, less control over the screenplay, less time to work with the actors, and no final director's cut. (Even with these limitations, TV movies tend to give a director more say than commercials, series, or long-form shows on streaming services, in which the style is set by an advertising agency or a "show runner" and the director follows a predetermined format.) Conditions were somewhat different with the more ambitious *The Wedding*. Burnett had qualified influence over the script and editing, plus the ability to consult about style with director of photography Frederick Elmes, who had worked with David Lynch, and production designer Geoffrey S. Grimsman, whose credits include *Blade Runner*. Burnett also had the benefit of the participation of composer Stephen James Taylor, who had become one of his most trusted collaborators, and several actors who had worked with him in the past. Still, Oprah Winfrey was frequently on the set, and (though Burnett has never said so) she is a producer who tends to micromanage. Furthermore, the cast was headed by one of Hollywood's major black stars, an Academy Award winner who could exert her own influence. Whatever difficulties Burnett may have faced, it should be easier to see a picture as good as this one. At this time the only available sources for the public are a DVD from England and a not very good YouTube version. It deserves better distribution.

Lisa Jones's screenplay is an intelligent adaptation of a novel by Dorothy West, a legendary figure of the Harlem Renaissance and its last survivor. Born in 1907 to a middle-class Boston family, West earned a graduate degree in journalism from Columbia University and in 1926 moved to Harlem, where she met Langston Hughes and Countee Cullen. An author of short stories, she was one of the first African American women to be published, at a time when such things were by no means easy. She and Hughes spent 1932 in the Soviet Union, writing a film about race relations, but the film was never produced. During the 1930s West also worked with the Federal Writer's Project and founded *Challenge*, a journal of black writing that featured early work by Richard Wright and Ralph Ellison. In 1948 she published her first novel, *The Living Is Easy*, about a young woman who aspires to rise socially into the black upper class. The novel was a critical success but sold little, and its lack of sales may have motivated her to move permanently to Martha's Vineyard, a large Massachusetts island known as a summer residence for presidents, artists, and the well-to-do, graced with lighthouses, sandy beaches, and a mild climate. She continued to write and publish short stories and in 1995 published her second novel, *The Wedding*, which deals with "colorism" (the superior attitude of the brown skinned toward the dark skinned) in a 1950s community of affluent blacks on Martha's Vineyard. Edited by Jacqueline Kennedy, to whom it is dedicated, the novel became both a critical success and a best seller. West died soon after its publication, in 1998, the year when the TV adaptation was broadcast.

The novel has been compared with works by William Faulkner, in part because West's prose involves some long, rolling sentences with complex syntax, and in part because the story centers on the culture of a small geographic area that has a complex generational history of race and class. But West's style is more graceful and lucid than Faulkner's, and her tightly unified plot is more compact than those of his novels, covering almost a century in roughly 250 pages. And although West's novel has certain things in common with many narratives about racial passing, it isn't one. Like the film derived from it, *The Wedding* is best described as a full-bore domestic melodrama, so long as the term doesn't imply condescension or denigration. It's a different sort of melodrama, however, from the Hollywood pictures of the type directed by Douglas Sirk or Vincente Minnelli in the 1950s (with the very qualified exception of *Imitation of Life*), because the family issues have less to do with patriarchy than with race, the psychological and social conflicts have greater historical dimension, and the world it represents is so rarely depicted in fiction or film.

The plot of the novel, set in 1953, centers on a Martha's Vineyard enclave of wealthy black homes known to residents as "the Oval," a term that suggests both an exclusive retreat and a circumscribed world segregated from both whites and poor blacks. Within this world, Shelby Coles, the beautiful, light-skinned daughter of successful doctor Clark Coles and his wife Corinne, is preparing to marry Meade Howell, a white, middle-class jazz musician from New York. The impending event is scandalous in the eyes of most Ovalites, who privately grumble that Shelby could have her choice of prosperous (preferably also light-skinned) black professionals but has chosen a white person of no social distinction and disreputable profession. Their disapproval is exacerbated because Shelby's older sister Liz eloped to marry a dark-skinned doctor, the son of a maid and a butler.

Shelby's parents, who have a strained but outwardly respectable married life involving hidden affairs, try to put on a good front in preparing for the lavish wedding while at the same time managing a variety of domestic tensions, including the fact that Meade's parents will not be attending. As the day of the wedding approaches, further complications arise in the person of Lute McNeil, a handsome, dark-skinned black man with three small daughters, who represents himself as a sculptor and architect from Boston and rents a summer house in the Oval. Lute appears to be a single parent, and when he sets eyes on Shelby he decides to seduce and win her over for marriage. "What did a white man have for her that he didn't have a hundred times over?" he asks himself in the novel. "He needed no more than an hour alone with her to break the crystal he could see through so clearly" (West 1995, 25–26).

Woven within these events and narrated mostly in third-person indirect inner monologues is an elaborate history involving the intermarriage of two family trees extending back to the end of the Civil War. Clark Coles is the Harvard-educated descendant of an Irish plantation owner in the South who impregnated one of his slaves and returned her to slavery. The son of this nameless "Ebony Woman" became a literate black preacher, who married "Butternut Woman." Their son, Isaac, moved north and married a white teacher and former abolitionist who had helped to educate him. He became a successful physician, and his son Clark went on to even greater success.

Clark's wife Corinne, on the other hand, is a black descendant of white southern colonel and plantation owner Lance Shelby, who lost all his money after the war and whose daughter Caroline, known as "Gran" by the Coles household (where she still lives), gave birth to a daughter named Josephine. Impoverished, widowed, and almost desperate, Gran allowed Josephine to marry Hannibal, a college-educated black who could support both wife and mother-in–law and who eventually became a college president. Hannibal and Josephine's daughter, Corinne, then made a dynastic marriage with Clark Coles, blending the family trees and producing two daughters of their own.

This history of what West calls "blue-veined" blackness results in a social caste that ironically mirrors the rarified manners and discriminations of Boston Brahmins and old-money eastern whites. "Though money was as important in the Oval as in any other upper-class community," West tells us, "it was not the determining factor in distinguishing between majors and minors. The distinction was so subtle, the gradations so fine drawn, that only an Ovalite knew on which level he belonged, and an outsider sometimes wasted a whole summer licking the wrong boot" (7). The most important, mostly unspoken, but not so "fine-drawn" distinction has to do with pheno-type or skin color rather than blood. In the "nighttime of love," for example, we're told that the light-skinned Corinne desires "the very darkness that repelled her in the light of day." Like others among the Ovalites, she feels superior to outsiders but at the same time half consciously ashamed of her own blackness. She thanks God for giving her two daughters who are as light as she is, but "Hannibal's half of her makeup" has not yet revealed itself on the skins of her children, and the chance that it might is "too slight for her to risk a third try at bearing Clark a son" (66).

The two-part, three-hour film closely follows the novel, differing in only a few ways. Out of necessity it expands and adds dialogue to many scenes that West treats in discursive fashion, and it renders the history of the two family trees through periodic, fully dramatized flashbacks. It deals only briefly with a lengthy episode that might easily have become one of West's short stories. In the novel, the child Shelby Coles loses her way while chasing a puppy and wanders into the white part of Martha's Vineyard, where everyone thinks she's a lost white child. After a great many complications, a woman who has heard that a child is missing from the Oval hesitantly asks Shelby if she's white. (Like some other whites in the area, the woman is a liberal, but she fears inquiring into race.) The innocent Shelby has heard the terms "colored" and "white," but doesn't know the answer to the question. When she's finally returned by the police to her panicked household, she asks Gran, "Am I colored?" and is told yes. Then she asks Gran the same question about her sister Liz, her mother, and her father. Again, the response is yes. "Are you colored too?" she asks, and is told simply "I'm your Gran." Shelby is greatly relieved because all the people she loves are like herself. "Oh, Gran," she says, I'm so glad we're all colored. A lady told me I was white" (79–80).

We don't need the full story because the gradations of skin color among the characters make the underlying issues visibly apparent; at one point two of the dark-skinned servants of the Coles are seen in private conversation, and one of them a bit derisively explains to the other that "these are the oldest black families—doctors, lawyers, it's all high yeller around here." A more significant difference from the novel is the way the film deals out information to the audience, particularly in regard to Lute McNeil (Carl Lumbly). In West's novel, we know almost from the beginning that even though Lute has three daughters and is very fond of them, he has a disturbing history with the three white women who were their mothers. The first was a promiscuous, amoral, "baby-faced tramp" whom he beat regularly and eventually threw out on the street to die in the gutter. The second was a "Polack waitress" from the country whom he treated as a servant and divorced when his serial infidelities narrowed down to a rich Beacon Hill woman named Della. After secretly marrying Della to keep the relationship from her parents, and after having a child with her, he has left her behind in Boston and taken his daughters and a girlfriend (masquerading as a household servant) to Martha's Vineyard, where he notices Shelby Coles and begins planning to have her as his fourth wife.

In the film, we're initially given none of this information. We see the handsome Lute, who at first claims to be a widower, arriving on the island via boat, observed with sexual interest by Corinne Coles (Lynn Whitfield) as she waits in her car for one of her lovers. Lute rents a cottage from one of the Ovalites, and Burnett provides charming views of his children at play. A kind of dramatic chorus made up of two light-skinned, white-haired ladies with pearls gossips about the new arrival. One of them (Ethel Ayler) remarks that "it used to be money alone couldn't buy you into the Oval" and complains that the cottage has been rented to "someone who doesn't come from the right family." Lute's wife Della (Patricia Clarkson) isn't revealed until later, and thus Lute appears sympathetic: a good, single father and a prosperous, self-made man worthy of Shelby but looked down upon by Ovalite snobs. His overtures to Shelby in the days leading up to the wedding suggest a burgeoning romance; she's clearly attracted to him, and the audience can think he might be a better partner for her.

The film is impeccably cast and from the beginning establishes a world of blue-skied, white-and-pastel summertime filled with good-looking people and tasteful opulence. An early scene introduces Shelby, a princess named after the white scion of one branch of the Coles family, who is trying on a gorgeous white wedding dress that offsets her flawless, light-brown skin. (She's played by Hallie Berry, an Oscar winner and one of the few women of color who crossed over into Hollywood stardom in the 1990s. She was even a Bond girl.) We're also given a sense of the Coles mansion, which has high ceilings and a ballroom space for parties and receptions; there's a fine antique grand piano that the family doesn't use, but we see Meade Howell (Eric Thal) approaching it, chatting unassumingly with one of the servants and playing a bit of jazz as he and Shelby anticipate their future. (Diegetic music in the film includes recordings by Nat Cole, Billie Holiday, and Charlie Parker, heard on radio.)

Soon the busy, cheery atmosphere of an impending wedding gives way to tension. The groom's family won't be attending the ceremony, and neither will Shelby's father Clark Coles (Michael Warren), who tells her that he objects to "high-society wedding business" redolent of the country club. That evening we see Clark and Corinne preparing for bed; she wears an alluring nightgown but he pushes their twin beds apart. Not long afterward we discover that they've been unfaithful to each other. She's a snobbish woman who complains about Meade Howell and suffers from a half-hidden neurosis. Clark's excuse for missing the wedding is a golf tournament with his fellow doctors, but he's actually going on a trip with his dark-skinned nurse, who has been his lover for several years. Further complications are revealed at the home of Shelby's sister Liz (Cynda Williams), her husband Lincoln Odis (Richard Brooks), and their child Laurie. Lincoln is a doctor, but unlike Clark Coles he has a practice that favors the poor. He, too, won't be attending the wedding, because Clark and Corinne have never approved of him; he's been treated, he says, as not good enough, or as too black. Liz and Laurie must go alone.

Much of the film takes place through conversations skillfully directed by Burnett with a moving, almost balletic camera that creates a serene counterpoint to the mounting problems of the wedding. On the day after talking with her husband, Liz meets Shelby and explains that Lincoln won't attend. The sisters resolve to avoid quarreling about anything, but when their mother Corinne is told the news she walks off in a huff to deal with a white workman. For the first time we meet Gran, the white grandmother (Shirley Knight). This is another example of the way the film creates narrative effects through the order in which it gives us information. In the novel, we learn about Gran through West's straightforward history of Corinne's ancestry; in the film, we've been told nothing about Gran, and her appearance as a genteel old white woman living with the Coles is both surprising and mysterious. Knight plays the role as a sweet-faced southerner who has long been affectionately tolerated even though she maintains the prejudices of her race and class. When she sees Liz's daughter Laurie, she worries openly that the little girl is beginning to look too dark.

While Liz and Shelby have lunch in a restaurant, Liz says to Shelby, "don't look, but the most handsome man is staring at you." It's Lute, who soon meets the sisters and gives them a lift when their car breaks down. His little girls are accompanying him, and Shelby is charmed by them. Lute explains that he owns "several manufacturing firms" and is a designer of furniture, although he's always wanted to be an architect. A rapport develops between the two, in part because Lute claims to be single and seems so gentle, unassuming, and open. When Shelby alludes to her family, Lute says that he's always thought of Martha's Vineyard as a place for "uppity lawn parties" given by snobbish colored people who drink tea (an indication that he isn't a

fortune hunter). Later, he tells her that until recently he was married to a Boston lady who was ashamed of being with a "negro." Shelby, about to be married to a white man, is sensitive to such matters, and the comment strikes home at her heretofore concealed worries and vulnerabilities. In a subsequent conversation with Meade, she talks about how years ago, in the white part of Martha's Vineyard, she was treated as a "lost little colored girl" and felt comfort only when she got back to the Oval. The placement of this much-abbreviated and less racially complex version of the childhood story here, in the context of a meeting of minds with Lute, shows indirectly that even though Shelby loves Meade, she fears the social and psychological conse-quences of interracial marriage. In committing to Meade and a life in New York, she'll be leaving the security of the Oval.

The film enters a new phase when Corinne, while putting away one of Clark's jackets, finds in his pocket two tickets to Paris for the same dates as his supposed golf tournament. She burns the tickets, and this motivates the first of *The Wedding*'s flashbacks, which is designed to reveal Corinne's family history. We go to Milledgeville, Georgia, in 1905. Caroline Shelby (the young Gran) has what she calls a "plain" daughter named Josephine (Maggie Welsh), who seems unable to save the two from poverty by attracting marriageable white gentlemen. But Josephine finds a love match in the person of Hannibal (Gabriel Casseus), a scholarly young black man whom we see reading Homer's *Odyssey*. Hannibal goes to Boston to further his education; two years later, after burying his mother, he sends a letter to Josephine with enough money for her to join him. Hannibal is now a college professor living in a comfortable middle-class home. He and Josephine marry, and Burnett stages one of his typically sensuous and moving love scenes, with the couple seen in a mirror as he raises her arm and kisses her softly on the neck. When their child Corinne is born, Gran comes to live with them and barely tolerates Hannibal.

Back in the present, the distraught Corinne, whose loveless marriage has been confirmed by the tickets she discovered, confronts Gran and blames her for "everything—what you've done to me, and my mother, and my father." The next flashback takes us to Washington, D.C., in 1915 and fully explains what Corinne means. Her mother, Josephine, becomes chronically ill, and although Hannibal is an affectionate father, much of the care and instruction of Corinne devolves on Gran, who pointedly avoids assuring the child that her mother loves her. When Corinne becomes a young woman, she's recognized as "the most attractive colored debutant in the city," and Gran impresses on her that she should marry someone "fair." The stage is set for her marriage to Clark Coles, but not necessarily for love.

Again in the present, Corinne has a heart-to-heart talk with Shelby and tells her, "I want to be sure you're marrying a man who loves you." The psychological pressures on Shelby continue to mount, and they become worse when she encounters Lute as she's walking along the beach. In a long, slightly low-level tracking shot framed against the blue sky, he tells her that he was also married to a woman he met in France, and the marriage was killed by the way whites treated his wife for being married to a black. "Have you ever had to drink from a colored only water fountain?" he asks. At this point, although we don't realize it fully, everything Lute says to Shelby has been calculated to undermine her resolve. In her protected world she's never had to drink from a public fountain, and she knows that as Meade's wife both she and he will have to deal with the overt or covert racists (including his parents) they will meet in New York. Her marriage could end just as his supposedly did.

A large prewedding reception at the Coles home is notable for the way Burnett blocks actors and camera so that all but a few of the important characters mingle with nicely individuated guests. Significantly absent are Lute, who hasn't been invited, and Meade's parents, who, Corinne explains,

aren't there because Mrs. Howell is "ill." Meade is of course present, but one potential problem with both West's novel and the film is that he's never established as a strong or sufficiently interesting character to challenge Lute. He's apparently a talented musician, and as the film has shown in an early conversation between him and one of the Cole servants, he's down to earth, free of class prejudice, and uneasy in the stuffy environs of the Cole mansion. His interactions with Shelby, however, don't have Lute's aura of power and sexual magnetism. Perhaps this is a strategy meant to intensify Shelby's conflict. At any rate, during the reception she receives a note from Lute asking to talk with her. She exits and meets him on the beach. He passionately kisses her, and she runs toward home, ending the first part of the film.

Suspicions about Lute begin to rise in part two, when we learn more about Emmaline (Margo Moorer), ostensibly his domestic helper, who is seen enjoying martinis with him. While Shelby sits at a table in a local bar-nightclub and Meade's combo plays a jazz composition dedicated to her, Lute enters, sits down beside her, and touches her hand. Meade and Lute almost come to blows over this, and Lute asks, "What makes you so sure you should be with Shelby . . . your color? Because it certainly can't be your money." In

the aftermath, Meade tells Shelby that he's having second thoughts: "boats and country clubs, I don't feel like I fit in."

Doubts about the coming marriage are expressed from every angle, including from Clark Coles, who, in a fatherly conversation with Shelby, worries that she will be sacrificing "our world—the Oval." Their conversation motivates another flashback, in which Clark's history is revealed. We return to Washington, D.C., in 1928, and find the successful young Clark and his dark-skinned girlfriend Sabina (Monica Ford) discussing his ambitions. They're in love, but the upwardly mobile Clark has been invited to a debutante ball in New York and confesses that he's always wanted to go back there. At the ball, he's introduced to Corinne, also from Washington, and privately told that she's "a prize for any up-and-coming doctor like yourself." When he demurs because of his love for Sabina, a fellow black doctor remarks, "Love is a luxury few of us can afford." He and Corinne dance, viewed from a camera crane that participates in the glamor of the occasion.

The flashback shifts to New York in 1934, where Clark, now married to Corinne, is enjoying a prosperous practice that attracts the interest of white colleagues. A white doctor at a party tells him that "our medical group" wants to "open up," and that "your wife" is "a very cultured and elegant woman." By this time Clark and Corinne have two children, but their married life is troubled. In their bedroom, she tries to be seductive, but he pulls away. We discover that he's begun an intense affair with his nurse, Rachel (Charlayne Woodard), who has been working with him for a year. Corinne, meanwhile, withdraws and goes through an emotional crisis; she has tried suicide because, she tells him, she fears having a black-skinned child, and "I just don't want my children to suffer for their color."

We return to the present. Clark gently asks Shelby if she's marrying Meade because he's white. "A wrong choice in marriage," he tells her, "is hard to undo." Moments later, Liz calls Lincoln, pleading with him to come to the wedding, and Clark receives a letter from Rachel, who has reached the age of forty and for the sake of security is going to marry a widowed city employee. Clark loves her, but he's been afraid of what divorce could do to his reputation and practice. There will be no trip to Paris. The melodrama intensifies when, on the heels of this development, the aged Gran has an apparent heart attack. As Clark checks her pulse, she whispers, "I told [Shelby that Meade] will make a fine husband." Clark replies, "You and everyone else said [to me] love will be a luxury."

Feeling repentant, Meade finds Shelby in a local flower shop and kisses her, much to the discomfort of the white shop girl. Meanwhile, Shelby's sister Liz has a conversation with Clark and tells him that it took all her strength to elope with Lincoln. Clark, sharply aware of the compromises he's made in his own life and chastened by Rachel's decision to leave him, confesses, "I've always admired you for that." A brief flashback takes us to Columbia, South Carolina, in 1891, the oldest date represented in the film, to show a conversation between Preacher (Paul Butler) and his son Isaac Coles, who will become the father of Clark Coles. Preacher wants the young man to go north and be educated. The sad parting between the two is emblematic of the generation of black "strivers" who left their birthplace and families in order to escape the oppressions of the post-Reconstruction South.

The emotional wounds within the Coles family begin to heal just at the moment when Shelby feels most insecure about marriage. Lincoln, Liz's husband, arrives at the Coles home and makes peace with Clark and Corinne, but at a restaurant called Dock Haven in the white area of Martha's Vineyard, Shelby waits for a lunch date with Meade, who hasn't yet arrived. The hostess (Claire Eye) won't seat her. Shelby is forced to sit in the entryway, the only person of color in the restaurant, while from the dining room we hear musicians playing "This Never Happened Before." When Meade appears, the humiliated and angry Shelby asks him, "What are we going to do if you get a job in Virginia or Georgia?" As if to emphasize problems of interracial marriage, the next scene takes us to Boston, where Lute's wife Della receives a letter from him. He wants a divorce because racial difference has destroyed the relationship. His actual reason is his growing confidence that he will be able to marry Shelby.

The eventful last episodes of the film are quite similar to West's novel and true to her general aims, but in my view they're flawed because they seem such an obvious attempt to wrap up problems and create a happy ending in which romantic love wins. Four things need to happen to achieve this happiness: Shelby needs to commit to Meade, Lute needs to be decisively eliminated as a possible alternative husband for Shelby, Clark and Corinne Coles need to try to salvage their long-damaged marriage, and the wedding must finally take place. Somewhat improbably, all four things happen in fairly rapid succession, though not quite in that order.

Shelby goes to her parents and talks with them about her increasing doubts: "Both of you have questioned my choice. I love Meade with all my heart, but I guess that's just not enough." Clark, standing near his wife and wearing white ducks and a blue blazer for the outdoor party before the wedding he now plans to attend, explains to Shelby that in his generation "love wasn't on the list." Another flashback takes us to Harlem in 1918, where we see the very young Clark (Deji Olsimbo) witnessing an argument between his parents over the conflict between material success and caring for the poor. Clark's mother says to him, "I want every possible advantage for you, Clark." Cut back to the adult Clark's conversation with his daughter, in which he retracts the advice he's previously given her: "You have a choice for love, and you can't let anybody take that away from you." When Shelby leaves, Clark has a tense discussion with Corinne and explains that despite all their problems he intends to work at reconciliation.

Shelby goes to Meade and tells him, "I don't think I want to spend my whole life fighting to prove who we are." On the morning of the wedding, however, she receives a gift of a necklace that's been passed down through three generations of her family and decides that her love for Meade can survive all obstacles. She visits the hotel where he's been staying and finds that he has checked out. Meanwhile (one needs to keep using this word to describe melodrama), Lute and his daughters are together at his cottage. Lute continues to feel sure he can win Shelby, but a taxi suddenly arrives at his front door bearing Della, who's determined to find out what made him write and ask for a divorce. "Everything you have is because of me," she shouts, and a fierce quarrel ensues, climaxing when Lute roughs Della up and throws her out the door onto the sidewalk. Grabbing her arm, he tosses her into his car, goes to the driver's seat, and backs up to head off toward the local airport, aiming to send her back to Boston. But his daughter Tina, who has been sent outdoors so she won't witness the inevitable fight, is behind the car and is run over. The death of the child is witnessed by many people, including Shelby, leaving everyone traumatized and Lute prostrate, revealed as a scoundrel, bent in grief over the body of his daughter.

Soon Shelby and Meade are reconciled, and the wedding goes ahead as planned. Gran, revived after her earlier collapse, is seen rocking Laurie, Liz's child, and singing her a lullaby; the old matriarch has apparently decided to abandon her fears that Laurie might be too black. The wedding ceremony has all the beautiful and elaborate trappings the father of the bride can provide. Meade's parents aren't there, but the minister declares that "love and loyalty alone will prevail." Shelby's reminiscent voice-over is heard, announcing "color is a false distinction, and so is class; in 1953 I married for love."

The ending of the film is sentimental; too dependent on accident and neat resolution, it avoids reference to problems that will surely continue to plague the interracial couple. But Like West's novel, which it closely resembles, it offers a strong statement of a powerful theme. West's epigraph for the novel comes from one of the most beautiful verses of the Bible, I Corinthians 13:4–7: "Love is patient; love is kind; love is not envious or boastful or arrogant or rude; it is not irritable or resentful; it does not rejoice in wrongdoing, but rejoices in the truth. It bears all things, believes all things, hopes all things, endures all things." We can and should strive for better social arrangements, but love of this kind would help achieve them.

NINE

The Annihilation of Fish *(1999)*

THE ONLY FEATURE THEATRICAL FILM Burnett directed for which he received no screenplay credit is *The Annihilation of Fish* (1999), a generic comedy, albeit a very unusual one on a subject risky for Hollywood. The film tells the story of a romance between an older couple of different races (James Earl Jones and Lynn Redgrave), both of whom suffer from schizophrenia. The title character, a Jamaican immigrant, is subject to wrestling matches with the Devil—or more precisely, with a demon that sneaks up behind him without warning. (The demon appears motivated by sex, because it first appeared to him as he looked up a woman's dress.) His eventual lover and mate is an elaborately costumed, severely alcoholic, crazy-looking woman who is having a hallucinatory affair with Giacomo Puccini. At night she listens to *Madame Butterfly* on an old record player and experiences orgasms. "One day you're going to kill me," she says to Puccini's ghost, "and I'll die a happy woman."

Critically underrated when it was shown at the Toronto Film Festival and a few other venues, *The Annihilation of Fish* never received distribution and at present is available for viewing only in university archives. Its death blow, one might say annihilation, was probably Todd McCarthy's review in *Variety* (1999), which described it as a "minnow of a movie," a "would-be charmer," and a "drear moment in the careers of all concerned." "Theatrical release other than via self-distribution is out of the question," McCarthy concluded, "with the odd TV date repping the only imaginable market." I don't think the film is as bad as McCarthy found it (though it has problems), and I hope one day it will be available in a revival or in a home-viewing format.

Based on a very short story by Anthony Winkler, a Lebanese Jamaican writer who also wrote the screenplay, *The Annihilation of Fish* was produced with a relatively low budget by entrepreneur Lawrence Dodge's American

Sterling Productions and Paul Heller, whose previous credits included *David and Lisa* (1962), *Dirty Harry* (1971), and *Withnail and I* (1987). Heller had worked with Winkler for nine years in the development of the script before it came into Burnett's hands. The original plan was to have Danny Glover and Anne Bancroft in the lead roles, but the casting of Jones and Redgrave is just as good. The picture was shot mainly at Hollywood's Occidental Studios, which date back to 1913, and at various outdoor locations in Los Angeles and San Francisco. Burnett did predictably fine things with nonactor extras and in postproduction was assisted by Nancy Richardson, an editor he respected, who had worked with him on *To Sleep with Anger* and would also edit *Selma, Lord Selma*. It's unfortunate that he had little control over the screenplay, which has only one black character and no families or children. The picture also suffers from an overly prettified production design and a surfeit of cuteness and whimsy alien to both Burnett's and Winkler's work. Winkler's story is concerned with impoverished characters and is marked by touches of dark humor; if more of these qualities had been retained in the film, *The Annihilation of Fish* would have been improved. Burnett was nevertheless attracted to the story of a couple in their seventies from different races, places, and backgrounds who, as he explained, "have to learn that they . . . need one another" (Kapsis 2011, 108). He did a fine job with the staging and helped imbue the action with moments of genuine tenderness and wit. Soon after he completed the picture, he told Terence Rafferty "I'd love to do my own films, but it takes so long. It just takes an extraordinary effort. . . . You have to pay the rent" (quoted in Kapsis 2011, 125).

In its opening scenes, *The Annihilation of Fish* establishes the two leading characters by crosscutting between them and developing a series of neat comparisons and contrasts. The first sequence is typical of Burnett in that it is set inside a church in a poor neighborhood. A funeral service is being conducted, and the preacher announces what will become one of the themes of the film, telling the congregation that "spirit" is more important among people than harmony or likeness. Fish says "amen," but during a moment of silence for the dead man he hears a slight, high-pitched sound like a bee or a fly, which causes him to collapse on the floor in a kind of fit. "Not here," he shouts. "It's not the time!" He's suffering from one of his frequent battles with the demon, and soon afterward we see him in conference with a psychiatric social worker who has lost patience. Fish is a soft-spoken gentleman wearing an old suit and a bow tie reminiscent of the 1950s. He explains that the demon has begun sneaking up behind him. The social worker replies, "There is no such thing as a demon, and if there were he wouldn't wrestle with a Jamaican immigrant, he'd wrestle with an American citizen!" He announces that Fish is being "de-institutionalized" because no treatment seems to help him: not shock, not pills, not group therapy, not unisex baseball, and not tapioca pudding.

Mourned by the other inmates, Fish steps out onto a New York street with his single small suitcase. The source of his income isn't clear, but he has enough money to travel by bus to Los Angeles, "the city of angels," and make his way to an attractive Victorian rooming house owned by an eccentric southern lady (played unconvincingly by Margot Kidder) who seems almost as out of touch with reality as he is. She identifies herself as Mrs. Muldroone and insists that the name always be spelled with a final "e." (In Winkler's story, she's simply Mrs. Muldroon, whose husband died of bowel cancer, and her boarding house is a dilapidated brick building with peeling paint.) He calls himself Obadiah Johnson but explains that his "real name" is Fish. "No final e?" she asks. She wonders if he has any hobbies. "I wrestle," he replies.

Meanwhile, Flower Cummings (aka Poinsettia) is in San Francisco attending an outdoor performance of *Madame Butterfly*. A garishly made-up woman wearing a flamboyant dress reminiscent of the 1920s or 1930s, she listens raptly until another woman tries to take the seat beside her. "The seat is taken," she says, and turns to apologize to the imaginary male companion on the empty chair. Soon she begins singing along with the performers and holding a conversation with the invisible friend, annoying everyone in earshot. After the opera, she goes to a wedding chapel and introduces her invisible companion as Puccini. The two want to get married, she says, because they're "tired of living in sin." When her plea is rejected, she goes to a new-age chapel, hoping to have a better reception. The minister says that unfortunately the groom must be "corporeal." In an apologetic tone, he explains that "things just haven't been right on planet earth since Richard Nixon was elected." Later, she walks alone near the Golden Gate Bridge, her scarf blowing in the wind, at almost the same spot where Kim Novak jumped in the water in *Vertigo*. Sitting on a park bench, she sorrowfully tells Puccini that they need to break up. Nearby, an Asian woman feeding pigeons ignores the conversation. When Poinsettia breaks into an aria, the pigeons scatter.

In the next scene, Poinsettia has gathered all her belongings and is taking a bus to Los Angeles. As with Fish, the source of her income isn't clear; in Winkler's story, she's a bawdy, cigar-smoking woman who lives on Social Security, but the film makes her more shabby-elegant and theatrical. At the Muldroone rooming house, Jamaican music ("Day-Oh") plays as Fish unpacks framed pictures of his family along with a portrait of Jesus. He carefully washes the toilet and the floors of his rooms, arranges furnishings he bought from a consignment store, and finds that a fan he purchased doesn't work. A neat, fastidious man, unlike the somewhat rough character in the Winkler story, he puts flowers on a table. Just then Poinsettia arrives and has a conversation with Mrs. Muldroone, who again explains how her name should be spelled. "My sweetheart is dead," Poinsettia laments, "I'm never going to laugh again." Mrs. Muldroone wants to know if she has any vices or "peculiar habits." "Opera," Poinsettia confesses, and breaks into an aria. Upstairs, Fish hears the singing and mutters, "I suppose no harm is done as long as you keep the door closed."

Poinsettia listens to a recording of Puccini while unpacking her flowery possessions, which include a cigar box full of makeup. After cleaning her room, she lights a cigarette in a long holder and reclines in her bathtub, singing an aria. Fish hears her and mutters "Heaven have mercy." Later, as he irons his clothes, he hears a slight whispering sound and doubles over, seized by the demon. Falling to the floor, he grasps his crotch and wallows in pain. "That move!" he cries. "Not in the book, you dirty dog!" He wrestles with the invisible opponent and tosses him out the window, shouting, "Next time fight fair!" Meanwhile Poinsettia, wearing a slip, sprawls in her bed with a bottle of Scotch. Getting up drunkenly, she looks in a mirror and decides "gotta get out of here." She puts on her grotesque makeup, dresses, and staggers out to a bar, where she encounters a handsome young gigolo. "Oh, excuse me," he says, "I thought you were somebody else." "I used to be," she tells him.

Later that evening Poinsettia somehow makes her way back to the rooming house and collapses on the floor outside her door. Fish hears loud snoring, comes out of his room in his underwear, pulls her into his room, and puts her to bed. After saying his prayers, he climbs into the bed beside her and mutters to himself, "At your age, why ain't you dead?" The next morning, while she's still sleeping, he does his daily pushups to keep in training for his bouts and is suddenly seized by the demon. Whirling around, he tosses his attacker out the window. Poinsettia awakes, sees this, and reacts in horror. "He rabbit punched me," Fish says conversationally, and asks, "Want some coffee?" She runs out and yells down at Mrs. Muldroone: "You got me living with a nut!"

By this point anyone who has seen a fair number of Hollywood romantic comedies will recognize that *The Annihilation of Fish* is following one of the oldest plot formulas in the book. Two opposites meet cute and become attracted to one another. There are many variations of the formula: she's a spoiled socialite and he's a butler, she's a wallflower and he's a playboy, she's a free spirit and he's a repressed scientist, and so forth. They connect, but something intervenes and splits them apart. Eventually their problem is solved and they live happily ever after. Old Hollywood shorthand for the plot was "boy meets girl, boy loses girl, boy gets girl." The big difference in this film is that the romantic couple is very unusual and the problem very difficult to surmount.

At first Fish and Poinsettia try to keep their distance, but her singing from the room across the hall disturbs him and brings back the demon. He tries to construct an elaborate model ark with matchsticks, but needs to put his hands over his ears to blot out the sound of her voice. One night she again comes home drunk and collapses in the hallway. He takes her to his room, putting her on his couch. When she revives, she remarks, "Hollywood's boring if you're not a fruitcake or a movie star." He says she shouldn't be so unhappy because she's a good-looking woman. These words immediately lift her spirits, making her friendly. Soon they begin visiting one another to play gin rummy. Burnett handles their card game by emphasizing the contrast between them: Poinsettia chain-smokes cigarettes in her fancy holder and repeatedly wins, while Fish looks gentlemanly but frustrated. "You got the goozoo on me," he says, and this makes her even more happily animated. One day she acts as "referee" for one of Fish's bouts with the demon, whose name, we learn, is "Hank"—one of the film's too-cute touches. That evening he asks her to go for a walk; she's been drinking again, and as they stroll along she makes a maudlin confession of her love affair with Puccini. To her surprise, he doesn't laugh and offers to make her a Jamaican dinner. "You won't laugh," she says, "and I can't cry any more. We might as well eat."

As the relationship between Fish and Poinsettia ripens, they go on excursions. Burnett stages an amusing scene at Echo Park, showing the two in a paddle boat, with Poinsettia vigorously paddling in her high heels as a mariachi band plays in the distance. But on the next day the demon attacks Fish again, and Poinsettia needs to come to his aid as referee. "Hell must be as perverted as Hollywood," she remarks at the end of the scuffle as she throws "Hank's" boots out the window. In return for the Jamaican dinner Fish has given her, she invites him over for a romantic, candlelit meal. While they eat, he plays a joke by pretending to choke on the food, and when she anxiously tries to resuscitate him he reveals his prank. They kiss. There follows a lovely sex scene, bathed in candlelight and played for both humor and sexiness. "I don't know if it works anymore," Fish says as they lie together on the bed. "I know how to make it work," she replies. In close-up, they kiss passionately. "I don't know where to put it," Fish confesses. She reassures him by climbing on top, a position she likes, and showing him. Afterward, she, too, makes a confession: all the men she's been with have beaten her.

Fish and Poinsettia take tango lessons and soak their sore feet together in her tub. She assists him in his building of his matchstick ark. One day Mrs. Muldroone discovers them coming out of Poinsettia's room together, but says nothing. Fish, however, is becoming depressed because his demon has stopped appearing. He talks with Poinsettia about his past life as a "train counter," a job he lost when the railroad disappeared, and about his marriage to a woman who died of cancer at the age of twenty-five. Poinsettia says that she has never been married: "I'm the kind men like to beat up." Turning to Fish, she impulsively declares, "I want to marry you. I love you."

Fish frowns and resists the idea: "I'm a black man. What we got in common?" Undeterred, she reminds him, "We got old!" Fish calls her sweetie and explains that because of his purpose in life, which is battling the devil (usually ready to fight because of sex), "the rassler can't sleep with the referee." She weeps and yells, "Don't sweetie me, you goddamned Jamaican rat!" Running out, she resigns as referee. Through her closed door, Fish says that "Hank" likes the prestige of having a referee, and that if one fighter sleeps with her so should the other. He needs her, he admits, and she has use for him because of her drinking. The problem, Poinsettia tells him, is that Hank can never die. Fish's response is another of the film's jokes, which, however funny, seems more like the voice of the screenwriter than the character. "Oh, yes," Fish says, "you can shoot him with a .22! You know why there's so much gun violence in America? Because all the demons work for the NRA, and the NRA know demons can be killed with a .22. They made a deal with the Devil not to shoot him."

Fish and Poinsettia go through their old routine—playing cards, strolling in the park—but because of his continuing need for his fantasy and her refusal to referee, they don't sleep together or even touch. Eventually he gives in: "You got me, woman. If you won't be referee, you be my wife." But soon after that he knocks at her door and asks her to referee a match. She comes out with a .22 pistol and starts shooting. "I got the son of a bitch," she cries, "I'm fighting back!" Fish is appalled and tells her she's done something wicked. "I have been annihilated," he says, and begins to weep. She curses him and goes to her room, where she starts drinking and playing her recording of *Madame Butterfly*. Fish sits alone, thinking. When Poinsettia later gets drunk and passes out in the hallway, he covers her with a blanket. She awakes and weeps, beginning a crying jag that goes on for a day. Fish's match-stick ark goes up in flames, and Mrs. Muldroone complains of the smell of "decomposing demon." Poinsettia seeks comfort from the landlady, who tells her she's "making a vulgar mistake if you think you need a body to have life." Just then Fish seems to have a heart attack on the stairway; actually, he has pneumonia, and Poinsettia begins feeding him and nursing him back to life. "I could kill you!" she says. "Eat!"

Winkler's short story ends without so many complications; after shooting Fish's demon, Poinsettia simply turns and shoots Puccini in the back, putting an end to both illusions. In the film, however, Poinsettia feels suicidal despair. Loving Fish is her only use in the world, she says, so she dresses as Madame Butterfly and gets out her .22 to use on herself. Fish intervenes, saving her, and the two are reunited. Puccini is renounced, a burial ceremony is arranged for "Hank" in Mrs. Muldroone's weedy front yard, and Fish and Poinsettia are married.

A running joke in the film has been a mailman who keeps slipping on the front steps of the Muldroone apartment house. Burnett wisely photographs this recurring accident from a great distance, making it look comically absurd. At the end of the film the mailman arrives and slips again in the process of delivering a picture postcard to Mrs. Muldroone. She reads it in her front yard, which is now free of weeds and pleasantly green. The card shows a photograph of Fish and Poinsettia, honeymooning in Jamaica. How they managed to pay for the trip is anybody's guess, but the postcard is in keeping with the spirit of fantasy in the story, and a nice way of concluding it with an image of the two likable stars.

TEN

Nat Turner: A Troublesome Property *(2003)*

HERE ARE SOME OF THE few things we know about Nat Turner. He was born a slave in Southampton County, Virginia, on October 2, 1800, the property of Benjamin Turner and later of Benjamin's brother Samuel. Intelligent and articulate, he learned to read at a young age, chiefly from the Bible, and was subject to visionary religious experiences. He preached to other slaves at Baptist ceremonies, influenced a local white man to become an abolitionist, and was regarded by some as a prophet. At the age of twenty-two he escaped, but he voluntarily returned to his owner because of a spiritual revelation. Then, on August 21, 1831, he led a rebellion of roughly fifty neighborhood slaves and free blacks, initially armed with nothing but farm implements, who killed about sixty white men, women, and children of the plantation-owner class, but none of the poor whites. Nat himself later confessed to killing only one person, a young woman named Margaret Whitehead.

This was by no means the only slave rebellion in the Western Hemisphere—the most successful was the 1791–1804 Haitian revolution led by Toussaint Louverture, which was fought by slaves and led to the establishment of a free state—but it was without question the most historically significant in the United States, sending shock waves throughout the South. It was soon quashed by an army of three thousand white vigilantes and Northampton militia, who went on a terror rampage and arbitrarily killed almost two hundred blacks. Black bodies were mutilated, and their heads were set atop poles for everyone to see. The names of the murdered blacks are unknown.

Over fifty blacks accused of taking part in the revolt were arrested, but Nat remained at large. He was described in a wanted poster as follows:

5 feet 6 or 8 inches high, weighs between 150 and 160 pounds, rather light complexion, but not a mulatto, broad shoulders, large flat nose, large eyes, broad flat feet, rather knockkneed, walks brisk and active, hair on the top of the head very thin, no beard, except on the upper lip and the top of the chin, a scar on one of his temples, also one on the back of his neck, a large knot on one of the bones of his right arm, near the wrist, produced by a blow.

The crude drawing accompanying the poster is the only image of Nat we have from the period when he lived. On October 30, 1831, he was found hiding in a hole by farmer Benjamin Phipps, who was hunting in the Southampton woods. Nat was armed with a sword, but Phipps had a rifle and a hunting dog. After he was arrested, manacled, chained, and placed in a cell, Nat was interviewed by Thomas Ruffin Gray, who had been doing research on the rebellion and hoped to profit by publishing a book. Gray became the author/editor of *The Confessions of Nat Turner*, which, whether or not it is a truthful account, has become the most often cited historical document pertaining to Nat's life.

Forty-five slaves and five free blacks were put on trial; nineteen were hanged, twelve were sold to out-of-state owners (they were too valuable as property to be killed), and the others were acquitted. Nat was hanged in Jerusalem, Virginia, a town that has since had its name changed to Courtland, probably because the locals wanted to obscure identification with Nat and his religious propensities. As revenge, and in order to create terror among blacks, his body was flayed, decapitated, and quartered. His heart was removed, and all the body parts were buried in unmarked land without a funeral.

There have been several films about Nat Turner, but Charles Burnett's absorbing television version occupies a special place, not only because of its quality but also because, like many important films, it doesn't fit neatly into a generic category. A fusion of dramatic reenactment (played by five different actors in the role of Nat), informative narration (spoken by Alfre Woodard), talking-head interviews, archival footage, and scenes of the making of the film, it's the most thoughtful and in my view the best picture on the subject. Interestingly, however, Burnett's original plan was somewhat different. When he and his cowriters Frank Christopher and Kenneth S. Greenburg first traveled to Northampton to start production, their aim was to make what Burnett called "a Truth and Reconciliation" documentary. He told interviewers: "We had hoped to get [black and white] descendants of families in a room together and have a discussion about where the community is now." But a newspaper reporter interviewed several of the people who would be talking to Burnett, promised them confidentiality, and then published what they said. "That caused a lot of hostility between neighbors," Burnett has explained. "At that point they didn't trust any outsider and especially one with a camera and recorder. So we had to make a different film" (quoted in Miguez and Paz 2016, 71).

The "different" film became an impressive, self-reflexive investigation into conflicting views of Nat and their social meanings. Burnett told me that "the idea of how to approach the subject was developed in a retreat. We worked on the new idea there. Frank [Christopher] should get credit for breaking the fourth wall. Ken [Greenburg] kept us focused on historical facts." There was plenty of material to consider. For most whites, especially in the nineteenth century, Nat's "confession" proved that he was an insanely evil religious fanatic (unlike all those nice darkies who worked under the supposedly benign arrangements of southern slavery), but for most blacks, he was a great and inspiring hero. Since his death he has been depicted in a variety of ways, not only by his quasi-amanuensis Thomas Ruffin Gray, but also by artists of fiction, theater, painting, and film and by historians, who have written many books and articles in an attempt to interpret his actions. The narrator of *Nat Turner: A Troublesome Property* sums up the situation in a kind of thesis statement that also serves as an epitaph for Nat: "His words became the property of others, as his body was during his life."

The film is interspersed with short interviews with blacks and whites from different backgrounds: historians Herbert Aptheker, Eric Foner, Eugene Genovese, Vincent Hardy, Thomas Parramore, and Peter Wood; cultural critic Henry Louis Gates Jr.; African American studies professor Ekewewume Michael Thelwell; English professor Mary Kemp Davis; novelist William Styron; Southampton County Historical Society director Kitty Futrell; Rick Francis (a descendant of the white victims); Bruce Turner (a descendent of Nat); law professor Martha Minon; actor/director/activist Ossie Davis; writer Louise Merriweather; Southampton painter James McGee; Race Relations Institute director Ray Winbush; and Pan-African Film Festival director Ayuko Babu (who acted in two of Burnett's short films). Burnett interweaves the remarks of these figures with dramatized, chronologically ordered scenes of the rebellion and its aftermath, as well as scenes based on several writers who tried to depict Nat in works of documentary and fiction. We see the beginning of the rebellion as a group of Nat's men invade a plantation house and use a hatchet to kill a husband and wife in their bed; white vigilantes rounding up and getting ready to butcher blacks; Thomas Ruffin

Gray's interview with Nat in his jail cell; Nat's execution (he's viewed in silhouette and appears to be the rather small man described in the wanted poster); a scene from abolitionist Harriet Beecher Stowe's 1856 novel *Dred: A Tale of the Great Dismal Swamp*; a scene from black novelist/orator William Wells Brown's Civil War–era, fictional rendition of Nat's speech to his men before battle; a Works Progress Administration (WPA) researcher interviewing an elderly ex-slave in the 1930s; a scene from Randolph Edmonds's 1935 play *The Nat Turner Story*; and scenes from William Styron's controversial 1966 novel *The Confessions of Nat Turner*.

In the dramatic scenes involving Nat, the use of different actors for the role serves to emphasize the fact that he has been imagined in different ways. When the film reaches the point of Nat's image in the 1960s and 1970s, we're shown newsreel and television footage of violence against civil rights protesters; an excerpt from James Baldwin's Oxford University debate with William Buckley; and clips from speeches by Stokley Carmichael, Huey Newton, and Malcom X, all of whom identified with Nat. Finally, Burnett and his collaborators and crew are shown working on the film we have been watching. His producer and co-screenwriter Kenneth S. Greenberg tells us that *Nat Turner: A Troublesome Property* is "a film about interpretation." He then asks rhetorically, "Isn't that film another interpretation?"

Indeed it is. The risk, as law professor Martha Minon remarks at one point in her interview, is that discussion of Nat might deteriorate into a mere catalog of varying opinions and hence a meaningless relativism. I believe, however, that the film's straightforward laying out of evidence and opinion with little overt judgment by the narrator serves not only to educate the audience but also to respect them. *Nat Turner: A Troublesome Property* isn't like Kurosawa's *Rashomon* (1950); it's about different opinions, not about relativism, and some opinions are more persuasive than others. When Burnett came to Southampton, he was disturbed by the fact that whites there were still fighting the Civil War; they were quick to condemn Nat for murdering whites in their beds, but unable to see or admit that black slaves were victims of even worse treatment. His film makes quite clear that nonacademic whites have responded to Nat's history differently than blacks, and that Nat's image has undergone changes in different historical circumstances. Some views of him have never completely changed, but that has less to do with relativism than with American racism.

In 2003 Scott Foundas reported to *Variety* that an earlier "work in progress" version of Burnett's film had been shown at a documentary festival in

2002; still in rough form, it was twenty-six minutes longer and, in Foundas's opinion, more overtly partisan. Courtesy of Johnathan Rosenbaum, I've seen a version that is twenty-nine minutes longer. I wouldn't describe it as more partisan, but I prefer it and wish it were widely available. It has a different narrator, more historical background, more dramatic episodes (including a scene adapted from William Styron in which we see Nat as a boy, thus making a total of seven actors who play the character), more interview material, more scenes of bloody white reprisals against rebellious blacks, and more scenes of Burnett and his collaborators at work on the film. It shows that before the Turner rebellion, legislators in Virginia had debated the possible abolition of slavery; it also has a brief scene dramatizing a speech by a prosperous, white, late nineteenth-century Baptist minister, who assures a group of genteel ladies that the rebellion was caused not by a desire for freedom but by a group of stupid heathen under the influence of liquor. In what follows, I concentrate on the film as it appeared on television, but I also describe several additional details from the longer version.

Time constraints imposed by PBS's *Independent Lens* program, which initially aired the film, may have been responsible for the final edit. The first dramatic scenes are reenactments of Thomas Ruffin Gray's interviews with the prisoner in his jail cell and are performed by two veterans of Burnett's *Nightjohn*: Carl Lumbly as Nat and Tom Nowicki as Gray. The speeches come straight from Gray's *Confessions of Nat Turner*. When the two men talk with one another, Burnett covers the action in shot/reverse shots, but when Gray/Nowicki interposes his opinions as editor of the confessions—for example, when he comments on Nat's education, intelligence, and apparently limitless potential—he turns and directly addresses the camera in the past tense. At one point he remarks on the "calm, deliberate" quality of Nat's confession and adds that he was disturbed by the expression on Nat's "fiend-like" face: "I looked on him and my blood curdled in my veins!" But nothing in these scenes looks fiendish or histrionically melodramatic. Nowicki avoids any overt suggestion that Gray was a smarmy opportunist (which he probably was), and Lumbly, a muscular, handsome man, plays Nat articulately, as if the character were in quiet awe of the religious vision that motivated his rebellion. Huddled on the floor in rags and chains, he recalls hearing a voice that told him, "Time is fast approaching when the first should be last and the last first." "While laboring in the field," he says to Gray, "I discovered drops of blood on the corn as if dew from the heavens, and communicated it to many, both white and black in the neighborhood." It was a sign from God, Nat says, and God determined his fate by telling him that "Christ had laid down the yoke he had borne for men and that I should take it on." When Gray asks Nat if he expected retribution, Nat responds with a rhetorical question: "Was not Christ crucified?"

Burnett cuts from these dramatized interview scenes to real-life interviews, in which talking heads express their opinions. We never hear the voice of an interviewer, but two questions naturally arise from what we've just seen: How accurate and reliable is Gray's report, and to what degree can historians ever achieve a full, true picture of Nat? Henry Louis Gates Jr. offers what I consider the best response. Without denying that Nat existed or that his rebellion was important, Gates remarks, "There is no Nat Turner back there whole, to be retrieved." Others more or less concur, especially in regard to the accuracy of the *Confessions*. English Professor Mary Kemp Davis says, "I do not believe for a moment that Nat Turner talked that way." For religious historian Vincent Hardy, "It is very clear by now that we cannot take Nat Turner's confession at face value. . . . But it is also clear that we cannot cast it aside. . . . Nat Turner must have eaten up the Christian and Hebrew testaments and begun to see himself as the embodiment of these." Still others have somewhat more faith in the record and/or the possibility of arriving at truth. Marxist historian Herbert Aptheker smiles in wonder and approval of Nat's comparison of his fate with Christ's crucifixion: "That's an astonishing statement!" (There is in fact something Christlike in the way Burnett and Carl Lumbly portray the imprisoned Nat's description of his mission and anticipation of his execution.) William Styron declares that "any intelligent reader [of the *Confessions*] would have to say this guy is a crazy lunatic." Historian Peter Wood doesn't make a judgment but has a rather optimistic view of historical scholarship, which has usually been written by the winners and always involves a decision about what events are historically significant. Nat Turner, he argues, has been shrouded in conflicting myths of saintliness and insanity, but "the historian has to find that real historical person."

Where judgments about Nat's rebellion are concerned, opinions are more at odds. Kitty Futrell of the Southampton County Historical Society, a rather sour southern white lady who looks as if she dislikes being interviewed, thinks the Turner rebellion shouldn't be dignified with the term "war." "That's declared!" she says, discounting not only the conditions of slavery but also the Japanese attack on Pearl Harbor and many other examples of surprise attacks: "You give people the choice that I'm going to fight you!" Almost reluctantly she adds, "Slavery was wrong, but murder is wrong, too."

Regarding the Futrell interview, it's worth noting that while making the film Burnett visited the small Courtland museum devoted to Nat, which had been established because at one point filmmakers from Hollywood were going to visit Southampton County and make a picture based on Styron's *Confessions of Nat Turner*: "I suspect that I'm the only black person up until then who was invited to hold Nat's sword and hold the rope that hung him," Burnett has said. "The white ladies that run the museum were nervous about me holding Nat's sword. I suspected they thought Nat's spirit was going to take over my body and use the sword on them. The [museum has] made a documentary about Nat . . . sold and shown in the local schools. The video characterizes Nat as a crazy murderer [who] killed innocent people, babies included" (Miguez and Paz 2016, 70).

Commenting on the murder of babies, another eminent Marxist historian, Eugene Genovese, argues, "Revolutions have to kill everybody. A revolution is either thorough or it's doomed." But Rick Francis, a descendant of the white victims, says "The murder of women and children sticks in my craw. . . . [Turner] would certainly be remembered better by history if he had limited the killing to . . . white adults." (Perhaps inadvertently, Francis's remark suggests that only men are adults.) Bruce Turner, a descendant of Nat, says, "The only way to do the rebellion was to make the price of resistance [from whites] too high." Law professor Martha Minon, one of the wisest interviewees, offers a plausible psychological explanation for the responses of southern whites: "I think that many white people identify with the innocents, the children. It's a position that's much more comfortable. People know they can't defend slavery morally, so they have to say there was something morally wrong in the uprising."

Having established a variety of present-day opinions, the film turns to a historical overview of Nat's changing image, showing how, as the narrator says, he has been "recreated by others to fit their needs." From the God-obsessed, crazy Nat portrayed by Gray in some parts of the *Confessions*, we move to Harriet Beecher Stowe's 1856 *Dred*, whose title character is based on Nat. Drawing on the sentimental tradition of nineteenth-century melo-drama from which she had achieved great success with *Uncle Tom's Cabin* (1852), Stowe depicts Dred as an innately gentle, kindly figure rather than a wild-eyed revolutionary or religious zealot; uneducated, he nevertheless has a poetic sensibility that "softens the heart toward children and the inferior animals," and a "flame" burning in his heart. In Burnett's dramatized scene from the novel, Dred is played by Patrick Waller, a sweet-faced, ursine actor who is seen wearing a red African turban, sitting in a forest, and cuddling a tiger cub; hearing a menacing sound, he grasps his sword and runs off along a forest stream.

Burnett cuts to William Styron, who remarks that Nat is a "boon" to writers because so little is known about him that he can be used as a metaphor or symbol for every sort of imaginative literature about slavery and black rebellion. This, however, could be said of any emblematic but politically controversial figure in history, no matter how well or little known. Where Nat is concerned, portrayals of him are always inescapably determined by a social and racial context. In the years leading up to the Civil War, Frederick Douglass often praised Nat as a powerful hero of black emancipation; as historian Eric Foner points out during his interview for the film, Douglass saw Nat as a worthy descendant of the original American revolutionaries, a man who was more true to the ideals of the nation than slaveholders who celebrated the Fourth of July. During the Civil War William Wells Brown (often described as the first African American novelist) delivered a speech in which he imagined what Nat must have said to his small army at Cabin Pond on the night of the rebellion. Burnett dramatizes the scene, casting the slender, intense Michael LeMelle in the role of Nat. "Friends and brothers," Nat almost whispers to his comrades in the silent woodland, "we are about to commence a great work tonight. Our race is to be delivered from slavery. And God has appointed us as the men to do his bidding."

In his interview, Ossie Davis recalls how black boys of his generation gloried in Nat and imagined scenarios in which he would triumph. This was especially true during the Great Depression, a period of intense political consciousness and a growing protest literature. Burnett shows a film clip from Orson Welles's celebrated 1936 "Voodoo" *Macbeth*, a WPA production with an all-black cast, which was set in the Haitian revolution and featured a rebel leader brandishing a Nat-like sword. He also dramatizes a WPA interview from the early 1930s in which Alan Crawford, an aged former slave, gives a sort of folkloric account of Nat regretfully killing a white baby. Then he dramatizes a closing scene from the most important representation of Nat during those years, Randolph Edmonds's *The Nat Turner Story*, a 1935 play intended to be performed mainly in schools. We see a small theater in which the play is being performed, with Tommy Hicks (who played Reverend Banks in *The Glass Shield* and would work again with Burnett) in the role of Nat. In a closing soliloquy, Nat becomes a tragic figure. Other slaves have called him a "beast," fearing white reaction. "But if I'm a beast," he asks, "who made me one?" Looking about at the death and blood on the stage, he cries, "My hands is bloody, too! Was I wrong, Lord?"

During the Civil Rights era and its violent aftermath, when Burnett was growing up, there was a resurgence of interest in Nat. In this period he was seen by blacks not as a tragic hero but as an emblem of angry, armed resistance to the brutality of white racism. After the assassination of Martin Luther King Jr., black leaders Stokely Carmichael, Huey Newton, and Malcom X all identified with Nat, as did the Afro-Caribbean intellectual Frantz Fanon. At the 1968 Mexico City Olympics, winning black athletes raised their fists in the Black Power salute while the US national anthem was played. But these were also the years of white author William Styron's *The Confessions of Nat Turner* (1966–1967), a controversial publication that remains to this day the single most ambitious attempt to portray Nat in fiction. Styron was a much-awarded southern white writer who was born less than a hundred miles from the site of Nat's rebellion. His best-selling novel, narrated in the first person by Nat and bearing the same title as Thomas Ruffin Gray's 1831 *Confessions*, won the Pulitzer Prize, landed him on the cover of *Newsweek*, and brought the Southampton slave insurrection to the attention of a white suburban culture that had barely if ever heard of it. Of course blacks also read the book. In Burnett's film, Henry Louis Gates Jr. says that as a young man he came home from school one day, saw that the novel had been delivered by the Book of the Month, and stayed up all night reading it. Just when it was on the verge of becoming a Hollywood movie starring James Earl Jones, however, a group of black scholars and writers reacted passionately against it and published a book of their own.

The longer version of Burnett's film goes into detail about 20th Century Fox's plans to adapt Styron's novel, and the reaction that ensued. The picture was to be produced by David Wolper (who is interviewed), directed by Norman Jewison, and written by black author Lou Peterson. Styron received $600,000 for the rights. When this was announced in the trade press, author Louise Meriweather organized a protest and purchased a full-page ad in the *Hollywood Reporter* containing many signatures of black professionals opposed to the picture. Wolper initially agreed to the demands of this group, who wanted the picture to be called simply *Nat Turner* and to be limited to historical records. But as soon as plans were announced to film in Virginia, white locals also protested, resenting the idea of Hollywood "outsiders" meddling with local history. All the old conflicting views of Nat had reemerged in highly public form. William Styron was content to keep his money and wash his hands of Hollywood's convoluted attempts to satisfy everyone. It soon became clear that the film was too controversial, and production was abandoned.

William Styron's The Confessions of Nat Turner: Ten Black Writers Respond (1968), edited by John Henrik Clarke, was a vitriolic attack on the novel, and for understandable reasons. Leaving aside the aesthetic merits of Styron's book and granting that he was a talented writer, any fiction about historical figures has a responsibility to be true to the historical evidence. In Nat's case, Styron overlooked parts of the history and filled the many historical lacunae with imagined motives and implied judgments that the ten black writers found racist. According to Styron (or perhaps one should say according to Styron's Nat, who, like any first-person narrator, might be, at least theoretically, somewhat unreliable), Nat was a reluctant, bumbling rebel who had been driven mad by the terrible impact of slavery on his native intelligence, religious conviction, and sexuality. His slaveholding owners were in many ways kindly, but the poor whites around him in Southampton were ignorant, deviant, and cruel. Essentially celibate, Nat had experienced only one sexual act, a homoerotic encounter with a young black male. When he became a house slave for the "saintly" Turner, his emotions churned with a mixture of gratitude, admiration, and cold hostility. And when he was befriended by Margaret Whitewood, the idealistic daughter of a slave owner, he boiled with a barely repressed conflict between love and hatred.

There is no historical evidence to support Styron's psychological speculations. John Henrik Clarke's introduction to *Ten Black Writers Respond* points out that according to some sources Nat had a wife on another plantation and was forbidden to visit her, a common situation for slaves, much like the fictional Outlaw and Egypt in *Nightjohn*, which could have provided one of several clear motives for his revolt. The proposed 1968 Hollywood movie based on Styron would in fact have eliminated most of the sex business with Margaret and given Nat a wife. Styron had seized upon a short passage in Gray's *Confessions* in which Nat straightforwardly describes killing Margaret and spun it into a lurid sexual drama. (He also dreamed up Nat's homosexual episode and a scene in which a female black slave enjoys being raped by an Irishman.) No matter how well-meaning Styron may have thought he was, he had indulged in the sexual fantasy of black lust for lovely, fair-haired, white womanhood that inspired Griffith's *Birth of a Nation*, the Klu Klux Klan, and a wave of lynching in the South. A few notable black intellectuals—among them Ralph Ellison and James Baldwin—came to his defense, but most others were furious and adamantly opposed to what he had written.

In the longer version of his film, Burnett dramatizes Styron's imagined sexual encounter between Nat and the young black boy. It's a tender scene in which Nat and the boy embrace and softly touch one another; when interviewed about it, Styron says that he didn't intend to suggest homosexuality, he wanted only to describe a "homoerotic" incident of a kind that many young men have experienced. In the shorter, TV version of the film, Burnett retains a couple of other scenes from Styron, using only Styron's language and doing cinematic justice to his novel. Nat is played by the tall, handsome, imposing Virginia stage actor James Opher and Margaret by the blond, blue-eyed, teenage Megan Gallacher. As they walk together down a wooded path, Margaret chatters excitedly, her head reaching only to the middle of Nat's shoulder. Nat remains silent. Burnett's camera looks down at her and up at Nat. She's a delightful young woman, enjoying what she seems to regard as an innocent friendship and a meeting of minds with a slave she admires, unselfconsciously talking with him about her love of books and her conviction that slavery is wrong. Over her talk, we hear Nat's inner, retrospective voice calmly confessing the riot of desire and hostility he felt when her arm inadvertently brushed against his and his barely contained temptation to take her sexually then and there. The next scene, in part from Styron and in part from Gray, shows the moment during the insurrection when Nat kills Margaret: he chases her across a field, catches her near a fence, and stabs her several times with his phallic sword. As she lies dying, she begs him to finish her. He asks her to close her eyes, seizes a fence post, and crushes her head.

It must be said in partial defense of Styron that this is not exactly the pure animal lust for white women that Griffith and other whites had depicted. Styron's Nat is a Freudian creation, an intelligent, sensitive man whose condition as a slave, obsession with religion, and repressed sexuality inflame him with a psychological need to exact vengeance upon the owners who have put temptation in his way. In his interview with Burnett, Styron says he wanted to "humanize" Nat and points out that his friend James Baldwin, who was living in Styron's house when he began the novel, encouraged him to use his imagination and plunge without reservation into the mind of a black character. (Baldwin had already made a similar but more successful experiment of his own in *Giovanni's Room* [1956], a novel told from the point of view of a privileged white American who becomes an expatriate in Paris and has a doomed homosexual love affair with a working-class Italian.) That, however, is an inadequate defense, as Ossie Davis observes in his interview when he asks exactly for whom Styron was trying to "humanize" the character. Davis had a black daughter and wanted her to know that she was beautiful; Styron was promulgating, in apparently more sophisticated form, the old idea that blacks adored and desired white womanhood.

Henry Louis Gates Jr. remarks that if not for its sexual themes Styron's novel would probably have passed muster with blacks. African American novelist Louise Meriweather, in her interview, says that that she was so angry with Styron that she flushed the pages of *The Confession of Nat Turner* down the toilet. Burnett himself was typically kind when Styron visited the set and watched the filming of the scenes from his novel. But Burnett confessed to interviewers that he had no admiration for the novelist: "[H]e was out of touch with the black community. . . . Styron said that he hoped his book would bring the races together, as we hoped we would in our film, strangely enough" (Miguez and Paz 2016, 71). Interviewed on the Nat Turner set by *Village Voice* reporter Gerald Peary in 2001, Styron remained unapologetic about his book: "I find almost all the complaints invalid, irrational, and hysterical, based on bigotry and prejudice. I don't want to seem self-assured, but I wouldn't change much" (Kapsis 2011, 127).

In the final moments of *Nat Turner: A Troublesome Property*, Burnett films James McGee, a black painter in Southampton, as he completes work on a large, heroic canvas representing Nat and his insurrectionary army. McGee says that he is trying to "illustrate what is said to me through my ancestors." In a very indirect way Burnett could be said to do the same thing, but he also places himself overtly and self-reflexively within the long history of art about Nat. The scene with McGee is followed by a montage in which we see Burnett at work on the film; directing the scene in which the rebellious slaves murder the Turner family; and conferring with his actors, cowriters, and crew. Interviewed while at work (by a crew member?), he emphasizes that "it is not that we are trying to reclaim Nat. We are just trying to present other artists' interpretations of Nat Turner . . . very faithfully, without interpreting their work." But as Jaqueline Najuma Stewart has pointed out, "the shots of Burnett in production cannot help but implicate him in the debates about what has motivated different artists in their approaches to Turner, particularly, as Burnett notes, how artists have 'interpreted [Turner's uprising] a certain way on racial lines'" (2015, 275).

At one point the film's narrator, Alfre Woodard, asks, "Can any work of art bring Americans closer to an understanding of Nat?" If by "understanding" one means a relatively unmediated knowledge of Nat's consciousness and personality, the answer to the question is no; we have too little historically reliable information about Nat. But if the question has to do with an understanding Nat's rebellion, the answer is yes. The problem has less to do with historical information than with who has the power of representation, what interests the representation serves, and whether or not the audience is willing to be persuaded. The racial divide in America continues to vex understanding of the 1831 rebellion in Southampton. Commenting on the ten black writers who attacked William Styron's interpretation, Henry Louis Gates Jr. gives black artists good advice: "If you don't like it, write your own." In 2016 a black filmmaker was at last able to mount a full-scale fictional representation of Nat that stands in vivid contrast to Styron's. Nate Parker's wonderfully titled *Birth of a Nation* portrays Nat as an intelligent and brave man of faith who became a martyr.

Burnett's film is no less important than Parker's and is arguably more important—this despite the fact that it shows different opinions of the Turner rebellion and has a relatively understated mode of representation. Burnett had no problem at all understanding Nat's actions, and he expected his film would help us understand. On YouTube, we can see him stating his purpose in response to an audience question after a screening of *Nat Turner: A Troublesome Property*: "As an African-American born in Mississippi, I can understand Nat Turner. I can understand anyone in those conditions who would want to be free. . . . It's very simple to me. If you've got your foot on someone's throat, I can't understand if you don't understand that someone's going to react to it."

ELEVEN

Warming by the Devil's Fire *(2003)*

BURNETT'S *WARMING BY THE DEVIL'S FIRE* was the fourth in a series of seven PBS films about blues music that were executive-produced by Martin Scorsese and directed by Burnett, Scorsese, Wim Wenders, Richard Pearce, Marc Levin, Mike Figgis, and Clint Eastwood. Burnett and Wenders took unorthodox approaches to the project by incorporating fictional elements into their films, but Burnett went further than Wenders, creating a fully developed fictional narrative interwoven with impressively selected archival footage. An early, extraordinary example of such footage is an archival clip of the black "Washboard Street Band," composed of musicians playing washboard, a toy trumpet, and tin cans, and a small boy dancer in a derby who performs a sort of proto-break dance. There are also documentary images of hard labor and lynching.

Of all the directors involved, Burnett had the most intimate experience of the blues, and he wanted to make a film with a blues-like form, less about the technical aspects of the music than about the culture and feelings out of which it emerged. In my opinion *Warming by the Devil's Fire* is miles better than any of the other films in the series, in part because, as Bruce Jackson has said in a fine essay, the narrative structure is loose and episodic, "at heart it is lyrical, like the blues" (2003). It's also Burnett's most autobiographical picture, mixing humor and history with the sad, sexual, sometimes raucous emotions of an old but still influential American art.

Burnett has often told the story of growing up in Watts to the sounds of his grandmother's gospel records and his mother's blues records. When he was a boy he sang spirituals in church, and the first tune he played on his trumpet was W. C. Handy's "St. Louis Blues." It wasn't until he reached adulthood that he realized how important both kinds of music had been, and

they clearly influenced many of his films. At a deep level, he understood that the two musical forms were symptomatic of a conflict between the strictures of fundamentalist religion represented by his grandmother and the sadness, sex, and rebellion represented by his mother. This conflict is apparent in the very title of *Warming by the Devil's Fire*, which suggests a kind of guilty pleasure. At one point in the film we're given the source of the title: we see old documentary footage of a southern black church service and hear the voice of a preacher admonishing his congregation to avoid their sinful pleasures, all of which, he says, are described in the fourteenth chapter of Luke as "warming by the devil's fire." (I asked Burnett where he found the recording of this sermon, and he couldn't recall; my guess is that it's a 1928 record by the Reverend Johnnie "Son of Thunder" Blakey.) As Burnett explained to interviewers, his film is an exploration of a partly forbidden art that had a complex impact on his upbringing: "I wanted to take more of a personal approach. I wanted to express my experience with the moral issues you might face growing up in a family that was divided on what is sin" (Miguez and Paz 2016, 80).

Burnett's grandmother and mother were the chief representatives of that division, but he also had two uncles who were opposites: a preacher in Mississippi who "believed in every word in the Bible" and an adventurous merchant seaman who "got along great" with his mother. The oppositions or dialectic within the family ultimately enabled him to see that spirituals and blues have a paradoxical relationship. "[I]f you really listen to the lyrics of some songs," he has said, "you can see why [blues music] is not appropriate for children. There are images of low life, hard drinking. You had the church trying to get you up from the gutter and here you are singing [the gutter's] praise." At the same time, there were blues songs "that make a profound observation about life. They are lessons in life . . . case studies of people who loved and failed, of people who were wronged and who died in fights. . . . Blues has a survival component that gives you a better perspective of life at an early age than any first year of school, I believe. It teaches lessons. So do folk tales. . . . [And] a lot of blues singers came from the church and a lot of blues singers towards the end of their lives went back to the church" (Miguez and Paz 2016, 80–81).

Burnett's interest in the blues was inseparably linked to his fascination with the South, where both his family's religion and the blues originated. He was an infant when he and his parents left Vicksburg, Mississippi, for California, but during the 1950s, when he was ten or eleven years old, his grandmother put him and his brother on a train from LA to Vicksburg so they could visit their southern relatives and make contact with old-time religion. In an interview presented as an "extra" on the DVD of *Warming by the Devil's Fire*, he recalls that the train made a stop in New Orleans, where he and his brother had a traumatic encounter with southern-style segregation. At the station was a playroom for white kids, and while waiting for a change of trains the two boys innocently wandered inside to look at the various toys. Suddenly everyone in the room exited and the place was surrounded by police. The boys weren't arrested, but they were shaken and extremely cautious when they finally arrived in Vicksburg.

Burnett's memories of that visit had largely to do with the climate and the unfamiliar aspects of southern poverty: stifling heat, humidity-laden air, and country outhouses that attracted rats and dirt-daubers (wasplike insects that build ping-pong-ball or even baseball-sized nests of mud). In his DVD commentary for *Warming by the Devil's Fire*, Burnett remarks, "When you're a city boy it's hard to go back to those things." He understood why many of the people he knew, including his mother, never wanted to return to the South, but the history and music of the South continued to exert a mysterious, romantic attraction for him. In the 1980s he returned to the area around Vicksburg to research a documentary that he never made, and during that visit he began to learn more about blues musicians.

Warming by the Devil's Fire is inspired by Burnett's visits to Vicksburg, but it also draws on his considerable knowledge of blues history. Set in the mid-1950s, it tells the story of an eleven-year-old boy named Junior (Nathaniel Lee Jr.) whose family sends him by train to New Orleans, where, because his relatives don't want him to ride a Jim Crow train to Mississippi, he's met by his Uncle Buddy (Tommy Redmond Hicks) and driven to Vicksburg in Buddy's shiny Chevrolet. Buddy is a blues aficionado, but also a dapper rapscallion and ladies' man who is disapproved of by the rest of the family; they openly wonder why he hasn't been sent to prison, killed in a fight, or lynched. In the course of the film he takes charge of Junior's visit, keeping him from the rest of the family and acquainting him with southern history and the lessons of life that blues music has to offer. All this is narrated off screen from the retrospective point of view of Junior as an adult (voiced by Carl Lumbly). Both of the principal actors in the story are charming and impressive, almost like a comedy duo: Nathaniel Lee Jr. maintains a stone-faced expression, occasionally frowning in bewilderment but quietly absorbing the strange new world in which he finds himself, and Tommy Redmond Hicks talks nonstop, behaving like an exuberant force of nature who is passionate about the history of blues and fond of his nephew.

The fictional parts of *Warming by the Devil's Fire* were photographed in color by John Dempster, who became Burnett's most frequent DP, on locations in New Orleans, Vicksburg, and Gulfport, Mississippi. Burnett was disappointed by the fact that he was unable to shoot in high summer, but the film's autumnal landscapes have a quiet beauty and are free of the cheap, gaudy, corporate chain stores that infest poor towns in today's America. Most of the documentary footage of blues musicians is in black and white, and Burnett occasionally segues from that footage into fiction by printing the opening moments of the color fiction sequences in black and white. Near the beginning of the film, after a grim montage of old newsreels and photos of southern black labor and lynching of blacks, a color fade takes us from archival footage of blacks exiting a New Orleans train to a shot of Junior alone with his suitcase in front of the station. He's neatly dressed in a 1950s-style coat and tie, looking like a polite boy on his way to church. Buddy soon arrives, wearing a sporty cap and two-toned shoes. He gives Junior a warm welcome, ushers him into a sparkling, almost new Chevy, and takes him on a quick guided tour of New Orleans before they depart for Vicksburg.

First they stop on Basin Street, which Buddy explains was once the location of the Storyville red-light district, later immortalized in Louis Armstrong's 1929 recording of "Basin Street Blues." "In those days you didn't need much money to have fun," Buddy says. (Burnett cuts to old photographs

and snippets of Armstrong's music.) Then they stop at Congo Square, located inside what is now Louis Armstrong Park. As we can tell from Buddy's enraptured speech, this is holy ground for anyone who regards blues and jazz as America's truly indigenous art forms. Dating far back into colonial times, Congo Square was originally a place where enslaved blacks were allowed to congregate on their Sundays off—not for church, but for market, music, and dance from Africa and the Caribbean. It was closed before the Civil War but reopened afterward, when it became a gathering place for Creoles and a source of the brass-band rhythms still associated with New Orleans. (Burnett cuts to old footage of the Eureka Brass Band in a funeral parade through the nearby Treme district, playing "Just a Closer Walk with Thee.") Its original name wasn't officially restored until 2011, long after Buddy supposedly makes his speech and even after Burnett made the film, but lovers of blues have always known its importance.

The film proceeds by this method, allowing Buddy to teach Junior blues history and initiate him into an adult world and giving Burnett the opportunity to show footage of musicians and the life that shaped them. One of the virtues of *Warming by the Devil's Fire* is that it says comparatively little about formal or technical aspects of the blues (which at least on the surface are relatively simple) and doesn't try to define the term; instead it does something better, showing how musicians described the blues and giving a clear sense of the trials, tribulations, and profane pleasures that were its emotional sources.

The film isn't simply an archive of great blues performances (though it is that) but also a meditation on black experience. It concentrates mainly on the harsh Delta blues that extended from Tennessee down to Mississippi and Louisiana, and without explicitly saying so it gives us subgenres of this music, all of them dealing with forms of trouble or desire. One kind has to do with the pains of sexual love. After playing "Death Letter Blues," a song about a man who gets a letter announcing "The gal you love is dead," Sun House (1902–1988) tells an interviewer, "Blues is not a plaything like people today think. . . . Ain't but one kind of blues, and that's between male and female that's in love. . . . Sometimes that kind of blues will make you even kill one another. It goes here [slaps his chest over his heart]." But there's another kind about the cruelty of the southern treatment of blacks. W. C. Handy (1873–1958) says, "When they speak of the blues . . . we must talk of Joe Turner." Handy's song about Turner ("They tell me Joe Turner's come and gone, got my man and gone") concerns a real-life character who lured Memphis black men into crap games and hijacked them for Deep South chain gangs, where they provided free labor.

Some blues are quasi-work songs, such as Mississippi John Hurt's "Spike Driver Blues," which Burnett accompanies with powerful footage of black labor: men using steel bars as levers to rhythmically nudge an entire railroad track from one position to another; a row of five men in prison stripes standing close together and digging a trench by swinging pickaxes in unison, the man in the middle flipping his axe in the air on the upswing and catching the handle for the downswing. Other blues are about weariness and soulful longing to be elsewhere. After playing "Nervous Blues," bassist Willie Dixon (born in Vicksburg in 1915; died in 1992) talks to his jazz quartet about the meaning of the blues: "Everybody have the blues . . . but everybody's blues aren't exactly the same. The blues is the truth. If it's not the truth it's not the blues. I remember down South, be on the plantation . . . and you would hear a guy get up early in the morning and unconsciously he's [singing blues] about his condition and [wishing] he was some other place . . . down the road." Still other blues, such as "Lonesome Road" by Lightnin' Hopkins (1912–1982), are about a deep loneliness and the wish to make contact with loved ones. We're given an example of these feelings when Buddy drives Junior down the Natchez Trace (a location Burnett wasn't able to photograph) and they pass an old man trudging down the empty road, who says no to the offer of a ride. Buddy explains that the old man is lost in thought, making one of his long, periodic journeys from northern Mississippi to Parchment Prison to see his son, who won't talk to him.

Parchment Prison was a source of blues music, as was Dockery Plantation, where blacks labored hard to pick cotton. Burnett shows documentary footage of the harvest at Dockery, and viewers of this footage can understand an observation Buddy makes when he takes Junior to Gulfport to view the Gulf of Mexico. Looking out at the vast, gray water and cloudy sky, Buddy seems relieved at the sight, just as Burnett's seafaring uncle probably was: "You can't pick damn cotton on the ocean," he says. The film makes very clear how much the blues can be related to backbreaking work on the land or to long hours of menial domestic labor. Standing on ground near the Mississippi River, Buddy tells Junior about the 1927 Mississippi flood, the most destructive in US history; he doesn't give statistics, but it left twenty-seven thousand square miles under water, in some places up to thirty feet, and displaced almost a quarter million African Americans from the lower Delta. (Burnett's grandmother, who experienced that flood, often talked about it.) We see documentary evidence of the devastation it wrought, and Buddy explains that black workers did a great deal of the labor needed to stem the floodtide. Archival scenes show black men in prison stripes trucked to work and trucked back in a windowless iron trailer with airholes on its sides. With help from the federal government, blacks also worked to construct the world's largest system of levees along the river, but they got little reward.

Given this environment, it's both understandable and amazing that nearly all the great blues musicians were self-taught. On the level of domestic labor, one of the most striking moments in the film, and one of the longest, is a documentary interview with the aged blues singer-guitarist Elisabeth Cotton (1895–1958), who, after singing "Freight Train" in a weak but beautiful voice, tells the story of how she acquired a guitar. When she was a very young woman, she went to white homes asking for domestic work. One lady invited her in and asked what she could do. Cotton proudly listed all her skills: cooking, setting a table, cleaning house, doing laundry, bringing firewood inside, bathing and looking after the lady's children, and so forth. The lady hired her at seventy-five cents a month. After a year, the lady was so satisfied that she raised the pay to a dollar. Cotton gave the money to her mother, who later bought her a guitar from a Sears-Roebuck catalog. She smiles when she remembers that she couldn't keep her hands off the instrument and almost drove her mother crazy learning to play it.

Of course blues music wasn't entirely about the woes of life. "With blues," Buddy says to Junior, "you either laughed or cried." A good deal of it, in fact, was about what the church called sin. We get a sense of this when Buddy takes Junior home with him to his tiny house, which looks like a blues museum. (In his commentary on the DVD, Burnett says that most of the old blues musicians, even the famous ones, lived in humble places like this, stacked with records and decorated with rare posters and photos; he also praises his production designer, Liba Daniels, for transforming an abandoned shack with very little money.) At night, Junior shares the narrow bed with Buddy, the two lying at opposite ends so that Junior's head is at Buddy's feet. Junior can't sleep because when Buddy isn't moving his toes to unheard music he suddenly jumps up and has a desire to put another record on the player. In the morning, Junior has his first experience of the horrors of the outhouse, made worse because the door won't stay shut (there's a blues poster on the inside of the door for convenient reading, and part of a broken 78rpm record on the wall). He finds a cat-gut string tacked to a post near the front door and strums it for a moment.

Buddy becomes Junior's teacher. He shows the "cut and run" razor he keeps with him in case of trouble and begins playing records to exemplify the history of blues. This gives Burnett an opportunity to show archival footage of the people Buddy mentions. Buddy starts the day, as he does every day, by almost prayerfully listening to Sister Rosetta Tharpe's "Precious Memories." (As we've seen, Tharpe [1915–1973] was a singer of both blues and gospel; her rendition of "Precious Memories" was used for the opening of *To Sleep with Anger*.) He then segues into a discussion of women artists, who were in great demand during the 1920s, before the recording industry began to dictate what could be heard. "So many women called themselves Smith," Buddy says, among them Mamie Smith (1883–1946), the first woman to record blues, and of course Bessie Smith (1894–1937), featured in a clip Burnett shows us from the sixteen-minute film *St. Louis Blues* (1929). A montage of other female singers and songs features Ma Rainey's "I Feel so Sad" (Rainey [1886–1939], the narrator tells us, was a successful stage performer who didn't play juke joints and who worked with such musicians as Louis Armstrong; she was also a writer of songs with lesbian themes.), "Four Day Creep" by Ida Cox (1896–1967), and a cover of "I Don't Hurt Anymore" by Dinah Washington (1924–1963). Buddy enthusiastically comments, "Those were some *mean* women, boy!" To reinforce his point, he plays a record by Lucille Bogan (1897–1948) and we hear a bit of the lyrics: "I got nipples on my titties big as my thumbs." Suddenly realizing this might be inappropriate, Buddy stops the record. The adult Junior's narrating voice informs us that he decided to pretend he didn't hear the words; Lucille Bogan, he says, had recordings that "would make the

Sister Rosetta Tharpe
"Up Above My Head"

Marquis de Sade blush." He adds that as a result of listening to blues, "I learned a lot about body parts."

Buddy is obviously a man who loves women and makes no secret of the fact. Soon after playing the records, he visits a lady friend's shotgun house and introduces her to Junior. "This is Peaches," he says, "one of the finest women God let walk on this earth." He and Peaches cozy up and head off to the bedroom, backed by the music of Sonny Boy Williamson. (Williamson [1914–1948], the narrator explains, was the star of the *King Biscuit* radio show who was later killed in Chicago; we also see a clip of another, equally talented harmonica player [1912–1965] who somehow got away with appropriating Williamson's full name.) Sullen, troubled, and beginning to disapprove of Buddy, Junior wanders outside. He gets in Buddy's car and pretends to drive, then explores the neighborhood, coming upon a small church atop a hill. This discovery may seem implausibly symbolic, coming as it does on the heels of Junior's increased uneasiness about Buddy's sinfulness; but God and the devil, like gospel and the blues, are never far apart in this film or in backcountry Mississippi. Junior goes into the empty church, which has a pulpit, pews, and a tapestry of the last supper. In his DVD commentary, Burnett says that the church was long abandoned and had to be fumigated for wasps before it could be decorated.) Sitting on one of the pews, Junior experiences ghostly memories of churchgoing and seems to hear voices singing ("Things I used to do I don't do any more") and a preacher's sermon, illustrated for us by old documentary footage.

When Junior and Buddy resume their drive, Junior pointedly asks about his other relatives in Vicksburg, whom he still hasn't seen. Buddy ignores the question and resumes his lessons in blues history by commenting on the large number of singers who were blind, among them Blind Lemon Jefferson (1893–1929), Blind Blake (1896–1934), Blind Willie Johnson (1897–1945), and Ray Charles (1930–2004). But Junior looks unhappy. Sensing this, Buddy tries to cheer the boy up. "Let's go see a movie!" he proposes. "Have you seen that movie *Shane*? I saw that one and *High Noon* about a dozen times!" Junior frowns and asks, "Why do you do bad things?" Buddy pauses, glances at him, and makes a prediction: "You'll be surprised who you find in Heaven and who you find in Hell."

Back at home, Buddy goes through a pile of old records and papers, including a yellowing, handwritten manuscript from a book he's been writing about the history of blues. The book is unfinished because he still doesn't have a beginning or end. The deep ancestry of the music, he explains, is in the early years of Reconstruction, in the era of Frederick Douglass, Ida B. Welles, and W. E. B. Du Bois, when southern blacks had greater freedom of expression. By the early twentieth century, mass production made guitars available through mail order, and distinctive forms of blues developed in the southeastern states, the Mississippi delta, and east Texas. The first blues musician to publish his songs was W. C. Handy, who could be considered the godfather of such later figures as Mississippi John Hurt (1892–1966), T-Bone Walker (1910–1975), and Muddy Waters (1913–1983), all of whom we see in performance. The life of blues musicians, Buddy says to Junior, was often tough and self-destructive: Bessie Smith bled to death in an accident, and Leadbelly and Sun House killed men.

As Junior's education proceeds, he begins to form an imaginative attachment to the music and stories he's heard. At one point we see him alone on a nearby dirt road, walking with his eyes closed, guiding himself with a long stick in order to experience what blindness must have been like for people like Blind Lemon Jefferson. Buddy takes him to visit a blind guitarist named Honey Boy (Tommy Tc Carter), who is sitting on his front porch with an aging, invalid gentleman named Mr. Goodwin. Buddy reverently explains that the invalid old man was once a player with The Red Tops (Vicksburg's most popular blues, jazz, and dance band of the 1940s, which entertained both white and black audiences). Junior is amazed that Honey Boy knows he's from California, and listens politely when the blind man tells him that blues musicians, if they live long enough, begin to mature and accept religion;

he explains that he ruined his eyes and health from wild living and drinking too much home brew and "canned heat."

Eventually, Junior becomes less concerned about Buddy's womanizing. Buddy takes him for a fried catfish lunch at the home of two pretty young women, who enjoy teasing him. Chucking Junior under the chin, one of them says he needs a better name and asks if he likes "Sweet Boy." "No ma'am," he says, "I like Junior." Broadly smiling and seductively looking him in the eyes, the other young woman tells him Junior isn't "a name for a man." She decides to call him "Sugar Stick." Buddy plays a slow blues record, and he and the awkward, shy, silent Junior begin to dance with the two women. Junior's partner, who is much taller, buries his head between her breasts, whispering that when he gets older she's going to teach him things. "I was backsliding into darkness," the narrating voice of the adult Junior tells us. "I was between heaven and hell."

Junior's full absorption into the imaginative world of the blues happens when Buddy takes him for another drive, stopping the car at a country crossroads of the kind where Robert Johnson and other blues greats supposedly sold their souls to the devil in exchange for a devilish style. (The legend of this Faustian pact, we recall, was especially important to Burnett's *To Sleep with Anger*.) Buddy tells Junior that they'll see the devil, but as night descends he falls asleep in the driver's seat. Junior stares ahead into the mysterious, moonlit darkness, where the ghostly image of a well-dressed blues musician appears standing and speaks to him in the voice of W. C. Handy (who was still alive in the mid-1950s). Fearful, certain that he's encountered an apparition of the devil, Junior shakes Buddy awake and tells him what he's seen. Buddy explains he was only joking and explodes into waves of loud laughter. (In his DVD commentary, Burnett remarks that it was ironically difficult for the film crew to find a country crossroad near Vicksburg. He also says, "One would think this scene would be about Robert Johnson, but it's not. It's about this kid's imagination.")

Going deeper into the devil's territory, Buddy climaxes his course of study by taking Junior to a local juke joint crowded with drinkers and dancing couples. Junior gets a fish sandwich on white bread and sits at a table, where he eats and observes the action while Buddy perches in lordly fashion at the bar, turning toward the room and saying hello to the regulars. The woman who owns the place rebukes Buddy for bringing a kid inside, but he begs for just one beer, and she relents. A sensible friend of Buddy's steps forward, declines the offer of a drink, and tells Buddy he's crossed a line by bringing a boy into the joint. Buddy laughs him off, and the friend says "I give up," exiting the place in disgust. Not long afterward a fight breaks out, viewed from over Junior's shoulder, and a man across the room is knocked to the floor. The owner and her bouncers put the unconscious man in a chair and relieve him of a switchblade. Buddy leans toward Junior and asks, "Having fun?"

Just then the disgusted fellow who walked out returns with Buddy's brother—he's Uncle Flem, Buddy's opposite, a preacher dressed respectably in a suit. Flem tells Buddy that Junior's family in LA and relatives in Vicksburg have been worried to death, and that Buddy is "crazy." Buddy knows that his time with Junior is up. He moves to the boy, gives him an intense look in the eyes, and hugs him. Flem announces that he's taking Junior to the decent members of the family elsewhere in Vicksburg. As Junior is led away, he looks back at Buddy. Burnett freezes the frame for a moment, holding on the boy's gaze, and then shows him leaving.

This is the end of Junior's association with Buddy, but not the end of Buddy's influence. As the film closes, Junior's narrating voice tells us: "I learned so much on that trip back home. I never forgot a second of it. I draw a lot from that time I spent with Buddy. . . . The years went by, and Buddy left the book for me to finish. I did, in my own way." In the last image we see a still photo of Buddy in a suit, next to Flem, holding a Bible to his heart. Junior's voice says, "Buddy ended up becoming a preacher, like so many of the blues players." In his "own way" Burnett himself has finished Buddy's book.

TWELVE

Namibia: The Struggle for Liberation *(2007)*

BURNETT'S LONGEST FEATURE FILM and one of his most elaborately produced, *Namibia: The Struggle for Liberation* won prizes at two African-centered film festivals (Best African Film and Best Director at Kuala Lumpur Film Festival; a Vision Award at Los Angeles Pan African Film and Arts Festival) but has rarely been screened in the United States. The only video available at this time is a German-produced Blu-ray without English subtitles. For that reason, my discussion of it is relatively brief.

A June 29, 2007, *Variety* review by Robert Koehler may have been *Namibia*'s commercial death knell, although the film would have been a problem to market even without the review. After praising Burnett's best-known work and lamenting that Namibian state sponsorship prevented him from making a personal film about Africa, Koehler pointed out that most US viewers can't find Namibia on a map; that Americans Carl Lumbly and Danny Glover aren't "major names" for young black viewers; that much of the picture's dialogue is in Afrikaans, Oshiwambo, OtjiHerero, and German; and that the running time is two hours and forty-one minutes. All this is true, but given that the film was aimed primarily at audiences in Namibia, it probably shouldn't be judged by the standards of Hollywood or US art-house ventures.

Namibia, budgeted at roughly $10 million (a paltry sum by Hollywood standards) is a Panavision spectacular, beautifully photographed in color by John L. Demps Jr. (who has photographed most of Burnett's films but sometimes appears in their credits as John, John N., and John Ndiaga); effectively scored by Stephen James Taylor; and using cinematic resources that Burnett has seldom had at his disposal: camera cranes, helicopters, incendiary special effects, and a cast of hundreds, if not thousands. It isn't, however a generic action film. It has short, vivid battle scenes, but the battles are necessary to an understanding of Namibian history. In making it, Burnett's approach wasn't entirely different from his approach to *Killer of Sheep*. He has often said that Basil Wright's advice to him as a student at UCLA—"respect your subject"—was especially important, and that he admires Wright's *Song of Ceylon* (state-sponsored by the British colonial government) because of its manifest respect for the people of what was then Ceylon. His ability to refrain from too much personal or political judgment of his characters is one of the things that makes *Killer of Sheep* so striking. Thus, when he accepted the Namibian government's offer to film a history of their long war of liberation from South Africa—a film they hoped might serve as a springboard for a planned Namibian motion picture industry—his chief aim was to respect their wishes and people.

The Republic of Namibia was overly optimistic about creating a national film industry, because it has a population of only 2.1 million. Located in the southwest corner of Africa, it borders on Zambia and Angola to the north, Botswana to the east, and South Africa to the south and east. Its western border is the Atlantic Ocean, and because most of its western territory is composed of the hyper-arid Namib and Kalahari Deserts, it is one of the least densely populated countries in the world. Its official language is English, but it also has ten officially recognized regional languages. The fifteenth-century Portuguese were the first Europeans to explore the land, and Germany colonized it in the nineteenth century, instituting a genocidal war against two of its rebellious tribes. After World War I British South Africa took control, and in 1948 control was transferred to the Afrikaans government of South Africa, which imposed apartheid, gave private ownership of virtually all arable land to the white minority population (0.2 percent white, according to the Wikipedia entry on Namibia on which my description of the country is based), and named the region South West Africa. In the second half of the twentieth century, black Africans in Namibia began a series of rebellions that resulted in the United Nations assuming official responsibility for the country, but South Africa resisted. The UN recognized black-nationalist SWAPO (South West Africa People's Organization, composed mainly of the Ambo, who are the majority black people) as a legal political party, but South African resistance resulted in a sustained war that lasted twenty-four years and took the lives of almost twenty-five thousand men, women, and children. In 1990 Namibia won independence, establishing a political party system and a democratic, parliamentary government with three branches similar to those in the United States. (These facts come from the Wikipedia entry on Namibia at en.wikipedia.org/wiki/Namibia.)

Burnett inherited a screenplay by Vikson Hangula and Femi Koyode based on Sam Nujoma's autobiography, *Nujoma: Where Others Waivered*. The founder of SWAPO and the country's first elected president, Nujoma was still in office at the time (the Namibian parliament had named him "Father of the Namibian Nation"), but his popularity was waning and a number of those who had participated in the War of Independence thought his memoir gave too little credit to others. Consequently, Burnett spent three months rewriting the screenplay with the help of story consultant Isaac Ikharuchab, giving it a wider focus and more epic scale. He described the overall production to me as "challenging and dangerous in many ways," but as "an unforgettable experience." Looking back on it, he recalled that at first it seemed "a nightmare," but that the Namibian people, to whom the production gave many jobs, were "great." Even though he thought of it as very challenging, he remembers it as "the best of times."

To avoid errors, Burnett needed to add a good deal to his knowledge of Namibian history, negotiate with various witnesses to the war, and cope with multiple languages on the set. He had Carl Lumbly and Danny Glover in leading roles, but the casting of locals for the roughly 150 speaking parts was difficult, in part because "every person in Namibia wanted to be in the film, to play a part, no matter what part, because they felt it was important" (Kapsis 2011, 173). It was necessary to find actors who spoke certain languages and dialects well enough to convince the African audience, and the problem was further complicated because a Namibian casting director had coached many of the applicants to behave in a highly theatrical style. Once Burnett got to know the actors, he found that they were quite good at realistic movie performances, but the sheer number of parts and his unfamiliarity with the many candidates caused him at one point to assign more than one role to the same people.

The completed film is nevertheless a reasonably clear narrative that follows the history of the war and takes full advantage of the highly picturesque Namibian landscape, which is so various and beautiful that it must have been fairly easy to point a Panavision camera in any direction and find a good composition. Burnett stages complex battle scenes and gives the war a heroic and tragic dimension. He makes the basic twists and turns of the politics behind the war apparent, although without English subtitles I couldn't make out some of the planning and strategy. Certain characters and reenacted

events will be much more familiar and understandable to an African audience than to Americans; the film often seems like a condensed, one-thing-after-another guide to a complex history that necessarily jumps over details.

The early scenes deal with Sam Nujoma's youth, showing him at age seventeen in 1946 (played by Joel Haikili), walking through Namibia's wide, sunbaked savanna and encountering a group of boys herding buffalo and singing a liberation song. Like many young boys, he experiences a rite of passage by traveling deep into the blazing white sands of the Namib. After moving to Walvis Bay, where he lives with his aunt, he looks for work near attractive white homes but is sternly warned by a policeman that the area is off limits to blacks. He eventually finds a ten-shilling-a month job in a white-owned general store. He can't speak Afrikaans, but by communicating in simple English he's able to persuade the gruff owner of his industry and honesty; eventually he becomes the owner's household servant and overhears white discussions about incipient rebellion.

During this period we meet Father Elias (Danny Glover), a Lutheran priest who sympathizes with the plight of blacks but thinks violent rebellion is anti-Christian. (Almost 90 percent of Namibia's population is Christian, originally converted by German and Finnish missionaries in the nineteenth century.) Elias, a fictional character compounded of several actual priests, provides the film with its only intimate scenes and psychological conflict. His faith makes war abhorrent to him, and at one point, during a quiet conversation in a church, he tells the young Nujoma, who is becoming radicalized, that only God can know what is good and evil. Nujoma replies, "That puts us at a disadvantage." Because Elias is black and understands the reasons for potential war, he's soon replaced by a white and moved to another assignment. Years later he returns and gives refuge and comfort to freedom fighters. Meanwhile the film shows a bit of Nujoma's education at an Anglican school in the capital city of Windhoek, where a white priest refuses to discuss politics but improves his English.

The film leaps over ten eventful years of Nujoma's life, omitting his work at a whaling station and the South African Railways; his encounters with politically knowledgeable soldiers from Europe, Latin America, and Scandinavia; his adult education by correspondence with a school in South Africa; and his visit to Cape Town, where he became cofounder with Andinmba Toivo ya Toivo of the Omamboland People's Organization (OPO), a Namibian independence movement (see Nujoma 2001). The adult Nujoma (Carl Lumbly) is seen returning to Walvis Bay with a fully developed political consciousness and an interest in Marcus Garvey's US black nationalism. Virtually all the useful land in the country has been appropriated by whites, and debates among blacks about violent rebellion are increasing. Burnett gives us an example of apartheid in action: a black mother sends her small son to a store for bread, but the boy becomes momentarily distracted by jars of candy and doesn't notice a customer taking the last dark loaf; unable to read the sign above a row of white loaves ("white bread for whites only"), he innocently takes one and is severely reprimanded by the store owner.

Nujoma writes to the *New York Times* and begins agitating to unite black South Africans under OPO's democratic-socialist agenda. He takes Che Guevara as his model and begins training a People' Liberation Army (PLAN) that drills with sticks in place of rifles, hoping to find real arms after an attack on a Portuguese port in Angola. An overwhelming majority of the membership in OPO, PLAN, and SWAPO was Bantu-speaking African of the Ovambo ethnicity (then, as now, they were a slight majority in the country and lived mostly in the north), but Nujoma sought to bring other ethnic groups into his movement. Some of the chiefs of these groups were puppets of the white South Africans (as we discover during battle scenes, the ground troops of the South African military, like those of other colonialist powers, were mostly black). In an amusing and suspenseful scene, Nujoma tries to woo one of the corrupt and alcoholic chieftains by bringing him a gift of whiskey. The visit comes to nothing because the more drunk the chief becomes, the meaner he gets; he enjoys dressing like a Harlem hipster, riding in a new American car, and ordering his thugs to tie his enemies to trees in

the wilderness. The more important chief is the aging and distinguished Hosea Komombumbi Kutako (Christian Appolus) of the Herero people, 80 percent of whom were exterminated when they rebelled against German occupation in the early twentieth century. Chief Hosea is the first black nationalist warrior in Namibia, a revered figure who, after negotiating with Nujoma, joins the new nationalist movement. He dies before the war ends. Burnett shows him supported by two of his retainers, hobbling off into the distance and dissolving away like a ghost.

A small, underarmed troop of PLAN soldiers, hoping to become the first colonized people to fight and defeat superpowers, begins combat with a long march that establishes a base at the village of Omugulugwombashe, where South African helicopters and heavily armed shock troops catch them by surprise and kill most of them. Burnett shows the attack in dynamic fashion, the camera situated in one of the copters and viewing soldiers as they disembark. The PLAN military scrambles for their few guns, and one fighter, armed with nothing but a small bow and arrow, takes a futile shot at the attackers. The date is August 26, 1966, which is remembered today as the first battle for Namibian independence. Afterward Nujoma holds a council with his officers and realizes that his army has been betrayed by spies. "We made mistakes," he says. "We won't do that again."

PLAN battle tactics shift to nocturnal guerrilla warfare and sabotage aimed at police stations and military installations, which Burnett renders as large, fiery explosions. The South African government responds by labeling the actions "terrorism," and the war continues even after the UN recognizes SWAPO as a legitimate political party. In an effort to sow discord among blacks, South Africa hires black killers to murder and rape African women and children. We see examples of captured rebels being tortured with systematic beatings and branding irons. (Recipe for improvised torture in the field: hold the captured rebel's head against the exhaust pipe of a truck while the engine is running.) All forms of communication between blacks are repressed; newsboys spreading information about the war and world reaction to it have to flee for their lives when police spot them, and the South African army captures Toivo y Toivo when he unsuccessfully tries to burn papers intended for insurgents.

In August 1967 Toivo and thirty-six other men (only a few of them seen in the film), along with eighty-one men still at large, are charged with terrorism and tried by a South African court. It's the first trial under the newly imposed South Africa Terrorism Act, which in this case is applied retroactively. The judge, a supercilious bigot, disregards defense arguments that the only evidence in the case has come from police who tortured the arrested men. In a swift decision, he sentences all the accused to imprisonment. As an example of their heinous terrorist actions, he singles out the man who used a bow and arrow against South African soldiers at the battle of Omugulugwombashe.

Given an opportunity to speak on behalf of the sentenced prisoners in the dock, Toivo, labeled "Accused number 21," rises and makes a short speech that made headlines around the world and has become one of the key moments of the war. Burnett gives us the speech in its entirety: "We are Namibians, and not South Africans. We do not now, and will not in the future, recognize your right to govern us; to make laws for us, in which we had no say; to treat our country as if it were your property and us as if you are our masters. We have always regarded South Africa as an intruder in our country. This is how we have always felt and this is how we feel now and it is on this basis that we have faced this trial." The film doesn't say so, but when he made this speech Toivo had already been in solitary confinement in Pretoria for over a year. In 1968 the Pretoria Supreme Court sentenced him to twenty years' imprisonment at Robben Island, near Cape Town. He was released in 1984. He went on to become a major figure in SWAPO and to hold various ministerial positions (among them the ministry of prisons) in Nujoma's government before his death in 2017.

In 1974 war in Angola and other Portuguese colonies in Africa contributed to a revolution in Portugal and the end of Portuguese rule over its empire. The next year was a turning point of the Namibian war. Cuba supported the newly formed communist government in Angola, and military supplies became much easier for PLAN to obtain. In response, South Africa stepped up its military action and began "Operation Reindeer," which involved indiscriminate aerial bombardment of Namibian villages. Burnett films huge planes dropping bombs and paratroopers, followed by slow-motion scenes of explosions and people running for safety. Some of the Namibian women hide in caves they have dug in the ground, and a paratrooper throws a grenade in after them. After the attack the camera pans over a field covered with dead bodies, and a high-angle crane shot shows South Africans piling them into a mass grave. Following classic counterinsurgency tactics, the South Africans also attack a safe-haven refugee camp near the border with Angola, killing seven hundred men, women, and children. When the UN tries to object, we see the United States and its allies refusing to offer support on the grounds that the camp was communist supported.

The war continues: PLAN stages a bazooka attack on a South African military camp; the South Africans raid a Namibian village, burning it to the ground because it supposedly harbors terrorists; a sabotage team blows up another police station; and trench warfare develops between the two sides. Consequently, low morale begins to affect the South African army. Father Elias, who has a young ward involved in battle, reluctantly accepts the need for armed struggle and has a quiet conversation in church with the young man and his fellow guerrilla fighter, who is named simply "Red" (Obed Emvula). When Red asks, "Where is God in all this?" Elias replies, "All around us."

As the fighting proceeds, Nujoma leads African representatives in negotiations with the Western Contact Group (WCG, composed of West Germany, Britain, France, the United States, Canada, and South Africa), which eventuate in the 1978 passage of UN Security Council Resolution 435, offering a plan for free and fair elections in Namibia. Nujoma, having grown a snow-white beard that vividly contrasts with the dark hair on his head, beams in satisfaction at his diplomatic success. (Carl Lumbly's beard in this and later scenes may seem artificial, but his looks and accent are quite true to Nujoma's.) The US and South African officials, however, are unhappy, as we see from their faces at the negotiating table. Their combined delaying tactics kept the resolution from being implemented for almost a decade, chiefly because the Reagan administration objected to Cuban involvement with the Namibian freedom fighters.

In conversation with his fellow African diplomats in the film, Nujoma jokingly refers to "the good old days, when Carter was president." Meanwhile, white South Africans and Europeans join with Namibians in street protests. Prominent among these is the South African lawyer Anton Lubowski (Louis Van Eeden), whom we see with a megaphone, leading a crowd that police roughly disperse in a style roughly similar to that used in Selma, Alabama, in the 1960s. Lubowski had been a social activist for many years and joined SWAPO in the 1980s. The film doesn't show us, but in 1989 he was assassinated by a South African hit squad in front of his home in Windhoek. Today there's a street in the city named after him (en.wikipedia.org/wiki/Anton Lubowski).

Recognizing that its power is slipping away, South Africa makes an all-out attempt at military invasion of Namibia, and the situation becomes desperate for the indigenous forces of PLAN. In a brief battlefield conversation with a female officer from Cuba, Nujoma explains that air support is essential, or all the struggles of the past years will come to nothing. The officer assures him that Fidel Castro will help, and not long afterward we see a group of Cuban MIG 25 jets executing a flyover of entrenched South African troops. At the end of their resources, the South Africans relent. The film doesn't go into the details of Cold War negotiation, but the historical record tells us that the ultimate solution to peace in Namibia and the implementation of Resolution 435 depended on a compromise in which Cuba withdrew forces from Angola and Namibia agreed to protect South African businesses in Windhoek. The film does, however, pointedly show that the US representative didn't join other nations in applauding the signing of the peace.

The film ends with Burnett's exciting re-creation of the celebration in Windhoek, which includes a large parade backed with African music and featuring a variety of dancers of different ethnicities in their traditional costumes. Most of the major and minor characters—Nujoma, Father Elias, Toivo, and even Red, who has lost a leg in the war—share in the excitement. We're given a brief, dreamlike scene with Nujoma standing on a battlefield and somberly viewing hundreds of dead Namibian soldiers, representing only a fraction of the deaths in the long war. The film doesn't give us details of the postwar transition to independence: almost fifty thousand SWAPO exiles returned home; the UN contributed a peacekeeping force, but hostilities broke out again and had to be quelled before the transition could proceed; one-person, one-vote elections were finally held in November 1989; and SWAPO won by a large majority, but their victory wasn't the two-thirds needed to completely unseat a South African–backed opposition party (en. wikipedia.org/wiki/Namibia). Burnett shows us a clip from a March 21,

1990, television news broadcast of the official founding of the new nation at Windhoek Stadium. F. W. de Kierk, president of South Africa, stands with his hand over his heart, his clearly unhappy wife beside him, as his country's flag is lowered and replaced by the flag of Namibia. Sam Nujoma, who has been elected president of the new nation, smiles with pride.

The closing credits are preceded by an announcement indicating that many important figures in the war were "left out in the retelling" because of time limitations. Three names are mentioned for special attention, but without explanation for foreign audiences of who they were: Anton Lubowski, Peter Nanyemba, and Tobias Hainyeko. I have identified Lubowski above. A Google search identifies Nanyemba as the commander of PLAN until 1983, when he was killed in an accident in Angola (a primary school in Angola is named after him today), and Hainyeko as a Soviet-trained, communist freedom fighter who created the first guerrilla force in the war of independence and was killed in action.

Whatever it may lack for commercial audiences in the West, and whatever simplifications and political issues it had to negotiate, *Namibia: The Struggle for Liberation* remains a valuable resource for its nation. In a 2007 interview with Diane Sippl, Burnett rightly took pride in his contribution: "It was a chance not only to play a supportive role but also to have a hand in getting a piece of work out that responds to a need. Namibians need to see themselves as members of a Pan-African culture and history" (Kapsis 2011, 173).

THIRTEEN

Two Screenplays

BLESS THEIR LITTLE HEARTS (1984)
AND *MAN IN A BASKET* (2003)

A COMPLETE FILMMAKER, BURNETT has not only directed but also written, produced, photographed, and edited many of his films (he took a brief turn as an actor in the fourteen-minute *Olivia's Story* [1999]), and in his role as director he often contributes to screenplays written by others. Most of his TV films, for example, have involved adjustments to the scripts he was given. "The TV movies that I did were Movies of the Week," he has explained. "I had more control as opposed to an episodic series, where the writer is at the top of the food chain.... I would go over the script with the [director of photography] and all the key department heads to exchange ideas, to find a better way of doing it. At this time, I would also talk about the mood with a composer" (Miguez and Paz 2016, 77). Like many filmmakers, Burnett has also experienced the frustration of writing scripts and script outlines that were never produced, either because he couldn't find sufficient funding or because producers wanted him to make changes he couldn't accept. Among the unfilmed projects are an epic film about Frederick Douglass; feature-length biographies of Paul Robeson and W. E. B. DuBois; *145th Street*, based on a collection of young adult short stories by the prolific black author Walter Dean Meyers; and *The William and Ellen Craft Story*, about two slaves who escaped from Georgia in 1848, the wife disguised as a white man and the husband as a servant (see Kapsis 2011, xxv–xxvi). In 2015 he was in Algeria, where he hoped to make a film about Emir Abd-el-Kader, the nineteenth-century Arab scholar and military leader who repelled a French colonial invasion and saved Christians in Damascus from being slaughtered by Arab tribesmen; unfortunately, financing for that film never materialized.

I have not seen screenplays for these films, but two others can serve to illustrate the range and excellence of Burnett's writing, which should get more attention, and which I want to emphasize here. First is an outstanding film he wrote but didn't direct, although it's very much in the style of his early pictures about Watts. Second is an adaptation of a novel by Chester Himes, which has yet to make it to the screen. Together, they exemplify not only his affection and concern for black lives, but also the range and inventiveness of his work at its most basic level of inspiration.

BLESS THEIR LITTLE HEARTS

In 1978–1979, during the period between *Killer of Sheep* and *My Brother's Wedding*, Burnett encouraged the Texas-born Billy Woodberry, whom he had come to know at UCLA, to direct a feature film. As incentive, he presented Woodberry with a seventy-page screenplay. The resulting film, *Bless Their Little Hearts* (1984), was also photographed by Burnett in 16mm black and white and used actors and family members who had previously worked with him. Like *Killer of Sheep*, it deals with a family in Watts who suffer from economic and emotional pressures, and it is one of the key examples of the distinctive style of black neorealism for which Burnett was largely responsible. (In my view, this style owes less to the Italians than to the Brazilian "cinema of poverty" and the films of Ousmane Sembene, which Burnett had seen as a student.) Rarely shown, it was restored by Milestone Films in 2017 and will at last be widely available on DVD, alongside *Killer of Sheep*. *Bless Their Little Hearts*, which in 2013 was selected for the National Film Registry, is in every way worthy to stand alongside the earlier picture.

Credit for the completed film goes primarily to Woodberry, who directed, edited, and slightly expanded the screenplay, putting greater emphasis on family relationships. But Woodberry retained most of the structure and dialogue Burnett had established. Both this film and *Killer of Sheep* are centered on poor black fatherhood, serving to refute the idea that inner-city families are typically matriarchal, lacking dedicated fathers. (As we have seen, however, Burnett's own father was absent for most of his childhood; he was raised by his mother and grandmother.) Also like *Killer of Sheep*, *Bless Their Little Hearts* is episodic, without the tight cause-effect plotting of Hollywood pictures and many social problem films. Most of the sequences are relatively self-contained vignettes illustrating a round of quotidian life that gradually drifts toward open conflict and near despair, and the ending is ambiguous, lacking full closure. The dialogue is typical of Burnett in its touches of humor and deft characterization; the strength of the screenplay, however, comes not only from language (some of which is improvised) but also from the eloquence and affective power of the activities and incidental details he chose to make up the story.

Killer of Sheep involved a laboring man who, however soul-destroying his work, was able to take a certain pride in supporting his family. In *Bless Their Little Hearts*, the situation is different; Charlie Banks (Nate Hardman) is equally committed to his family but has been without permanent work for almost a decade and can only scratch out temporary menial labor. His wife, Andias (Kaycee Moore, even more impressive here than in *Killer of Sheep*), works as a domestic (as Burnett's mother once did) and has become the breadwinner. The couple has three kids, aged twelve, ten, and six (Angela, Ronald, and Kimberly Burnett), the oldest of whom looks out for the others when the parents are away. We never see Andias at work, but she's shown in somber close-ups as she takes long bus rides to and from her place of employment, sometimes nodding off to sleep, sometimes gripping the bar atop the seat in front of her in a restless gesture, sometimes pensively and sadly holding her chin in her hand as the city passes outside her window.

Early in the film we see Charlie in a series of telephoto shots as he visits an employment office; a burly fellow and a heavy smoker, he slowly and carefully fills out forms with a lead pencil, studies a sign on the wall labeled "Casual Labor," and wanders around the office until closing time, his actions backed by a saxophone and piano jazz version of "Nobody Loves You When You're Down and Out." (The nondiegetic music functions much as it did in *Killer*; a compilation score made up chiefly of jazz and blues, it comments on the action and isn't mixed with ambient sound.) Then he exits, walking through the decayed Watts rail yard with the closed and shuttered factory buildings of Goodyear and Firestone Tire and Rubber visible in the background. In the evening he arrives home to find his kids in the kitchen, the oldest cooking sweet potatoes while the others play cards. In the bedroom, his exhausted wife is in bed. When he asks if she's asleep, she says, "I wisht I was."

Stan in *Killer of Sheep* suffered from depression induced by his job, but Charlie in *Bless Their Little Hearts* suffers from depression, shame, and repressed anger over his joblessness. His sense of masculinity and self-worth are under threat. His wife is too tired to offer him emotional or sexual comfort (he lies beside her in bed at night, staring at the ceiling), and as a result he becomes alienated. He hangs out with a group of men who sit around drinking Colt 45 and cheap bourbon, listlessly debating such topics as who has the lightest skin and commiserating over their joblessness. At one point a member of the group suggests that they could maybe take up robbery like the kids are doing. "We're smarter than they are," he says. Charlie declares that he would never do anything to lose his family and tries to view his situation as a spiritual crisis to be overcome. One of the drunken men thinks of using guns to hunt for food, but another remarks, "You know how far you have to drive to kill a rabbit?"

In the evening Charlie gets into bed with the half asleep Andias, who mumbles "you eat sumthin'?" He tries to kiss her on the shoulder, but she doesn't respond. Later we see Andias and the children cleaning the kitchen while Charlie, who never seems to help with domestic labor, is smoking and lying atop the hood of a car outside the Compton All Star Fish Market; a pal brings him a piece of fried fish, and nondiegetic blues can be heard on the sound track. When he's at home Charlie reads want ads in the newspaper. One of the most impressively written and acted scenes involves his attempt to assert male authority by disciplining his small son, who hasn't cut his fingernails. Charlie and Andias are having coffee at the kitchen table, and he talks about how low he is because of being out of work. She tries to give him encouragement, and he suddenly calls for his son to bring him cigarettes and an ashtray. Covering his vulnerability, he lectures the child. "Boy, didn't I tell you to keep your fingernails cut?" he says. "Girls and sissies have long nails. Are you a sissy?" As he cuts the boy's nails, the boy quietly cries. Charlie repeatedly jerks the boy's arm hard, ordering him to stand straight and stop crying, and the boy does his best to comply.

An equally painful but more poignant scene shows Andias preparing the kids for Sunday school. She tells them to wait for their father, who will give them money for a tithe. Then she goes out to the hallway, where Charlie is waiting in obvious discomfort. She opens her purse and gives him money, silently admonishing him to act the patriarch. Trying to conceal his humiliation, he goes to the kitchen and gives each of the children a coin.

Another of the memorable domestic scenes has only a single line of dialogue. Charlie is in the bathroom shaving, and director Woodberry makes brilliant use of a wide shot to show the entire process. Charlie hums to himself as he carefully, methodically shaves his thick beard. His oldest daughter enters, wanting to use the bathroom. He gently tells her to wait. She exits. He rinses his face, and a tight close-up shows him grimly looking at himself in the mirror. He slowly turns off the tap water with a force that, as Alessandra Raengo has observed, makes his hands seem to indicate "the struggle they are both expressing and holding back" (2015, 302). He exits. After a moment the daughter enters and tries to turn on the tap. She can't. She exits again. A moment later she comes back with a monkey wrench almost as big as she is and turns on the water.

Eventually Charlie finds temporary piecework with a local contractor. One of the outstanding qualities of the film is its tendency to document the process of both domestic and outdoor labor. We see Andias and the children preparing food and washing the walls and surfaces of the kitchen, and Charlie proves to be something of a jack-of-all-trades. In a montage that conveys the repetitiveness and sheer discomfort of hard physical work, he and another man swing scythes to clear brush on a vacant lot. Burnett shoots the action with a telephoto lens, and the camera seems to be positioned deep down in the thick brush, which almost swallows the two men. At the end of the long, hot, hazy day, Charlie, who has no proper work clothes, piles the chopped brush in the center of the field. He sits on a hillside and waits for his employer, who drives up in a battered truck. Charlie explains that his coworker gave up in the heat and went home, and the employer promises to pay him. As they drive back toward Watts, Charlie sits in the passenger seat, quietly smoking. To the sound of blues, we see the cityscape passing outside his window and we eventually travel through the old industrial area of Watts, with its shuttered buildings and skeletal factory remains. Thom Andersen's celebrated essay film, *Los Angeles Plays Itself*, pays tribute to Billy Woodberry by closing with these scenes. Andersen observes that when Watts had industrial jobs, visitors and the people of the city could tour the nearby Goodyear plant to learn how tires are made; now, they go on tours of movie lots. As David E. James puts it, "the manufacture of images has replaced the manufacture of material goods," and the social costs of this transformation have been represented not in "Hollywood's false, manufactured spatialities," but in "modes of film production opposed to the industry that grow out of the working class itself" (2005, 422).

At home after clearing the field, Charlie reclines in a full bathtub and snores—this to the discomfort of his son, who knocks on the bathroom door and can't get a response. Somewhat later Charlie gets a job painting over the graffiti on a storage building ("Fuck all Bruins" and "East Side Crips") and does good professional work, carefully cleaning off the gutters, trimming certain areas with a small brush, and putting away his ladders and tools with efficiency and pride. That evening he brings home ice cream for his kids, smiling and teasing them with his power to bestow a special treat. But things take a troubling turn when, still happy with himself, he meets an old girl-friend, Rose, a single mother who has a couple of kids, one of them almost grown. With her, Charlie can drink beer, have sex, and feel important, and he spends his money to show off. He brings the rest of the money home to help Andias pay bills, and when she notices some of it is gone he makes a lame excuse. She immediately senses his infidelity and talks with a neighborhood woman about philandering husbands who have had their "little egos" hurt. One evening after work she returns home to find the place empty and the kitchen dirty. "Lord have mercy!" she cries. "I would think *somebody* in this house would have hands besides me!" Her kids come in bearing groceries, and her mounting fatigue, pain, and anger cause her to snap. Ranting at everybody for sitting on their "well-rested behinds," she begins unwrapping a whole chicken from the groceries. "We could be *dead* as far as he's concerned!" she shouts, then throws the chicken hard against the wall.

Charlie, meanwhile, is having a conversation with Rose, who sits on his lap and tells him she needs a man to take care of her boys, especially the teenager, who is too big to whip. Her interest in Charlie is obviously motivated by something other than his sex appeal. He explains that he has kids of his own to raise and just wants a bit of comfort. "I thought I could have peace," he whines. "I'm tired, baby!"

Charlie's complaint comes back at him with a vengeance in the film's most powerful sequence: a ten-minute, handheld, long take in which Kaycee Moore and Nate Hardman provide a virtual master class in improvisational acting. Improvisation in film is of course somewhat different than on stage, because scenes can always be reshot if the results are unsatisfactory; nevertheless, this sequence has a vérité quality that can be obtained only when actors approach a scene existentially, relying on their immediate instincts to escape what Ed Guerrero has called "the illusionist narcosis so prevalent in Hollywood films" (1991, 320). Woodberry has said that Nate Hardman was reluctant to perform it and quit the production for almost two months because he believed—wrongly—that Moore had revealed secrets of his private life to Burnett, who used them to create the situation (see Sheppard 2015, 235–36). In the event, both actors seem to be drawing on reserves of personal feeling that give their behavior unusual authenticity.

Charlie comes home in the evening wearing a crisp white shirt and gets a cold reception. "What's wrong with everybody?" he asks. "It ain't *everybody*, it's *me*!" Andias cries, finally releasing all her pent-up anger and grief. An especially effective aspect of the scene is the ebb and flow of emotional energy between the two actors. At first Andias is disgusted and furious. Confronting Charlie with his infidelity, she gets in his face, tells him he's smelling of "ten-cent perfume," and shoves him away whenever he tries to touch her. He softly pleads, trying to sweet talk, telling her she's "crazy . . . just cause things ain't going right." Then, as a result of her unyielding scorn, he gives in, swearing in typical wayward-husband fashion that the woman "meant nothing." "I'm *tired*, Charlie, *tired, tired, tired, tired*!" Andias keeps shouting the words like a whiplash or a broken record. Charlie says that he's trying all the time to find permanent work. "Don't try," she says, "*do* it!" Guilty, backed into an emo-tional corner, humiliated and angry at his many job frustrations, he roars back at her, and at one point it looks as if the shouting match is going to turn into a knock-down, drag-out fight between the big man and his slender wife. Andias is tearful and unforgiving. Charlie relents, and the scene ends when he quietly asks to sleep apart for the night, giving them both time to calm down.

All the conflict of the film has been unleashed, and while one's sympathy is mostly with Andias, it's typical of Burnett that Charlie, flawed but equally miserable, is also worthy of respect. He spends a night on the couch, contem-plating the state of his marriage. Soon afterward, the contractor he's been working for explains that at present there aren't any piecework jobs. For once, Charlie doesn't aimlessly drift. We see him digging madly through the family's crowded storage closet, looking for his fishing rod and tackle. Andias comes to his aid, and for the first time she smiles. (The moment is almost equivalent to the scene when Stan smiles near the end of *Killer of Sheep*.) Charlie takes his tackle box into the kitchen. In a series of close-ups Woodberry again shows him at work, his big hands untangling fishing line and using pliers to repair hooks and small lead weights. He has the delicacy and skill of a craftsman and experienced fisherman. The next day he joins other black fishermen near the seacoast, where a yacht sails past in the distance.

Charlie's nadir comes in the next scene. For unexplained reasons, his old-est daughter has broken her arm and is wearing a cast. The family sits around the table in the kitchen, and Charlie dissolves into tears because of his inabil-ity to give his family a better life in a better place. Hardman touchingly conveys a big man's helpless anguish. Andias stands behind Charlie, puts her hand on his shoulder, and offers comfort.

Next Charlie visits a roadside market where black fish sellers are waving at passing cars and offering fresh, river-caught catfish. He can't compete. The film ends as he walks away from the camera toward the rail yards in Watts. Grim as his situation is, it's far from unique. Everywhere in the United States, working-class blacks have always been the last hired and the first fired, and their pay has always been lower than whites'. There was a time when Watts had industrial jobs; in those days Charlie operated forklifts and drove trucks. Now the factories are shells, and he returns home to the same conditions and threats to the survival of his family that he has suffered before. *Bless Their Little Hearts* brings us much closer to complete despair than *Killer of Sheep*, but at least its protagonist is going back to his family.

MAN IN A BASKET

The screenplay for *Man in a Basket*, unlike the one for *Bless Their Little Hearts*, must be discussed to some degree conditionally. Written in 2003, it's a straightforward adaptation of a 1959 detective novel by Chester Himes (published in the United States in 1973 under the title *The Crazy Kill*) and seems especially well-suited to Burnett's talents as a director of darkly humorous ensemble pictures about communities of the black underclass. It could, and probably would, make an outstanding film noir, but has yet to receive financing. In 2016 Burnett told Spanish interviewers that he was interested in the novel because it's "the Himes story that comes close to a love story." He had hoped to get support from Harvey Weinstein on the coattails of the Denzel Washington picture *The Great Debaters* (2007), which Weinstein had distributed, but when *The Great Debaters* did poorly at the box office Weinstein lost interest (Miguez and Paz 2016, 89.) Since then Burnett has twice come close with other production companies, and as of this writing he is still trying.

Burnett's title is derived from the original French version of the novel, *Couché dans le pain* (roughly, "Laid Out on Bread"; the first English title was *A Jealous Man Can't Win*). Like all of Himes's crime fiction involving Harlem detectives Grave Digger Jones and Coffin Ed Johnson, it was initially published by Gallimard in its *Série noire* paperback editions. Although now considered a major African American novelist, Himes didn't achieve widespread literary success until he moved to Paris during the period when Richard Wright and James Baldwin were there. He was born in Jefferson City, Missouri, in 1909, the son of middle-class academics who were in deep conflict with one another. His youth was rebellious and violent, and when he briefly attended college at Ohio State University he became an outlaw; he led black fraternity boys to a party at a local brothel, dropped out of college, passed bad checks, stole guns from a National Guard Armory, and was eventually convicted of the armed robbery of an elderly couple in the relatively affluent Cleveland neighborhood of Cleveland Heights. At age nineteen he was sentenced to twenty to twenty-five years of hard labor at an Ohio prison. While there, he began writing short stories, one of which was published by *Esquire* using his prison number—59623—as a nom de plume. In the late 1930s he was paroled and moved to California, where he worked in wartime industries in Los Angeles. On the basis of that experience, he wrote his first novel, *If He Hollers Let Him Go* (1945), which Mike Davis has aptly described as a "brilliant and disturbing analysis of the psychotic dynamics of racism in the land of sunshine" (1990, 43).

Himes's early novels were influenced by Richard Wright and can be categorized as social protest fiction involving criminal themes, although they have a distinctively mad, nightmarish quality. Underappreciated in America, Himes migrated to Paris in the early 1950s (leaving a wife behind) and made contact with Marcel Duhamel, the celebrated editor of the *Série noire*, who was also the French translator of *If He Hollers Let Him Go*. Duhamel commissioned him to write a crime novel in the hard-boiled manner of Hammett and Chandler, advising him to create vivid scenes and concentrate on action rather than psychology. Himes never acquired French (certainly not enough to write in the language), but Duhamel provided him with translators. Himes quickly wrote *La reine des pommes* (1958; later published in English as *A Rage in Harlem*), and as a result became the first non-French author to be awarded the *Grand Prix de la littérature policière*. This book inaugurated the series of Gravedigger/Coffin Ed detective novels, which, as Robert Polito (2001) has written, constitute "his most incisive, radical, and enduring fiction."

Himes never lived in Harlem for any length of time. The Harlem setting for his crime novels is largely imaginary and hallucinogenic, though he gives us accurate street names and convincingly realistic details. (For an informative essay about the place by one of its natives, written not long before Himes arrived in Paris, see Baldwin 1955.) "The Harlem of my books was never intended to be real," he recalls in *My Life of Absurdity*, his 1976 autobiography. But the question of realism is complex. At first, Himes says, "I thought I was writing realism. It never occurred to me that I was writing absurdity. Realism and absurdity are so similar in the lives of American blacks one cannot tell the difference." Ideas about the "Absurd" were of course au courant in Paris at the time Himes lived there and had influenced the work of Sartre, Camus, and Beckett. But the absurdity in Himes's novels isn't philosophical or abstract in the manner of the French; the surreal or blackly comic quality of his work originates in all-too-real social and political conditions that he and other black Americans experienced. His Harlem novels are steamy caldrons of prostitutes, junkies, thieves, alleyway killers, fake preachers, brutal cops, stool pigeons, chorus girls, ex-cons, hucksters, and characters with names like Deep South, Pigmeat, Baby Sis, Doll Baby, Acey, Deucy, and Chink Charlie. ("I would swear this is a list of circus acts," a cop says in Burnett's screenplay.) The atmosphere is carnivalesque and the plots zany, but the novels succeed as metaphors for the violence of American life. Whatever he intended, Himes was writing social realism by another means.

Some of the Harlem detective novels were adapted by black directors in Hollywood before Burnett wrote his script, but none of the adaptations fully conveys the tough, edgy, dark-side-of-town quality that makes Himes a noir master; on the contrary, they have more in common with the blaxploitation cycle that Burnett and his UCLA cohort rebelled against. The best is Ossie Davis's *Cotton Comes to Harlem* (1970), which was shot on location and has documentary value because of its colorful, detailed picture of the Harlem streets of that period. Unfortunately, it portrays Coffin Ed and Gravedigger (Raymond St. Jacques and Godfrey Cambridge) as extremely well-dressed types who look as if they've just stepped out of a Bond movie, and it contains too many 1970s-style car chases and flashy action. Its sequel, Mark Warren's *Come Back, Charleston Blue* (aka *The Heat's On*, 1972), is more of the same. Bill Duke's *A Rage in Harlem* (1991), starring Danny Glover, Gregory Hines, Forest Whittaker, and Robin Givens, might have been an important exception, but it was shot in Cleveland and suffered from tension between Duke and his producers.

We can only imagine what kind of film Burnett would be likely to achieve, but his screenplay gives every indication that he wants to capture the original period flavor (one of the characters watches *Queen for a Day* on TV) and the gritty, almost claustrophobic feel of Himes's novel, which for all its absurdity has certain things in common with the ghetto James Baldwin had described in his well-known essay on Harlem: "The buildings are old and in desperate need of repair, the streets are crowded and dirty, there are too many human beings per square block. . . . All of Harlem is pervaded by a sense of congestion, rather like the insistent, maddening, claustrophobic pounding in the skull that comes from trying to breathe in a very small room with all the windows shut" (1955, 57). Burnett is also much better than previous adapters at retaining and often enhancing the particular kind of wit and dark humor in Himes's work.

Burnett's screenplay is a straight rendition of the plot of *Couché dans le pain/The Crazy Kill*, preserving some of Himes's dialogue, adding or substituting equally good lines, and in places condensing the action. It is, however, more pointedly concerned with racism. One striking difference is that the best-known characters, precinct detectives Coffin Ed and Gravedigger, are named "Ice Water" and "Sharecropper." When Burnett sought rights to the novel, they were owned by the Goldwyn Company, which at one point had wanted to produce a picture based on *The Crazy Kill*. Goldwyn was no longer interested in the film and told Burnett that he could get the rights from Himes's literary agent, Roslyn Tag; the only catch was that Goldwyn wanted to retain the rights to the names Coffin Ed and Gravedigger for possible future use. Burnett had to invent new names, but this is no great loss, because his conception of the characters is much truer to Himes than previous movies have been. Far from the natty dressers depicted in *Cotton Comes to Harlem* and *Come Back, Charleston Blue*, the Himes duo are "tall, lanky colored men dressed in black mohair suits that looked as though they'd been slept in" (Himes 1973, 29). Almost half of Coffin Ed's (Sharecropper's in Burnett) face has been horribly scarred by an acid thrower, and his temper is so violent that his partner repeatedly needs to calm him down. This is not a good cop/bad cop act. Both men are as jaded and tough as they look, and they have no problem with using "extra-legal" measures, such as a punch to the mouth or solar plexus, to get information. In Himes and in Burnett's screenplay, the two detectives put handcuffs on a suspect's hands and ankles, suspend him upside down from the top edge of an open door, and apply pressure with their feet to his armpits until he talks. All the while, other cops are calmly at work beyond the open door.

Gravedigger and Coffin Ed (hereafter Ice Water and Sharecropper, and all quotes are from Burnett's screenplay) are more prominent characters in some of the Harlem novels than in others. In this novel, as in Burnett's screenplay, they have important roles but aren't the center of interest; in fact, they're a step behind in the discovery of a murderer. The more important character, and the reason for Burnett's interest in the novel as a "love story," is Johnny Perry, a veteran of a Georgia chain gang who, in his youth, killed his stepfather. Johnny has become a figure to be reckoned with in Harlem: a smooth, smart, laconic, bejeweled gambler who owns a small club named Tia Juana at the corner of 124th and Madison. He drives a cream-colored Cadillac convertible, and Harlem kids gather around in awe whenever he appears. He has an intelligent Harlem lawyer, and the police defer to him. Everybody else drinks booze, but he drinks lemonade. You wouldn't want to play cards with him and wouldn't want to make him angry; nevertheless, he doesn't cheat at cards and has a sense of personal ethics. In some ways he resembles the shady heroes of Raymond Chandler's early pulp fiction, who behave with sangfroid under pressure. His only problem, besides being a suspect in a murder he didn't commit, is his wife Dulcy, a sexy, heavy-drinking young woman who dresses to please men; a former cabaret singer, Dulcy loves Johnny but makes him very jealous, and she, too, is a suspect. Ultimately, he needs to become a sort of detective to find out who committed a murder and just how innocent she might be.

Burnett's screenplay, like Himes's novel, begins at 4:00 A.M. in front of an A&P grocery in Harlem, where a robbery takes place. A truckload of groceries has just been delivered outside the store, including a big wicker basket full of bread, and a black cop is guarding the groceries. The cop sees the nearby robbers and gives chase. Johnny Perry's Cadillac convertible pulls up to the curb (Burnett notes that a small shrunken head is hanging from the rearview mirror) and Val Valentine Haines, Dulcy's so-called brother and a friend of Perry, gets out of the passenger side. Meanwhile, three stories above in Mamie Pullen's crowded living room, a wake is being held for her husband, Big Joe. Describing the scene, Burnett writes, "It would look more like an after-hours party catering to gamblers, numbers men, and women who have been used up by life and men, if it were not for the open casket." Ten people are present, including a musical trio playing a blues version of an old spiritual, "Steal Away." (No doubt one reason Burnett is attracted to the project is the jazz, blues, and spiritual music that permeates the novel; he adds more of it.) A good deal of sexual tension circulates among the women in the room because a handsome fellow named Chink Charlie has been paying too much attention to Dulcy. As Chink Charlie exits to find a few sticks of marijuana, one of the "mourners," a Holy Roller preacher named Reverend Short, who has been imbibing from a bottle of "nerve medicine," stands at a bedroom window and observes the robbery taking place below. When the thieves take flight, he leans out too far and falls from the window, dropping three stories and landing in the basket of bread. After a few moments he revives, adjusting his glasses and making his way back up to the wake. When he explains what happened, the party guests are skeptical and go to the bedroom window to have a look. Down below, a dead body is lying atop the bread basket: it's Val Haines, with a hand-tooled English dagger in his heart.

The party from the wake runs out to the street and cops arrive, followed by Ice Water and Sharecropper. Three characters see the two Harlem detectives coming toward them:

PIGMEAT: Detectives Ice Water and Sharecropper.

CHINK: Yeah, Buck and Bubbles.

DEEP SOUTH: Man, you're asking for an ass whuppen.

A cop turns to the crowd gathered around the body: "Anybody see anything? [Before anyone can answer he quickly gives up in disgust.] Of course not." Johnny Perry and everyone at the wake are taken in for questioning, and we meet the chief characters, who are called one by one into a small interrogation room, where an Irish detective named Brody is assisted by Ice Water and Sharecropper. Mamie Pullen, Big Joe's wife, recognizes Ice Water as "little Timmy Waters," a kid she knew long ago. Reverend Short claims he's had a "vision" of the killer. Alamena, an attractive older woman who was Johnny Perry's first wife, can't help with anything. Chink Charlie tries to act like a smart aleck ("You're going to find yourself tripping down some stairs," Brody says). Chink's girlfriend Doll Baby, a nightclub dancer who dresses provocatively, tries to give him an alibi. Dulcy, also a provocative dresser, is accompanied by Johnny Perry's lawyer and defends Johnny. At one point Burnett cuts away to a holding tank for the suspects, where Johnny Perry glances at Chink Charlie across the room:

Johnny sits with his legs crossed, with his eyes half-closed, yet still very much awake. The band [from the wake] is staying in practice doing a little a cappella blues. Deep South and Susie Q. beat out a ham bone rhythm on their legs. The white cop is irritated by the noise.

COP: You people just can't sit still.

DEEP SOUTH (*looking at the cop, decides to be nice*): That's how I make a living, young man.

COP: In some hole in the wall joint where people get their throats cut?

DEEP SOUTH: Mister, ain't no call for that.

Johnny, giving one leg a rest, crosses the other leg very neatly. He holds his hands out in front of him, looking at them for a moment, and puts one hand back in his coat pocket.

COP: I grew up in the South.

PIGMEAT: We knew that without you telling us.

Chink leans over, fingering his hat, stares at the pocket Johnny's got his hand in.

Eventually Johnny is called into the interrogation room, accompanied by his lawyer. Brody asks questions, without much result:

Brody and Johnny exchange stares for a moment, both poker-faced and unmoving.

BRODY: Okay, boy, you can go now.

JOHNNY *(getting to his feet)*: Fine. Just don't call me boy. I'm a man, and if anybody wants any peace they will remember it.

BRODY *(face turning red)*: Is that a threat?

JOHNNY *(Points to Ice Water and Sharecropper)*: Ask these gentlemen

Given that *Man in a Basket* is a detective story, I won't spoil things by saying much more about the plot. In any case that isn't necessary, because Chester Himes is the kind of artist (as are Hammett, Chandler, and Burnett) for whom scene is as important as, if not more than, plot. One of the many excitements of Burnett's screenplay is the opportunity it would give him to stage sinister and humorous scenes dealing with Harlem culture and the unforgettable minor characters that populate Himes. By way of illustration, I offer a description of a couple of scenes that not only contribute to plot development but also provide Harlem atmosphere and interaction among several characters. Notice the prevalence of music in both; it occasionally serves as indirect commentary on the characters' feelings, in nearly the same way as classic Hollywood musicals.

Just before Big Joe's funeral, Johnny, his lawyer, Dulcy, and Alamena go to lunch at Fats' Down Home Restaurant, a small, narrow place with a neon sign depicting a man shaped like a hippopotamus. Inside are a bar, a dining room with eight tables, a juke box, and a sawdust-covered floor. The place is populated by what Burnett calls "people of the trade." "What say, Pee Wee," Johnny says to the extremely tall bartender. "Just standing here and moaning low, Pops," the bartender replies as he flourishes a glass and offers Johnny a drink on the house. Johnny orders a pitcher of lemonade. Fats, the owner, a completely hairless man wearing a silk shirt with a diamond collar button and pants that aren't big enough, greets Johnny with a wheezing whisper: "They tell me big Joe got a smile on his face." Johnny answers, "I guess he likes it, wherever he is." The cook sticks his head out of the kitchen and waves at Johnny: "Hiyuh, Pops." When Johnny and his companions sit in the dining room, Dulcy wants a Singapore sling. Johnny glares at her and she settles for brandy and soda. The lawyer wants iced tea and an order of brains and eggs with biscuits. Johnny asks for "the same as always." The waitress puts a nickel in the juke box (music unspecified), and everybody watches as a couple begins to dance.

Chink Charlie comes in with Doll Baby, who is wearing a dress exactly like Dulcy's, and they sit at a table across the room. The entire joint becomes tense, but Johnny ignores the newcomers. Dulcy says she wants the waitress to play Jelly Roll Morton's "I Want a Little Girl to Call My Own." Doll Baby begins talking loudly to Chink: "After all, Val was my fiancé. . . . And if truth be known, he was just knifed to keep me from having him." This drives Dulcy into a fury, and Johnny has to grab her and push her back down in her chair; looking at Chink, he shouts, "Keep her damn mouth shut!" Chink says, "Keep her quiet your damn self." For a moment it seems like an incipient fight or shoot-out in a Western saloon; Johnny stands up, Doll Baby runs for the kitchen, and Pee Wee moves toward Johnny, saying "Easy, Pops." Fats appears, waddles over to Chink, and orders him out: "And never come in here no more either." He pushes Chink to the door: "You're lucky, lucky, lucky. Get out of here before your luck runs out."

Not long afterward all the suspects attend Big Joe's crowded funeral at Reverend Short's Holy Roller church. Reverend Short jumps up and down behind the pulpit, working up a sweat; the Grand Wizard of Joe's lodge, dressed in gold braid, presides over a group of pallbearers; middle-aged church women in white uniforms pass out fans; and Ice Water and Sharecropper stand at the back of the church in dark glasses, "looking mean." Reverend Short begins a eulogy with his regular churchgoers chanting choral support ("Lord have mercy, the trouble I've witnessed"), but the Reverend soon begins screaming in a frenzy, accusing Dulcy of being a murderess and a fornicating adulteress. Dulcy yells back at him, and Johnny restrains her, remarking, "Somebody needs to throw some cold water on these holy rollers." The Reverend keeps pointing a finger at Dulcy as the organist begins playing "Nearer My God to Thee" and the congregation calms down. Mourners file by the casket, and the pallbearers, led by Johnny, carry it out to a hearse. The band plays "The Coming of John," changing the beat to swing time and causing the departing congregation to step to the music. Ice Water and Sharecropper are left alone in the church. "These are your people," Ice Water says, and Sharecropper replies, "No they ain't."

These tense confrontations cause trouble between Johnny and Dulcy; as the plot takes twists and turns, he not only becomes suspicious of her (in the past he had given her a fancy knife exactly like the one used to stab Val Haines) but also begins to feel that she or somebody else is trying to frame him for the murder. Dulcy's drinking accelerates, followed by an almost violent fight—Johnny breaks his glass of lemonade, knocks over a table, and tries to kick Dulcy's dog, Spookie—and later by a sex scene in which Dulcy creates a sultry mood by singing the blues. Frustrated by her behavior, Johnny suspects that she's trying to get money from him and run away with Chink Charlie. He's willing to let her leave, but she doesn't try. All this causes him to investigate the crime while Ice Water and Sharecropper are conducting their own investigation. Ultimately, he locks the drunken, sleeping Dulcy in her room, gets in his Cadillac, and drives at high speed all the way to the south side of Chicago to find out something about Dulcy's life as a singer before he met her.

Arriving in the morning, he visits The Dynamite Club, where blues singer Stavin Chain is onstage in his underwear, ironing his suit and singing to himself ("The Blues met me this morning, Lord, my baby told me she loves another man . . . cause my cream kaint lighten her coffee and my jelly roll ain't sweet no more"). "You came all the way to Chicago about a woman," Chain observes. "Man, you got it bad." Next Johnny goes to the Club Alabam and talks with Big N Small, who is armed with an ice pick:

JOHNNY: You don't need that ice pick.

BIG N SMALL: You don't know this neighborhood.

JOHNNY: Why don't you get a gun?

BIG N SMALL: In my years of experience, this will make a fool straighten up faster than a gun will.

Then Johnny goes to see a sixty-year old musician named Blind Billy, who shares his tiny apartment with a parrot in a towel-covered cage. To Johnny's delight, Blind Billy happens to have lemonade. He advises Johnny to go on about his life. "If life wasn't so damned crazy, I could," Johnny says. Blind Billy replies, "Boy, life never made any sense."

The information Johnny gets in Chicago clears up certain mysteries but not others. He finally discovers the chief culprit, arriving at the scene just before Ice Water and Sharecropper and barely preventing another murder. Like many noir narratives, this one ends in relatively spectacular fashion. I've left out a great deal of information and skipped over many excellent scenes, merely trying to indicate that the screenplay is exceptionally promising as an adventure, a muted social commentary, and a kind of love story. It may seem odd that a writer/director who began his career in rebellion against movies about blacks as gangsters, prostitutes, and drug dealers would later want to make a film centered on the black underworld. Burnett's film, however, would be different. In his screenplay the sex is consensual; the violence, except for the violence of cops plus one scene involving a shotgun in which nobody gets hurt, is sparing; the vividly demotic and often humorous dialogue has almost no cursing or profanity; and the only evidence of drugs is a bit of marijuana and a police stoolie who is a heroin addict. All the emphasis is on environment, atmosphere, and character. One can only hope that this, the most brilliant adaptation of Himes, will someday be seen by audiences.

FOURTEEN

In His Element

THREE SHORT FILMS AND AN EPILOGUE

IN A 2007 INTERVIEW WITH James Ponsoldt, Burnett remarked, "I see film as more of an art form than a commercial thing." He brought that attitude to student filmmaking at UCLA, and it still motivates his work. As we have seen, that doesn't mean that he's been unwilling to compromise with commercial interests. No filmmaker who isn't independently wealthy or supported by governments, foundations, or patron-controlled museums can afford to be indifferent to investors or ticket sales. Nor does it mean that Burnett regards art as somehow beyond entertainment and above politics. In the same interview, he elaborated on his position: "To share experiences— that's what art is for. . . . I think because I come from a segregated experience, there's a need to tell stories other than mainstream stories" (Kapsis 2011, 159).

Apart from his early films, Burnett has been farthest from commercial dealings and most free to share his experiences and convictions when he has made relatively short pictures involving a minimal crew. These pictures are important not only because they have artistic value, but also because they rise out of what might be called Burnett's original or instinctive element: they're street-level narratives produced with few resources, centering on people whose lives are outside the mainstream. In some cases they have reinvigorated his love of the medium. In a discussion with Susan Gerhard about *When It Rains*, he commented on the pleasure that short film gave him: "When you finish a [commercial] film, you want to do something that's yours. We had the use of a camera, and a group of us just shot this film over a couple of days. It was kind of therapeutic and refreshing" (Kapsis 2011, 179). In an interview with Aida A. Hozic, he pondered the reasons the group he worked with at UCLA no longer work collectively to make inexpensive, personal films:

Perhaps we are all trying to be practical, trying to survive.... If there was some institution or just a house where we could all get together and make movies—perhaps it would be different. Perhaps. That's what I would like the most.... The other thing that happened—I was talking to Haile [Gerima] recently—is that as you start making bigger movies, you get caught up in a certain way of doing things and removed from the independent friends that you had earlier. You forget how much you could do with how little and have to be reminded of how much can be done without this whole steamroller and budgeting behind you. And realizing it you start looking around and finding other avenues. (Kapsis 2011, 92)

Here I discuss three examples of Burnett's "other avenues." The three are different from one another but have important features in common: they were written, directed, shot, and edited by Burnett; they deal with poor people struggling to survive in a mostly uncaring world; and their anger at social injustice is given strength by sweetly melancholic humor and savage wit.

WHEN IT RAINS (2007)

The best of Burnett's short films and one of his best films period, the thirteen-minute *When It Rains* was shot in Watts and in Leimert Park, a virtually all-black community in south Los Angeles that has poor to middle-class residents and a somewhat bohemian atmosphere. The film is a friends-and-family affair, with a cast that includes Burnett's two sons, Billy Woodberry, Charles Bracy (who worked with Burnett on *Several Friends* and *Killer of Sheep*), and Bracy's wife and two children. The philosophical, good-hearted narrator and central character is acted by Ayuko Babu, the founding director of the Los Angeles Pan-African Film Festival, who is a large, gentle man with a pleasant face and a deep, resonant voice. A self-styled griot (the West African term for traveling musicians, poets, storytellers, and oral historians), this character tells the story of his New Year's Day travels around Leimert Park and its environs in an attempt to raise cash contributions for a single mother and her daughter who are about to be evicted because of overdue rent. Although the story concerns a troubling situation, it has humorous elements, and like many good jokes or folktales, it ends with a surprise twist and a kind of punchline.

When It Rains could also be termed a jazz fable. Burnett told Terence Rafferty that it was "just a little movie about blues and jazz I made with some friends of mine: we got a camera, put all the equipment in a Volkswagen, and we shot here and there and took advantage of everything we saw." Rafferty describes it as a movie that "feels improvised but, as in a great jazz solo, every note counts and the shape of the whole is irreducible, inevitable. It's a song about survival—that's the blues component—and you can't get the melody out of your head" (Kapsis 2011, 123–24). Music is both a theme of the story and a pervasive element: the griot is a jazz player; African drums accompany jazz at a local festival; a virtuoso trumpeter plays jazz on the sidewalk; and Burnett's frequent collaborator Stephen James Taylor provides musical support for the whole, composing a jazz number over the closing credits. Jonathan Rosenbaum, an early champion of Burnett and a jazz aficionado, has called *When It Rains* one of the best examples of jazz aesthetics in the movies: "It's one of those rare movies in which jazz forms directly influence film narrative" (2004, 286).

The film begins with a sadly amusing shot: a partly decorated Christmas tree is tossed over a red, graffiti-covered wall and lands on a curb. "Christmas gift!" a deep voice shouts from behind the wall, and gold tinsel on the tree flickers in the sunny California breeze. Next are three successive close-ups of nonactors, a couple of them in African garb, who give the film a quasi-documentary flavor. They look straight into the camera and say, "Don't take my picture!" The voice of the griot narrator (the same voice we heard from behind the wall) comments, "Obviously they don't want their pictures taken. You'd be trying to steal their soul." His story proper then opens with a mother banging on her landlord's door as her daughter stands behind her. "A new year," the narrator says. "Trouble already." When nobody answers the door, the mother instructs her silent, frowning daughter to wait and not move while she goes for help.

"We live with contradictions," the narrator comments as the mother crosses a Watts bridge and catches a local train (the Watts Towers can be glimpsed in the distance). "How do you mix jazz and blues together? Part is in darkness, the other half faces the sunlight." He laments that young people today don't seem to know that both jazz and blues have their roots in African percussive music. At this remark we cut from the mother's plight, which is a blues subject, to the main square of Leimert Park, where a New Year's Day flea market and jazz concert are in progress. Burnett covers the event like a documentary, with a montage of convivial faces in the crowd. A row of drummers in African dress and a boy in jeans beat out a rhythm, and one of the spectators—a very heavy woman in a loose, African-patterned blouse—launches into an amazingly graceful dance. The distraught mother finds the griot in the midst of this gathering, having a friendly chat with another spectator, and pleads for his help. A tall, bespectacled figure in a dashiki and dreadlocks, he immediately comes to her aid, leaving the festivities and going with her to meet the landlord. After more pounding on the door, the landlord answers. "Brother, I'd like to talk to you about this sister's situation," the griot says. "Her situation is she's behind in her rent," says the landlord. "I can't take it no more. I just can't take it!" The landlord says he'll wait until the end of the day and closes the door. The griot turns to the mother and calms her. "Forget about this fool," he advises and goes in search of the rent money.

The remainder of the film is concerned with the griot's travels around the area, sometimes in his car, sometimes on foot, to ask different people for contributions. He has a charmingly sincere demeanor and the gift of gab; narrating offscreen and chatting with potential contributors, he provides a vocal bass line for individual, largely improvised "solo" performances. As Rosenbaum puts it, "Each person he goes to see registers like a separate chorus in a 12-bar blues" (2004, 286). First he goes to the woman's ex-husband Charles, who, he explains to us, "was never right in the head" after serving jail time for "resisting the draft and refusing to go to Vietnam and joining the Black Panther Party." Charles, wearing a suit and tie as he polishes his car, simply mumbles incoherently. "I can see the brother's somewhere else," the griot tells us, and proceeds to a man named Soul, who has a heart weighing "less than a feather" and is "good people." Soul is in his back yard working on a wrecked car while his young son puts a hand in his armpit and flaps his arm to make fart sounds. Soul contributes some money and says, "Glad I had a little left over." Next the griot goes to an unseen lady's apartment; we hear only her voice as she shouts through the door and forces him to beat a quick retreat: "Don't tell me about other people in need! No, I can't help you. You're always looking for a handout!"

Walking past a playground, the griot meets a mother holding the hand of her small child. She can't talk about money because the child starts screaming and she needs to find him a bathroom. A kid with a basketball comes along and the griot tells him, "You gonna keep playing ball, you gonna get dumb." The kid says, "Shut up, old man." On the street, the griot approaches a slender, gangster type in coat, tie, and dark shades who is engaged in an intense conversation with another man. The griot and the gangster exchange a bit of jive talk, and when the gangster hears about the woman in need he says smoothly that he can solve the problem: "I gotta guy owes me a favor. We'll take him out!" The griot cautiously extricates himself from the

conversation and goes farther down the street, where he finds a friendly man in African garb standing in front of a shop he runs. The shopkeeper makes a contribution, but just then we hear a shout: "Hey, man! You owe me money!" The voice belongs to a fellow who has obviously loaned money to the griot, and the griot has no choice but to turn over his cash.

The griot's last encounter is with "my main man, Juno," a little old man in a fancy hat and fur coat who stands on a street corner and blows an unusual trumpet that has a twisted shape and three separate horns. The griot asks if he can have his horn back, and the little old man pleads, "I'm not finished yet." "Just a couple of dollars," the griot says, and the trumpeter reaches under his arm and offers a record album instead. Taking the album, the frustrated griot goes back where he started, hoping to persuade the landlord to delay the eviction. He stands outside the landlord's door with the mother and child and starts to make a speech, when the landlord notices the album; it's John Handy's 1965 alto sax performance at the Monterey Jazz Festival, which jazz buffs regard as an important moment in alternative or vanguard music (several of the cuts on this album are much longer than Burnett's entire movie). The landlord smiles. "I'm hip to John Handy," he says, and the griot gives him the album in exchange for the rent.

The Good Samaritan-griot's quest ends not with money but with a bartered exchange typical of poor communities, not unlike the ones Burnett had illustrated in *Killer of Sheep* and the original screenplay of *To Sleep with Anger*. The woman and her daughter are saved not by the cash the griot has failed to raise, but by something of his own that he freely gives. It's a moment of happy chance and jazz serendipity. "Damn!" the griot says in the last line of his narration. "I'm glad I didn't have a rap album in my hand!"

Burnett cuts to the little old man with the trumpet. Still on the street corner, he plays a masterful solo full of tricky passages that are far better heard than described.

THE FINAL INSULT (1997)

Financed by South German television's *Das Kleine Fernsehspiel* (The little teleplay) and shot on digital video, *The Final Insult* is a grim, fifty-five-minute film about homelessness in Los Angeles, combining documentary and fiction in unorthodox, experimental fashion. The fictional story centers on Box Brown, a part-time accountant named after a legendary slave who escaped by mailing himself north in a box. As in *When It Rains*, the central character is played by Ayuko Babu; he narrates the story and his deep-voiced line readings give the already effective language a poetic quality.

At the opening of the film, Brown, his hair neatly trimmed, dressed in the white shirt and conservative tie of an office worker, is driving into Los Angeles in his rattling old Dodge sedan and singing snippets of the blues: "The eagle flies on Friday, / and Saturday I go out and play. / Sunday I go to church, / and I kneel down to pray." As Brown segues into a few bars of "See, See Rider" and enters the city, the camera tracks a considerable distance along the sidewalk to show disturbing documentary footage of dozens of homeless people sleeping on the concrete, some under shabby blankets, some in makeshift tents, and a few in cardboard-box shelters. "If a whale is beached up," Brown's voice says, "everybody cries in alarm. When I was beached up, everybody looked the other way." More documentary footage shows the homeless waking to a new day, putting their few possessions in plastic bags, and moving toward a huge line outside a food center. Brown continues: "When O.J. was found guilty, the landlord raised my rent." He tells us that the IRS also charged him with fantastically high penalties for five-year-old unpaid taxes. But he doesn't blame his situation entirely on white backlash. "It was my fault, abandoning the tools my mother gave me," he says. He only wonders how a sharecropper's son could have found himself in such huge debt. "It was so easy to lose everything," he laments. "Between heartbeats you could be on the street."

When Brown reaches the busiest, most prosperous area of Sunset Boulevard, his rattletrap car breaks down. Here, as in much of the rest of the film, the sound track is filled with the ambient noise of traffic, recorded wild and contributing to a tense documentary atmosphere. The scene is photographed with a telephoto lens, so that people on the sidewalk are less aware of the presence of a camera. Stopped in the middle of the street near Tower Records and in front of Sunset Plaza, Brown gets out of the car, raises the hood, and begins working on the engine while other vehicles circulate around him. An affluent crowd dining outside under umbrellas completely ignores him. A passerby offers assistance, but Brown manages to start the car and goes on his way to work.

Arriving at a small branch office of The Bank of America, Brown sits at a desk and goes over accounts. "I have to tell these people how to make money and I don't have a dime to my name," his narrating voice says. He nevertheless plays the role of a loyal slave to capital, ironically showing the bank "how to save by laying off permanent employees." After checking through a pile of papers on his desk, he tells the bank manager in a sincere voice totally lacking in irony that she can avoid paying health insurance for workers and get tax benefits if she changes to temporary staff. "It's perfect for our setup," he explains, because there are plenty of job candidates out on the street. "Just bring them in here, send them out there, work 'em like everybody else does." In his offscreen narration, he confides, "People I work for don't even know my home is in my car. My biggest fear is ending up pushing a shopping cart."

Grim as the film is, there are moments of humor. Brown goes into a small liquor store to play the lottery and asks the Hispanic clerk, "Señor, what's the lucky numbers today?" Hesitantly, the clerk replies, "I'm liked three and nine." Jazz can be heard in the shop as Brown fills out the lottery slip and then wanders over to examine a long row of skin magazines: "Look at some of these girls! Lord, lord, lord!" He pulls out one of the zines and complains, "They started putting plastic over them." Going down the row, he notices, "The white girls looking good today. The white girls' butts getting bigger! Maybe that's a trick photograph."

A more sweetly amusing scene involves a recurring character, a bearded fellow who collects aluminum cans in a shopping cart and sells them for a bit of change at a recycling center. Early in the film we see him wearing sun-glasses, a pair of old striped Bermuda shorts, flip-flops, and a shirt that barely covers his belly. He comes down a sidewalk with his cart, checking a garbage can, and notices three nicely dressed young Korean ladies who are standing at the corner, talking to one another in Korean. He stops nearby and begins singing a traditional Korean song in a beautifully trained voice. Stunned, the ladies listen with amazement and begin giggling. They ask where he's from and he smiles and says "around here." They want to know how he learned Korean, and he tells them that he simply memorized some old records. "You have very good pronunciation!" one of the ladies says. He repeats a couple of Korean proverbs and says he can't remember the one that goes, "You always meet your enemy on a narrow bridge." They instruct him how to say it and giggle wildly.

At other places in the film we hear this same fellow singing a German *lied*, the French "Cantique de Noël" ("O Holy Night"), and "Danny Boy," all in a powerful voice. Is he for real? Is he homeless, or an impoverished eccentric who wanders the streets? The credits for the film identify him simply as Misha. His scenes were clearly staged, using nonprofessional actors, but they have an improvised quality and an air of documentary authenticity that make their exact status unclear. Similar ontological questions arise with another recurring character, a sweet-faced old lady on the street, identified as Maya Dawson in the credits, who tries to sell a random, pathetic mixture of things she has collected: a bowl, a broken candle, a piece of origami, a half-empty bottle of bubble-blowing solution, and a few other items. She spreads her wares on a blanket, obsessively arranges and rearranges them, and smiles at passersby, most of whom ignore her. She's harmless and appealing, but she seems mentally ill. A Korean lady eventually stops and charitably behaves like an interested customer, allowing the old woman to demonstrate bubble-blowing. She buys the almost empty bottle of suds.

The question of the status of these two characters arises because they occupy an ambiguous position between the fictional and documentary poles of the film. Box Brown's fictional story gives the film an overarching unity but is often interrupted when Burnett cuts away for a series of talking-head interviews with people on the street. In these cases we're entirely in a documentary world. The filmed subjects acknowledge the presence of the camera, but we don't hear the questions they're asked. When they speak, there's no reason to suspend disbelief in their reality and think of them as actors. Following are four examples.

A shirtless young man who might be of Polynesian ancestry stands at a freeway entrance near beggars who are trying to get money from passing motorists and makes a speech to the camera in solidarity with them: "There's something wrong with America today. . . . We're in dire need of help here. Go to a welfare unit and ask how many veterans are in line. The freeway in front of me, this morning they came and cleared it out because they knew this film company was going to come here. I believe the film's name is *The Final Insult*. And if you ask me if I was to vote for the next President I might as well vote for Jerry Lewis."

A white woman of indeterminate age who has, dark, fatigued rings around her eyes sits on a bench beside a shopping cart piled with newspapers. She tells the camera that her husband left her and got custody of their children; she could live with her sister, she says, but the sister is "too religious" and "I'm a free spirit." She's better off than some, she insists, because she has epilepsy and gets a monthly check for health expense. The camera zooms in as she turns her head away and withdraws into a solitary world of despair.

Beside a highway, a young white man holds a cardboard sign asking for money and the woman with him, who sounds Hispanic, makes a slurred, histrionic speech to the camera. Wearing a Betty Boop T-shirt and baggy shorts, she holds a pair of flat shoes in her hand: "I can't get a job. Where's my pills? Where's my home at now? See my shoes? . . . I would appreciate it if I get my pills back and my clothes back. My husband passed away about four months ago. Taking my kids away, that hurt me a lot. . . . Will you help me? Hunh? We had to move up that way, where the drug addicts are."

A black man with a graying beard, several missing teeth, and a cigarette-husky voice sits near a curb in his undershirt and talks eloquently about the loss of manufacturing jobs. "Most people are probably a couple of paychecks away from being in this same situation," he says. "There is no genuine sense of community. Some people lose their faith and integrity. People are maligned because of drugs and alcohol." Credit cards contribute to the problem, he explains, because "we Americans are accustomed to immediate gratification."

The film mixes scenes such as these with the story of Box Brown, shifting back and forth between two clearly marked registers that complement one another. In addition to documentary footage of homeless people sleeping on the street, it includes a tour of an aid facility where food is handed out to indigent men, women, and children. "Hey, we're going to be on TV!" one of the men shouts. "How much are we getting paid?" But the documentary and fictional parts of the film have an uneasy relationship with the scenes involving the multilingual singer and the old lady selling trinkets, which raise questions about their veracity. (There is also a scene that looks like convincing documentary evidence but, according to the credits, was acted. In it a mother sleeps on an empty bench near a bus stop while her small child restlessly hangs around the edge of the bench; the credits to the film identify her as Florence Bracy and her son as Brad Bracy, both of whom were actors in *When It Rains*.) Burnett has often made films that mix documentary and fiction or that blur the boundaries between them in interesting ways, but in this case, even though there's no reason to doubt the film's sincerity and the fact that poverty and homelessness are an appalling disgrace to America, I can't decide whether the acted/not acted distinction should have been more evident.

The Box Brown story is a convincing demonstration of the struggle to survive in a hostile environment in which one can lose everything "between heart beats." He sleeps in his car, bathes from a plastic bucket, and makes sandwiches with Wonder Bread and baloney. His brother Reggie, who has recently been tested for AIDs, lives under a highway overpass, and in order to persuade Reggie to go to the doctor Brown crawls up a dangerous, forty-five-degree concrete buttress wearing business clothes and carrying his briefcase. But Reggie refuses to talk, saying he's going to die anyway. At another point Brown is making a sandwich on the hood of his car when a burly young black man approaches with a shopping cart (the film's most persistent motif). The fellow asks for money, and Brown says he hasn't any, but can offer food. This enrages the young man. "All you got to do is give me the money!" he says and slams a big fist into Brown's rib cage. Brown falls and the man keeps beating him. "Where's the money, man?" the assailant says, going through Brown's pockets and looking around to make sure there's no witness. "Old-ass motherfucker, give me the money!" Frustrated, he throws the bread and baloney on Brown's prostrate body and walks away.

The greater disaster and penultimate insult comes when Brown's car breaks down completely in a quiet, prosperous-looking neighborhood where nobody comes to his aid. Somehow both he and the car wind up in a hobo camp of older men, where he loans a box of salt to a communal cook and has friendly conversations with one of his fellow campers. Soon, however, the film shifts into a new mode, more Godard-like than realistic. We've already had a portent of this change in an earlier scene, when a couple of aggressive young rappers, unrelated to the rest of the film, face the camera and go into an angry, almost nihilistic routine. Here at the end, a group of young men are drinking beer when Brown approaches them and argues that a revolutionary,

Watts-like "burn down" is needed to overcome the forces arrayed against the poor. In response, they and the rappers we've seen before attack Brown and lay his dying body on a shopping cart. Unlike the earlier attack, this one looks unreal, as if the film were making an emblematic or purely allegorical comment on the self-destructive alienation of poor black youth. A dreamlike scene follows, showing Brown atop the cart in his white shirt and tie. The hands of a couple of unseen people hold candles over him in memoriam. The film doesn't seem to be advocating a Watts-style conflagration, but it implies that the social fabric has deteriorated even more than in the days of the Watts riots, and that without some radical, communal action the inevitable result is death.

QUIET AS KEPT (2007)

The shortest and most amusing of the three films is the five-minute *Quiet as Kept*, which deals with the US government's response to Hurricane Katrina, a disaster in 2006 that devastated poor areas of New Orleans and permanently uprooted many black families. At one point in the film, a beleaguered father, who with his wife and son has been displaced by the storm, says, "I'd like to know what idiot said that laughter is the best remedy for pain." I don't know who the idiot was, but several people who weren't idiots—among them Hegel and Freud—have argued that a certain kind of humor, sometimes called (ironically in this case) "black humor," is an important, even noble way of surviving amid "outrageous fortune." This film proves their point and is also a pointed, self-reflexive comment on the movies.

Quiet as Kept was Burnett's contribution to a series of films in honor of Mable Haddock, the head of the New Orleans Black Film Consortium. It takes the form of a mini, alternative-style situation comedy in which a Louisiana father, wife, and teenage son have a conversation about their new life in Texas. Like other black residents of New Orleans, they have been scattered around and given insufficient money to get back home or even pay day-to-day expenses. They feel trapped, unfamiliar with their surroundings, and fearful of strangers or drive-by shootings. The short, three-way dialogue that constitutes the entire film is both sad and funny, and the three actors are an actual family from Mississippi: the teenager is Nathaniel Lee Jr., who played the boy in *Warming by the Devil's Fire*; the father is Nathaniel Lee Sr., who was also in that film; and the mother is Sharial C. Lee.

At the opening, the father is working on his car outside a small apartment while his son, a typical bored adolescent in a baseball cap, is sitting on the front step. We hear the son's weary offscreen narration, giving us his thoughts about the father, who, he says, is always talking about "little-ass this and little-ass that," as in "his little-ass check to buy groceries and put in his big-ass ice box." The mother returns from a trip to the grocery store, and the father goes inside to the kitchen, asking, "Where's my change? I need to buy an oil filter." But the mother has no change. Looking at the grocery receipt, the father says, "This can't be no hundred dollars' worth of groceries! That little-ass FEMA check sure don't go very far." He looks at the "little-ass" loaf of bread, which he's amazed to find costs six dollars, and remembers the good old days when such things cost seventy-five cents. Back outside, he returns to work on the car, telling the son that they can't go to the movies tonight because his mother has spent all their money on groceries. "Can I go to the mall?" the son asks. The father asks how he's going to get there, and the son says he can take the bus. "No!" says the father. "That's how people get shot on them buses. . . . We're an endangered species!"

The son complains, "I want to go to the movies. I'm tired of sitting around the house." The father says, "Movies cost too much. It's eleven dollars now!" The mother steps outside and suggests family entertainment the old-fashioned way, by going for a walk around the block. But that, too, is deemed too dangerous. She then joins in the conversation about movies. Katrina, she says, might has well have been called *Gone with the Wind*. "We better have a Plan B," she warns. "Them rich white folks, they don't want us in New Orleans." The son pipes up, "I want to see *Star Wars*." The father, still working on the car, frowns. "There ain't no black folks in *Star Wars*," he argues, and says his son would be better off watching "classics" like *The Mack* or *Superfly*. The mother objects: "Those aren't kid movies! They need to go see a *black* movie, something to make them proud—something like *The Cosby Show*!" The father scoffs: "That's like de-caffeinated coffee! You wouldn't know a good show if you saw it. I grew up on *Beulah* and *Amos and Andy*. Good stuff! Then, before that, we had *The Bronze Buckaroo*, *The Blood of Jesus*, and so forth. . . . We used to sit up in that area they called the crow's nest [the balcony of segregated theaters in the South]. Whole lot of fun if you could get over the lynching that was taking place."

The mother gets the last word in the argument, and Burnett is no doubt speaking through her about his own aims as a filmmaker. "A black movie," she says, "would have told us what's going to happen when Katrina hit. It would have told me where I stood in this country—just like Emmet Till told my father where he stood!" The father wants to drop the topic. "Why you want to blame all our problems on a little-ass movie?" he asks, and the film ends.

The father's dismissive comment at the end of *Quiet as Kept* has an obviously ironic relation to the picture we have been watching: a "little-ass" comic movie, but one that makes a strong comment about the state of the nation. Only one year later, the United States experienced its worse economic recession in history and elected its first black president, who accomplished many good things. But the presence of a black (in fact mixed-race) man in the White House set loose forces of reaction. Although the economy improved, a conservative Congress and Supreme Court stalled or reversed most attempts at progressive legislation; gun sales increased; a wave of police and civilian shootings of unarmed blacks spread across the country; the economic disparity between rich and poor grew larger than since the Gilded Age; skinheads and white supremacists became more visible and vocal; and in 2016 a neofascist administration was elected.

In such an environment, the films of Charles Burnett are more important than ever. He still has youthful energy, flexibility, and future projects in mind. As I write these words, he's been working on three films inspired by his social activism. The first is a documentary about the little-known history of the civil rights movement in US hospitals, which until 1965, especially in the South, were segregated and gave black patients inadequate treatment for serious injury and illness. (The same cruel racism was true of mental hospitals.) The second film is also a documentary, made for the Watts Community Action Labor Center to spread information about the extraordinarily high levels (over two hundred times the allowable amount) of mercury, lead, and other contaminants in the water supply of South Central Los Angeles—a problem that also affects Flint, Michigan, East Chicago, and other black-populated areas in the country. The third film, which Burnett has wanted to make for some years, began as a film about Barack Obama's mother, who was an early proponent of using microfinancing to help raise the status of women in developing countries. At one point Burnett and Albert Maysles were going to work together on a version of this film, which had the working title *Stanley Ann Dunham, a Most Generous Spirit*. Backers were enthusiastic, but according to Burnett the enthusiasm waned. As a result, he decided to write a more completely fictional screenplay on microfinancing, entitled *Faith and Credit*. He has described this film to Spanish interviewers as the story of a small town in the United States in which corporate money and politicians conspire to limit economic competition; a young female activist takes a job designed to help locals get microfinancing, but runs into opposition from established business interests (Miguez and Paz 2016, 89). Burnett's producer on the film is Carolyn Schroder, who was also his producer on *The Glass Shield*. She has told me that if things go as planned, production could begin at some point in 2017.

Burnett's career hasn't given him widespread fame, but as I hope this book has shown, it has developed against odds with a remarkable dignity, honor, and consistency. His artistry, his ability to treat American racism with an angry intelligence but without hate, his sense of humor, his humane respect for his audience, his interest in the ordinary lives of people largely unrepresented in the media, and his commitment to providing symbolic knowledge all give his work enduring value. He remains one of the most important American filmmakers. We are indebted to him for his past work, and anything he does in the future will deserve our attention.

FILMOGRAPHY

Several Friends (1969)
Producer: Charles Burnett
Director: Charles Burnett
Screenplay: Charles Burnett
Cinematography: Jim Watkins
Editor: Charles Burnett
Cast: Andy Burnett, Gene Cherry, Charles Bracy, Cassandra Wright, Donna
    Deitch, Deloras Robinson, James Miles, L. E. McGraw, Ernest Cox, E. R. Canan,
    Arthur Boot, Alan Jurgens
16mm black and white, 21 mins.

The Horse (1973)
Producer: Charles Burnett
Director: Charles Burnett
Screenplay: Charles Burnett
Cinematography: Ian Conner
Editor: Charles Burnett
Music: Samuel Barber, "Knoxville: Summer of 1915"
Cast: Gordon Huston (William), Maury Wright (Ray's boy), Gary Morrin (Walter),
    Roger Collins (West), George Williams (Lee), Larry Clark (Ray)
35mm color, 13:50 mins.

Killer of Sheep (1977)
Producer: Charles Burnett
Director: Charles Burnett
Screenplay: Charles Burnett
Cinematography: Charles Burnett
Editor: Charles Burnett
Sound Recording: Charles Bracy, assisted by Willie Bell, Larry Clark, Christine
    Penick, Andy Burnett

Music: George H. Clautsam, "My Curly Headed Baby"; Allan Robinson, "The House I Live In"; "Going Home," performed by Paul Robeson; Cecil Gant, "I Wonder"; William Grant Still, "Afro American Symphony"; George Gershwin, "Lullaby"; Maurice White, "Reasons," performed by Earth, Wind, and Fire; Elmore James, "I Believe"; Serge Rachmaninoff, "Piano Concerto Number 4"; Otis, "This Bitter Earth," and Gordon, "Unforgettable," performed by Dinah Washington; "Shake Hands," performed by Faye Adams; Walter Jacobs, "Mean Old World," performed by Little Walter; Lowell Fulston, "It's Your Fault, Baby"; Arthur Crudup, "Mean Old Frisco Blues"; Franz von Suppe, "Poet and Peasant Overture"; Scott Joplin, "Solace"; King Oliver, "West End Blues," performed by Louis Armstrong
Cast: Henry Gale Sanders (Stan), Kaycee Moore (Stan's wife), Charles Bracy (Bracy), Angela Burnett (Stan's daughter), Eugene Cherry (Gene), Jack Drummon (Stan's son)
Also: Slim, Dolores Farley, Dorothy Stengal, Tobar Mayo, Chris Terrill, Lawrence Pierrot, Russell Miles, Homer Jai, Johnny Smoke, Paul Reed, Steven Lee, Charles Davis, Cecil Davis, Carlos Davis, Dorothy Daniels, Jannie Whitsey, Bill Williams, Calvin Walker, Sammy Kay, LeRoy Seibert, Cassandra Wright, Junior Blaylock, Charles Cody, Sheila Johnson, Lisa Jonson, 300 Pounds, Menorie Davis, Tony Davis, Carl Davis, Roderick Johnson, Crystal Davis, Peggy Corban, Vincent Smith, Susan Williams, Saul Thompson, Pat Johnson, Bobby Cox, Cadillac, Arthur Williams Jr., Calvin Williams, Alvin Williams, Patricia Williams, Brenda Williams, Bruce Warren, Dian Cherry, Latishia Cherry, Jonathan Cherry, Vernell Cherry, Margrenet Clark, Ronnie Burnett, Regina Batiste, Henry Andrews, Danny Andrews, Marcus Hamlin, Divinoni Hamlin, Ricky Walsh, Gentry Walsh, Michael Harp, Derek Harp, Reggie Williams, Robert Thompson, Ray Cherry, Verrane Tucker
16mm black and white, 84 mins.

My Brother's Wedding (1983; director's cut 2007)
Charles Burnett Productions, *Zweites Deutsches Fernsehen* (Milestone Film & Video, 2007)
Executive Producer: Gaye Shannon-Burnett
Producer: Charles Burnett
Associate Producer: Brigitte Kramer
Supervising Producer: Earl C. Williams Sr.
Director: Charles Burnett
Screenplay: Charles Burnett
Cinematography: Charles Burnett
Editor: Thomas M. Penick
Executive Editor: Charles Burnett (director's cut by Charles Burnett and Ed Santiago)
Assistant Directors: Julie Dash Fielder, Ronald Hairston, Camelia Frieberg
Music: "Amazing Grace," performed by Dr. Henry Gordon; "Take Me to the Water"; "Never Let Me Go" and "Any More," performed by Johnny Ace; "Taru-

reg Medicinal Chant" and "Hausa Street Music," recorded in Africa by Stephen Jay; "Bear Dance," performed by John Briggs Consort

Cast: Everette Silas (Pierce Mundy), Jessie Holmes (Mrs. Mundy), Gaye Shannon-Burnett (Sonia Dubois), Ronald E. Bell (Soldier), Dennis Kemper (Mr. Mundy), Hobert Durham Jr. (Mr. Richards), Sally Easter (Mr. Richards), Angela Burnett (Angela), Tim Wright (Big Daddy), Cora Lee Day (Big Mama), Monte Easter (Wendell), Francis E. Nealy (Mrs. Dubois), Sy Richardson (Mr. Dubois), Garnett Hargrave (Walter), Maria Rodriguez (Maria), Jackie Hargrave (Hattie), Ross Harris (Mr. Bitterfield), Julie Bolton (rape victim), Charles Bracy (Walker), Lucious Walker (Jack Ace)

Also: Stacey Evans, Nate Hardman, Debbie Williams, Henry G. Sanders, Helena Springs, Taglito Atpay, Ed Prevost, Gene Cherry, Dian Cherry, Tony Brown, Brilla Cherry

35mm color, 118 mins. (director's cut, 81 mins.)

To Sleep with Anger (1990)
SVS Films/Samuel Goldwyn
Executive Producers: Edward R. Pressman, Danny Glover, Harris E. Tulchin
Producers: Caldecot Chubb, Thomas S. Byrnes, Darin Scott
Director: Charles Burnett
Screenplay: Charles Burnett
Cinematography: Walt Lloyd
Editor: Nancy Richardson
Art Direction: Troy Meyers
Music: Stephen James Taylor
Cast: Danny Glover (Harry), Paul Butler (Gideon), Mary Alice (Suzie), Carl Lumbly (Junior), Vonetta McGee (Pat), Richard Brooks (Babe Brother), Sheryl Lee Ralph (Linda), Ethel Ayler (Hattie), Julius Harris (Herman), Sy Richardson (Marsh), Davis Roberts (Okra Tate), DeVaughn Nixon (Sunny), Reina King (Rhonda), Wonderful Smith (Preacher), Jimmy Witherspoon (Percy)
35mm color, 102 mins.

America Becoming (1991)
Public Broadcasting Service
Producer: Dai Sil Kim-Gibson
Directors: Charles Burnett and Dai Sil Kim-Gibson
Screenplay: Charles Burnett and Dai Sil Kim-Gibson
Editors: Baylis Glascock and Judy Reidel
Narration: Meredith Vieira
35mm color documentary, 90 mins.

The Glass Shield (1994)
CiBy 2000/Miramax
Executive Producer: Chet Walker

Producers: Thomas Byrnes, Carolyn Schroder
Director: Charles Burnett
Screenplay: Charles Burnett (partly based on the screenplay *One of Us*, by Ned Walsh)
Cinematographer: Elliot Davis
Editor: Curtiss Clayton
Music: Stephen James Taylor
Cast: Michael Boatman (J. J. Johnson), Lori Petty (Deputy Deborah Fields), Richard Anderson (Commander Clarence Massey), Elliott Gould (Mr. Greenspan), Ice Cube (Teddy Woods), Erich Anderson (D. A. Ira Korn), Bernie Casey (James Locket), Wanda De Jesus (Carmen Munoz), Victoria Dillard (Barbara Simms), Don Harvey (Deputy Jack Bono), Tommy Hicks (Reverend Banks), Michael Ironside (Det. Gene Baker), M. Emmet Walsh (Det. Jessie Hall), Natalija Nogulich (Judge Helen Lewis), Gary Wood (Sgt. Chuck Gilmore), Sy Richardson (Mr. Taylor)
1.85:1 screen ratio, color, 114 mins.

When It Rains (1995)
Leapfrog Productions (Milestone Film & Video, 2007)
Producer: Chantal Bernheim
Line Producer: John Oh
Director: Charles Burnett
Screenplay: Charles Burnett
Cinematography: Charles Burnett
Editor: Charles Burnett
Music: Stephen James Taylor
Cast: Ayuko Babu, Florence Bracy, Kenny Merritt, Juno Lewis, Charles Bracy, Soul, Billy Woodberry, R. Ray Barness, John Rier, Barbara Bayless, Jonathan Burnett, Brad Bracy, Damon Ray Ritchie, Sandy Shaw
color, 13 mins.

Nightjohn (1996)
RHI Entertainment, Disney Channel Productions, Sarabande Productions, Signboard Hill Productions/Disney Channel Productions, Hallmark Entertainment
Executive Producer: David Manson
Producer: Dennis Stuart Murphy
Coproducers: John Landgraf, Bill Cain
Director: Charles Burnett
Teleplay: Bill Cain, based on the novella by Gary Paulsen
Cinematography: Elliot Davis
Editor: Dorian Harris
Production Design: Naomi Shohan
Art Director: Jim Hill
Music: Steven James Taylor

Cast: Carl Lumbly (John), Allison Jones (Sarny), Beau Bridges (Clel Waller), Lorraine Toussaint (Dealey), Bill Cobbs (old man), Kathleen York (Callie Waller), Gabriel Casseus (Outlaw), Tom Nowicki (Dr. Chamberlaine), John P. Ford III (Jeffrey Waller), Monica Ford (Egypt), Robin McLamb-Vaughn (Sarny's mother), Jordan Williams (James G. Waller), Danny Nelson (Rev. Rush), Gerald Brown (Joe), John Herina (Homer), Shannon Eubanks (Fanny Bowen)
35mm color, 70 mins.

The Final Insult (1997)
Documenta X, Arte, ZDF
Producer: Charles Burnett
Director: Charles Burnett
Screenplay: Charles Burnett
Music: Stephen James Taylor
Cast: Ayuko Babu (Box Brown)
Digital video, color, 70 mins.

The Wedding (1998)
Hamdon Entertainment, Harpo Films/American Broadcasting Company
Executive Producers: Kate Forte, Oprah Winfrey
Producer: Doro Bachrach
Associate Producers: Daniel Schneider, Valeria Scoon
Director: Charles Burnett
Teleplay: Lisa Jones, based on the novel by Dorothy West
Cinematography: Frederick Elmes
Editor: Dorian Harris
Art Director: Geoffrey S. Grimsman
Music: Stephen James Taylor
Cast: Halle Berry (Shelby Coles), Eric Thal (Mede Howell), Lynn Whitfield (Corinne Coles), Carl Lumbly (Lute McNeil), Michael Warren (Clark Coles), Marianne Jean-Baptiste (Ellen Coles), Shirley Knight (Gram), Cynda Williams (Liz Coles Odis), Patricia Clarkson (Della), Richard Brooks (Lincoln Odis), Gabriel Casseus (Hannibal), Ethel Ayler (Eunice), Paul Butler (Preacher), Peter Francis James (Isaac Coles), Carl Gordon (Mr. Hawkins), Claire Eye (Dockhaven hostess), Margo Moorer (Emmaline)
35mm color, 180 mins.

The Annihilation of Fish (1999)
American Sterling Productions/Regent Entertainment
Executive Producer: Kris Dodge
Producers: Paul Heller, William Lawrence Fabrizio, John Remark, Eric Mitchell
Line Producer: Arlene Albertson
Director: Charles Burnett
Screenplay: Anthony C. Winkler, based on his short story

Cinematography: John Ndiaga Demps
Editor: Nancy Richardson
Production Design: Nina Ruscio
Music: Laura Karpman
Cast: James Earl Jones (Fish), Lynn Redgrave (Poinsettia), Margo Kidder (Mrs.
  Muldroone), Tommy Redmond Hicks (New York minister), David Kogen (social
  worker), Ronald Hoiseck (Reno minister), Philip Kato (hippie minister), Hoyt
  Richards (man in bar)
35mm color, 108 mins.

Selma, Lord, Selma (1999)
Espara/Katz Productions, Walt Disney Television/American Broadcasting
  Company
Executive Producers: Moctesuma Espara, Robert Katz, Julian Fowles
Producer: Christopher Seitz
Director: Charles Burnett
Teleplay: Cynthia Whitcomb, based on the book by Sheyann Webb, Rachael West
  Nelson, and Frank Sikora
Cinematography: John Simmons
Editor: Nancy Richardson
Production Design: Naomi Shohan
Music: Stephen James Taylor
Cast: Jurnee Smollet (Sheyann Webb), Clifton Powell (Martin Luther King Jr.),
  Mackenzie Astin (Jonathan Daniels), Ella Joyce (Betty Webb), Yolanda King
  (Miss Bright), Elizabeth Omilami (Amelia Boynton), Brett Rice (Sherriff Pots),
  Tom Nowicki (Mayor), Danny Nelson (Father Whitaker), Stephanie Zandra
  Peyton (Rachel West)
35mm color, 94 mins.

Olivia's Story (1999)
Producer: Dai Sil Kim-Gibson
Director: Charles Burnett
Screenplay: Dai Sil Kim-Gibson
Cinematography: Steve Schecter
Editor: Charles Burnett
Music: Steven James Taylor
Cast: Charles Burnett (Umpire), Sungia Moon (Grandmother), Ilyon Woo (Olivia)
Digital video, color, 14 mins.

Finding Buck McHenry (2000)
Lin Oliver Productions/Showtime Networks
Executive Producers: Robert Halmi Jr., Lin Oliver, Bobby Heller
Line Producer: Stephen J. Terbull

Director: Charles Burnett
Teleplay: Alfred Slote and David Field, based on the novel by Alfred Slote
Cinematography: John L. Demps Jr.
Editor: Dorian Harris
Production Design: Kathleen Climie
Art Director: Marilyn Kiewiet
Music: Stephen James Taylor
Cast: Ossie Davis (Mr. Mac Henry, Buck McHenry), Ruby Dee (Mrs. Henry), Ernie
    Banks (Ollie Johnson), Michael Schiffman (Jason Ross), Duane McLaughlin
    (Aaron Henry), Megan Bower (Kim Axelrod), Kevin Jubinville (Chuck Axelrod)
35mm color, 94 mins.

Nat Turner: A Troublesome Property (2003)
Subpix, in association with KQED Public Television/ITVS California Newsreel
Producer: Frank Christopher
Coproducer: Kenneth S. Greenberg
Associate Producer: Cynthia Griffin
Director: Charles Burnett
Writers: Charles Burnett, Frank Christopher, and Kenneth S. Greenberg
Cinematography: John Demps
Editors: Michael Colin, Frank Christopher
Production Design: Liba Daniels
Music: Todd Capps and Stephen James Taylor
Cast: Alfre Woodard (Narrator), Carl Lumbly (Nat Turner-Gray), Tom Nowicki
    (Thomas R. Gray), Tommy Hicks (Nat Turner-Edmonds), James Opher (Nat
    Turner-Styron), Megan Gallacher (Margaret Whitehead), Michael LeMelle (Nat
    Turner-Brown), Reshara Coleman (Lucinda), Mark Joy (Judge Jeremiah Cobb),
    Justin Dray (Thomas Moore), Michael Kennedy (James Trezevant), Harry Kol-
    latz (Benjamin Phipps), Laurel Lyle (Harriet Beecher Stowe), Tony Miratti (Gov.
    John Floyd), Billy Dye (Nat Turner) Patrick Waller (Nat Turner-Stowe), and
    interview subjects Herbert Aptheker, Charles Burnett, Kenneth Greenberg,
    Ossie Davis, Henry Louis Gates, Eugene Genovese, William Styron, Eric Foner,
    Vincent Hardy, Thomas Parramore, Peter Wood, Ekewewume Thelwell, Mary
    Kemp Davis, Kitty Futrell, Rick Francis, Bruce Turner, Martha Minon, Louise
    Merriweather, James McGee, Ray Winbush, Ayuko Babu
35mm color, 58 mins.

Warming by the Devil's Fire, **film 4 in the series** The Blues (2003)
Road Movies Filmproduktion, Vulcan Productions/Public Broadcasting Service
Executive Producers: Martin Scorsese and Ulrich Felsberg
Episode Producer: Paul G. Allen
Producers: Margaret Bodde and Alex Gibney
Coproducers: Wesley Jones and Mikaela Beardsley

Line Producer: Daphne McWilliams
Director: Charles Burnett
Writer: Charles Burnett
Cinematography: John Demps
Editor: Edwin Santiago
Production Design: Liba Daniels
Original Score: Stephen James Taylor
Cast: Carl Lumbly (narrator), Tommy Redmond Hicks (Uncle Buddy), Nathaniel
   Lee Jr. (Junior), Susan McWilliams (herself), Nathaniel Lee, Dr. (W. C. Handy),
   Sonny Boy Williamson (himself).
35mm color, 106 mins.

For Reel? (2003)
Public Broadcasting Service
Producers: Charles Burnett and Skye Dent
Director: Charles Burnett
Writers: Bill Plympton, Charles Burnett, Skye Dent
Cinematography: John Demps
Digital video, color, 12 mins.

Namibia: The Struggle for Liberation (2007)
Namibia Film Commission, Pan Afrikan Center of Namibia
Executive Producer: Uazuva Kaumbi
Producers: Abius Akwaak, Steve Gukas
Associate Producer: Edwin Kanguatjivi
Line Producer: Antoinette Parkinson
Director: Charles Burnett
Screenplay: Charles Burnett, expanded from an original script, "Nujoma: Where
   Others Waivered," by Vikson Hangula and Femi Koyode
Story Consultant: Isaac Ikharuchab
Editor: Ed Santiago
Music: Stephen James Taylor
Cast: Carl Lumbly (Sam Nujoma), Danny Glover (Father Elias), Joel Haikali
   (Nujoma at age sixteen), Christian Appolus (Sam Hosea), Obed Emvula (Red),
   Simon Karipangua Petrus (Nujoma at age thirteen), Salmo Danie (Nujoma at age
   nine), Dhameer Gaingob (Sam Hosea at age seven), Andimba Tovio ya Tovio
   (Lazarus Jacobs), Peter Mweshihange (Muhinda Kaura), Kovambo Nujoma
   (Johanna Shikongo), Young Kovambo (Sevelier Namghama), Abri le Roux
   (Prime Minister Botha), Louis Van Eeden (Anton Lubowski)
Panavision, color, 161 mins.

Quiet as Kept (2007)
Milestone Film and Video
Producers: Charles Burnett and Jon Oh

Director: Charles Burnett
Screenplay: Charles Burnett
Cinematography: Charles Burnett
Editor: Charles Burnett
Cast: Nathaniel Lee, Sr. (The Father), Sharial C. Lee (The Mother), Nathaniel Lee
  Jr. (The Son)
Digital video, color, 6 mins.

Relative Stranger (2009)
Larry Levinson Productions; LG Films/Hallmark Channel
Executive Producer: Larry Levinson
Coexecutive Producers: Randy Pope and Michael Moran
Producers: Erik Olson and Brian Martinez
Director: Charles Burnett
Teleplay: Eric Haywood
Editor: Craig Bassett
Cinematography: Todd Barron
Production Design: Laird Pulver
Music: Nathan Furst
Cast: Eric La Salle (Walter Clemons), Michael Michele (Charlotte Clemons),
  Michael Beach (James Clemons), Dana Davis (Denise Clemons), Sherri Saum
  (Nicole Tate), Cicely Tyson (Pearl Clemons), Carlos McCullers II (Andy Clem-
  ons), Dan Castellaneta (Father Gary)
Digital video, color, 88 mins.

BURNETT'S MISCELLANEOUS CREDITS

Welcome Home Brother Charles (1975)
Director: Jamaa Fanaka
Camera Operator: Charles Burnett
color, 91 mins.

Passing Through (1977)
Director: Larry Clark
Camera Operator: Charles Burnett
color, 105 mins.

Bush Mama (1979)
Director: Haile Gerima
Cinematography: Charles Burnett (as Charles Burnette) and Roderick Young
black and white, 97 mins.

Your Children Come Back to You (1979)
Director: Alile Sharon Larkin
Cinematography: Charles Burnett
black and white, 27 mins.

A Different Image (1982)
Director: Alile Sharon Larkin
Cinematography: Charles Burnett
color, 51 mins.

Illusions (1982)
Director: Julie Dash
Editors: Charles Burnett and Julie Dash
Cinematography: Charles Burnett
black and white, 34 mins.

Bless Their Little Hearts (1984)
Director: Billy Woodberry
Screenplay: Charles Burnett
Cinematography: Charles Burnett
black and white, 80 mins.

Crocodile Conspiracy (1986)
Director: Zeinabu Irene Davis
Cinematography: Charles Burnett
color, 124 mins.

Young at Hearts (1994)
Director: Don Campbell
Cinematography (documentary): Charles Burnett and others
color, 73 mins.

Silence Broken: Korean Comfort Women (1999)
Coproducer: Charles Burnett
Director: Dai Sil Kim-Gibson
Editor: Charles Burnett
Cinematography (documentary): Charles Burnett
color, 88 mins.

Wet Sand: Voices from L.A. Ten Years Later (2004)
Director: Dai Sil Kim-Gibson
Editors: Charles Burnett and Richard Kim
Cinematography (documentary): Charles Burnett
color, 57 mins.

REFERENCES

The following list is confined mostly to items cited in the text. A more complete bibliography devoted to Charles Burnett, compiled by Janet Cutler, is available at *Oxford Bibliographies Online.*

Baldwin, James. 1955. "The Harlem Ghetto." In *Notes of a Native Son.* Boston: Beacon Press.

Burnett, Charles. 1986. "Film as a Force for Social Change." *Black Film Review* 2, no. 4: 12–14.

———. 1989. "Inner City Blues." In *Questions of Third Cinema,* edited by Jim Pines and Paul Willeman, 223–26. London: British Film Institute.

———. 1991. "*Killer of Sheep,* screenplay." In *Screenplays of the African-American Experience,* edited by Phyllis Rauch Klotman, 99–116. Bloomington: Indiana University Press.

———. 1996. "*To Sleep with Anger.*" *Scenario: The Magazine of Screenwriting Art* 2, no. 1: 96–99.

Cain, Bill, S.J. 1996. "*Nightjohn*: A Diary." http://www.companysj.com/v142 /Nightjohn.html (last accessed in 2016; not found in June 2017).

Chandler, Karen. 1999. "Folk Culture and Masculine Identity in Charles Burnett's *To Sleep with Anger.*" *African American Review* 33, no. 2 (Summer): 299–311.

Clarke, John Henrick, ed. 1987. *William Styron's Confessions of Nat Turner: 10 Black Writers Respond.* New York: Praeger.

Corbin, Amy. 2014. "Charles Burnett's Dialogic Aesthetics: *My Brother's Wedding* as a Bridge between *Killer of Sheep* and *To Sleep with Anger.*" *Black Camera* 6, no. 1 (Fall): 34–56.

Cunningham, Phillip Lamarr. 2011. "The Haunting of a Black Southern Past: Considering Conjure in *To Sleep with Anger.*" In *Southerners on Film: Essays on Hollywood Portrayals since the 1970s,* edited by Andrew B. Leiter, 123–33. Jefferson, NC: McFarland.

Davis, Mike. 1990. *City of Quartz: Excavating the Future in Los Angeles.* New York: Random House.

Diawara, Manthia, ed. 1993. *Black American Cinema*. New York: Routledge.

Ellison, Mary. 2005. "Echoes of Africa in *To Sleep with Anger* and *Eve's Bayou*." *African American Review* 39, nos. 1/2: 213–29.

Espinosa, Julio Garcia. 1979. "For an Imperfect Cinema." Translated by Julianne Burton. *Jump Cut*, no. 20: 24–26.

Evry, Max. 2007. "*Killer of Sheep*: Interview with Charles Burnett." April 9. http://www.blackfilm.com/20070406/features/charlesburnett.shtml.

Field, Allyson Nadia, Jan-Christopher Horak, and Jacqueline Najuma Stewart, eds. 2015. *L.A. Rebellion: Creating a New Black Cinema*. Berkeley: University of California Press.

Foundas, Scott. 2003. "Review: *Nat Turner: A Troublesome Property*." *Variety*, March 4. Variety.com/2003/film/reviews/nat-turner-a-troublesome-property-1200542996/.

Gillespie, Michael Boyce. 2016. *Film Blackness: American Cinema and the Idea of Black Film*. Durham, NC: Duke University Press.

"The Glass Shield." 1995. *Time Out London*, August 5. https://www.timeout.com/london/film/the-glass-shield.

Goddu, Teresa A. 1997. *Gothic America: Narrative, History and Nation*. New York: Columbia University Press.

Grant, Nathan. 2003. "Innocence and Ambiguity in the Films of Charles Burnett." In *Representing Blackness: Issues in Film and Video*, edited by Valerie Smith, 135–55. New Brunswick, NJ: Rutgers University Press.

Guerrero, Ed. 1991. "Negotiations of Ideology, Manhood, and Family in Billy Woodberry's *Bless Their Little Hearts*." *Black American Literature Forum* 25, no. 1: 315–22.

Himes, Chester. 1973. *The Crazy Kill*. New York: Vintage Crime/Black Lizard.

Hoberman, J. 2007. "L.A. Story." *Village Voice*, March 20. https//www.villagevoice.com/2007/03/20/l-a-story-e/.

Horak, Jan-Christopher. 2015. "Tough Enough: Blaxploitation and the L.A. Rebellion." In Field et al., *L.A. Rebellion*, 119–55.

Jackson, Bruce. 2003. "On Charles Burnett's *Warming by the Devil's Fire*." www.counterpunch.org/2003/10/11.

James, David E. 2005. *The Most Typical Avant-Garde: History and Geography of Minor Cinemas in Los Angeles*. Berkeley: University of California Press.

Kapsis, Robert E., ed. 2011. *Charles Burnett Interviews*. Jackson: University Press of Mississippi Press.

"Killer of Sheep." 1982. *Variety*, October 7, 22.

Kim, Nelson. 2003. "Charles Burnett." *Senses of Cinema*, no. 26 (May). www.sensesofcinema.com/burnett.

Kleinhans, Chuck. 2010. "Charles Burnett." In *Fifty Contemporary Filmmakers*, 2nd ed., edited by Yvonne Tasker, 60–69. London: Routledge.

———. 2015. "Threads and Nets: The L.A. Rebellion in Retrospect and in Motion." In Field et al., *L.A. Rebellion*, 57–82.

Klotman, Phyllis Rauch, ed. 1991. *Screenplays of the African-American Experience.* Bloomington: Indiana University Press.

Klotman, Phyllis Rauch, and Janet K. Cutler, eds. 1999. *Struggles for Representation: African-American Documentary Film and Video.* Bloomington: Indiana University Press.

Koehler, Robert. 2007. "Review: *Namibia: The Struggle for Liberation.*" *Variety,* June 29. Variety.com/2007/film/reviews/namibia-the-struggle-for-liberation-1200558217/.

Kridler, Chris. 1995. "Police Look Different through '*The Glass Shield.*'" *The Baltimore Sun,* June 2, 77. http://articles.baltimoresun.com/1995-06-02/entertainment/1995153170_1_michael-boatman-charles-burnett-lori-petty.

Martin, Adrian. 2008. "Teeming Life." *Film Quarterly* 61, no. 4 (Summer): 72–73.

Martin, Michael T. 2015. "Struggles for the *Sign* in the Black Atlantic: Los Angeles Collective of Black Filmmakers." In Field et al., *L.A. Rebellion,* 196–224.

Martin, Michael T., and David C. Wall. 2013. "The Politics of Cine-Memory: Signifying Slavery in the Historical Film." In *A Companion to the Historical Film,* edited by Robert A. Rosenstone and Constantine Parvulescu, 445–67. Oxford: Wiley-Blackwell.

Martin, Michael T., and Eileen Julien. 2009. "Interview: Charles Burnett—Consummate Cineaste." *Black Camera* 1, no. 1 (Winter): 143–70.

Maslin, Janet. 1978. "Screen: 'Killer of Sheep" Is Shown at the Whitney: Nonprofessional Cast." *New York Times,* November 14, C10.

Massood, Paula J. 1999. "An Aesthetic Appropriate to Conditions: *Killer of Sheep,* (Neo)Realism and the Documentary Impulse." *Wide Angle* 21, no. 4: 20–41.

McCarthy, Todd. 1994. "Review: *The Glass Shield.*" *Variety,* May 30. Variety.com/1994/film/reviews/the-glass-shield-1200436941/.

———. 1999. "Review: *The Annihilation of Fish.*" *Variety,* September 22. Variety.com/1999/film/reviews/the-annihilation-of-fish-1117752169/.

Miguez, Maria. 2016. "Girls with Watchful Eyes: Charles Burnett's Cinema for Children." In Miguez and Paz, *Charles Burnett,* 117–26.

Miguez, Maria, and Victor Paz, eds. 2016. *Charles Burnett: A Troublesome Filmmaker.* Galicia, Spain: Play-Doc Books.

Mitchell, Monica. 1998. "Maker of Films: Charles Burnett." *Director's Guild of America Magazine* 23, no. 2: 89–91.

Nujoma, Sam. 2001. *Where Others Waivered: The Autobiography of Sam Nujoma.* London: Panaf Books.

"On Now." 1982. *Sight and Sound* (Summer): 216.

Paulsen, Gary. 1995. *Nightjohn.* New York: Bantam Doubleday Books for Young Readers.

Polito, Robert. 2001. "Hard-Boiled." *New York Times,* March 18. www.nytimes.com/books/01/03/18/reviews/010318.18politot.html.

Raengo, Alessandra. 2015. "Encountering the Rebellion: *liquid blackness* Reflects on the Possibilities of the L.A. Rebellion Films." In Field et al., *L.A. Rebellion,* 219–318.

Raines, Peter. 1995. "*Glass Shield*: Pursuit of Manifesto Cloaks Cop Drama." *Los Angeles Times*, June 2. Articles.latimes.com/1995-06-02/entertainment/ca-8828_1_glass-shield/.

Reid, Mark A. 1993. *Redefining Black Film*. Berkeley: University of California Press.

———. 2005. *Black Lenses, Black Voices: African American Film Now*. Lanham, MD: Rowman and Littlefield.

———. 2016. "Charles Burnett's Urban Blues as Agency." In Miguez and Paz, *Charles Burnett*, 100–107.

Rocha, Glauber. 1983. "The Aesthetics of Hunger." Translated by Burnes Hollyman and Randal Johnson. In *Twenty-Five Years of the New Latin American Cinema*, edited by Michael Chanin, 12–14. London: Channel Four Television, BFI Books.

Rosenbaum, Jonathan. 1997. "The World According to Harvey and Bob." In *Movies as Politics*, 159–65. Berkeley: University of California Press.

———. 2004. "Chains of Ignorance: Charles Burnett's *Nightjohn*." In *Essential Cinema: On the Necessity of Film Canons*, 285–90. Baltimore, MD: Johns Hopkins University Press.

Sheppard, Samantha. 2015. "Bruising Moments: Affect and the L.A. Rebellion." In Field et al., *L.A. Rebellion*, 225–50.

Smith, Valerie, ed. 2003. *Representing Blackness: Issues in Film and Video*. New Brunswick, NJ: Rutgers University Press.

Stewart, Jacqueline Najuma. 2005. *Migrating to the Movies: Cinema and Black Urban Modernity*. Berkeley: University of California Press.

———. 2015. "The L.A. Rebellion Plays Itself." In Field, et al., *L.A. Rebellion*, 251–90.

Styron, William. 1993. *The Confessions of Nat Turner*. New York: Vintage Books.

Taylor, Clyde. 2015. "Preface: Once Upon a Time in the West . . . L.A. Rebellion." In Field et al., *L.A. Rebellion*, ix–xxiv.

Thompson, Clifford. 1997. "The Devil Beats His Wife: Small Moments and Big Statements in the Films of Charles Burnett." *Cineaste* 23, no. 2: 24–27.

Webb, Sheyann, Rachel West, and Frank Sikora. 1980. *Selma, Lord, Selma: Girlhood Memories of the Civil Rights Days*. New York: Morrow Quill.

West, Dorothy. 1995. *The Wedding*. New York: Anchor Books.

Widener, Daniel. 2010. *Black Arts West: Culture and Struggle in Post War Los Angeles*. Durham, NC: Duke University Press.

Winkler, Anthony C. 2009. *The Annihilation of Fish and Other Stories*. Oxford: Macmillan Education.

INDEX